The Shared World

The Shared World

Perceptual Common Knowledge, Demonstrative Communication, and Social Space

Axel Seemann

The MIT Press
Cambridge, Massachusetts
London, England

This book was set in Stone Serif and Stone Sans by Jen Jackowitz. Printed and bound in the United States of America.

Library of Congress Cataloging-in-Publication Data

Names: Seemann, Axel, 1969– author.
Title: The shared world : perceptual common knowledge, demonstrative
    communication, and social space / Axel Seemann.
Description: Cambridge, MA : The MIT Press, [2019] | Includes bibliographical
    references and index.
Identifiers: LCCN 2018035669 | ISBN 9780262039796 (hardcover : alk. paper)
Subjects: LCSH: Perception (Philosophy)—Social aspects. |
    Communication—Social aspects. | Space perception—Social aspects.
Classification: LCC B828.45 .S44 2019 | DDC 302/.12—dc23 LC record available at
https://lccn.loc.gov/2018035669

10 9 8 7 6 5 4 3 2 1

Contents

Acknowledgments

My introductory course in philosophy often begins, not very originally, with Descartes's First and Second Meditations. Few other texts are capable of similarly sparking the undergraduate imagination, immediately catapulting students into the dizzying heights of disembodied minds, forever separated from the matter that may or may not surround them. It usually does not take long for the at-first-exotic notion of radical skepticism to establish itself as a strangely credible possibility in the philosophical beginner: half an hour into the class, the adventurous first-year will be quite enamored with the idea that the great wide world may be nothing but a confabulation by the Evil Demon. But when the time comes for critical reflection, the intellectual heat in the classroom tends to cool considerably. It is less exciting to try to poke holes into the *Cogito* than it is to let yourself be carried away by it; also, the critical business turns out to be surprisingly hard work. As not only undergraduates have found, once you allow yourself skeptical indulgence, it can be very hard to dislodge it. However, there is one objection to Descartes's argument that my students almost never fail to voice: *What about other people?*

Well, what about them? It is not that the bloody-minded Cartesian would exempt fellow minds from skeptical treatment: if nothing necessarily exists except your own mind, neither do the minds of others. Still, even students who enthusiastically endorsed the skeptical doctrine just a moment ago are often moved by the objection. We may be prepared to shed, for the length of a philosophy lecture, our everyday realism about the objects that surround us; letting go of our realism about other minds seems significantly harder. If you are a mind, capable of hallucinating your surroundings, why not grant the same privilege to others?

The intuition that our everyday realism about the world is grounded in the presence of others is at the heart of this essay. People matter for the constitution of our world; they also matter in the writing of books. My list of those who deserve thanks begins with my students, for their curiosity, good cheer, and insistence that I keep it real. My employer, Bentley University, has patiently supported my endeavors with a sabbatical, a Valente Arts & Sciences Fellowship for a one-course teaching release and several summer grants. My colleagues in the philosophy department have helped create a conducive and supportive work environment. In particular, Bob Frederick, its long-standing former head, did everything in his power to enable me to pursue my work unencumbered by institutional and administrative burdens that he heroically took on for all of the department's members for almost two decades. That I ever managed to finish this book, whose entire draft he read and commented on, is in no small part due to him.

Other people who have provided support, debate, and inspiration over the years include Steve Butterfill, Shaun Gallagher, Dan Hutto, Hans-Bernhard Schmid, Corrado Sinigaglia, Karsten Stueber, and Mike Wilby, as well as the organizers of and participants in various iterations of the Joint Action Meeting and Collective Intentionality conferences. The Social Ontology Group at UC Berkeley repeatedly gave me the opportunity to present and discuss my ideas early on. I have benefited from feedback from audiences at the Universities of Milan, London, Connecticut, Copenhagen, Lisbon, Ahmedabad, and Ankara. I am grateful to all.

Three anonymous reviewers provided careful, detailed, and sympathetic comments, resulting in a much-improved manuscript. Not everything valuable they said made its way into the final draft, often because a serious engagement with their suggestions would have required more space than I had; their ideas may well resurface again in future work. Thanks are due to these readers, as well as to Phil Laughlin, editor for philosophy and cognitive science at MIT, for his patience over the years during which this book took shape, and to Paul Fisher Davies for the wonderful cover drawing.

The intellectual debt to various philosophers and psychologists will be obvious. Reading Timothy Williamson's *Knowledge and Its Limits* (2000) enabled me to finally articulate the idea, which had long been sloshing about in the shallow depths of my philosophical half-conscious, that making progress with the notion of perceptual common knowledge required conceptualizing it as individuated by the environment of its subjects; it was only once I saw this that the core argument presented in this work finally came together. I rely significantly on the experiments and findings of various psychologists, without which the inquiry could not have proceeded. Shaun Gallagher's unique capacity to integrate empirical insights into a philosophical account of the embodied mind was supremely useful at various junctures.

I reserve the most important of these debts for last. As will, again, be obvious, the line of thought presented here owes much to John Campbell's work. It was John's papers on joint attention, and the way in which he accounted for that notion from within his views on perceptual experience and demonstrative thought, that proved essential for my purposes. They enabled me to see the beginnings of a theory in which joint perceptual capacities would occupy a central role in, rather than be relegated to the sidelines of, a more general account of the relation between mind and world. Wherever I may have gotten with this hefty project, beginning it would not have been possible without his groundwork.

Introduction

I.1 The Raft of the Medusa

You can imagine nicer places to be than on the tragic vessel that is the subject of Théodore Géricault's painting *The Raft of the Medusa*. The survivors of a shipwreck, huddled together against the ferocious waves of a hostile ocean, are stuck on a makeshift contraption that might fall apart at any minute. They have long run out of food and drink; they are parched and starved and have endured atrocities beyond the limits of the human imagination. Mutineers have been killed, the weakest slaughtered, and the dead eaten. Those still alive had to join forces to survive, but insofar as their efforts can be called cooperative at all, they warrant this label only in the thinnest sense.

And yet they would not have made it thus far had it not been for the others sharing their fate. None of them could have built the raft, however shoddily tied its planks may be, on their own. They are propping each other up, clinging to each other's limbs, mutually providing scant protection from the elements. They are also jointly scanning the choppy waters for rescue. They have spotted a ship, barely discernible on the horizon, and are frantically signaling: rags, arms, bodies form one dramatic human wave, possessed of desperate force, an ultimate effort to escape an otherwise certain demise.

They don't know yet that they will be rescued, 15 out of an original 150 or so set adrift (Laborie 2017), but they have seen the ship. Perhaps the man at the front of the raft spotted it first, this dot at the intangible meeting point of sea and sky: could it be? He will have looked again, more carefully now; leaned forward as far as the raft allowed, squinted, extended an arm. He will have turned around, caught the eye of his mate: could it be? They will have doubled their efforts, a tautening of muscles, a tightening of their grip on each other; a ship, a savior. The discovery will have spread, gestures, bodies united in one attentive effort. And this effort procures survival in the end.

The overarching topic of this book is the role of others in the perception and cognition of our surroundings. Its first goal is to show that joint perceivers and agents stand in a particular relation to their environment and that this relation can be marshaled to address a range of questions arising in the context of the discussion of the social aspect of the mind. A second aim is to make progress toward the integration of this discussion into the larger philosophical debate about the nature of mind.[1] The last three decades or so have seen a welcome increase of interest by analytic philosophers in its social dimension.[2] One focus of the discussion here is the topic of collective intentionality—the question how to think of the action intentions of plural agents.[3] Then there is the philosophical and psychological debate about mindreading—the question of how individual perceivers can be in a position to glean knowledge about another creature's mental life.[4] Both of these research programs are, at their core, individualist in outlook. The debate about collective intentionality begins, almost without exception,[5] by taking for granted the individual agent's capacity to form intentions for action. The discussion of mindreading begins by stipulating the individual's ability to form a general theory of mind, or her grasp of her own mental life. It is from this individualist vantage point that the question about the social variants of these capacities is then addressed.

But the strategy reaches its limits when you think about perception and perceptual knowledge in joint contexts. It is not promising to begin with some account of ordinary perception and then ask how the account can be brought to bear on scenarios in which two (or more) individuals perceive an object together. The problem is that all perception is from somewhere and all perceptual knowledge is informed by the perceiver's standpoint. Distinct perceivers, even co-attending ones, occupy distinct locations that inform their perceptual experiences. How, then, could there be a form of perception of, and perceptual knowledge about, the environment that is enjoyed by two individuals together? It seems as if, strictly speaking, there simply could not be such a thing; we do not enjoy qualitatively identical experiences when looking at some object together, and neither of us knows exactly what the character of the other's experience amounts to. So there is a methodological problem facing the inquiry into joint perception that does not arise for theories of collective intentionality or mindreading. One possible move at this juncture is to start with the consideration that some social capacities are inherently interpersonal, as proposed by intersubjectivity research in developmental psychology.[6] But this tradition is predominantly concerned with the sharing and attunement of agents' feelings and emotions; and while there can be little doubt that paying tribute to the subjective aspect of mental life is crucial for an account of sociality, it is not obvious how it can be put to use for an explanation of the role of others in shaping the perception of ordinary, nonminded objects. Neither does it seem promising to bite the bullet and propose a collective mode of perceiving, since such an approach would be hard to reconcile with the perspectival nature of perception.

It appears that what is needed, in the attempt to work out a theory of joint perceptual phenomena, is a strategy that is neither individualist nor collectivist in nature. A promising approach will aim to overcome this dichotomy; it will regard neither the individual nor the collective as the basic building block of the eventual theory. To that end, I begin in part 1 with a reflection on a form of knowledge that can be enjoyed only in joint forms of perception, although it is entertained by individuals. This knowledge is of a common kind: it isn't just that each of the perceivers on the raft knows that there is a ship on the horizon, and it isn't either that each of the perceivers knows perceptually that there is a ship and each also knows that the other knows this. Their way of knowing the perceptual fact together is more fundamental than these iterative descriptions convey; it is embedded in the perceptual constellation itself.[7] For the survivors on the raft, the triadic nature of this constellation is of the utmost importance. Suppose the ship were gleaned by only one of them (perhaps the foreman at the front of the vessel) while none of the others could discern it, however much they strained their eyes: the event would not carry the same significance at all. Initial hopefulness would soon give way to disappointment, renewed despair. If the lone perceiver maintained that the ship was approaching and that rescue was near, but the fourteen other pairs of eyes could not verify his claim, his report would be dismissed as the fantasy of a crazed mind. It is a stricture on perceptual common knowledge that it be available to others looking at the same scene. Correspondingly, it is a stricture on such knowledge that the experience of its object make available public evidence in support of the knowledge claim to those others. "There's a ship!" the foreman exclaims, pointing and waving, and now the others can see it too: there really is a ship, and they may be rescued after all.

The particular epistemic power of perceptual common knowledge gives rise to a question: How does our world have to be if its perception, in joint constellations, is to produce common knowledge about it? The question is not easy. The environment of the raft's occupants includes physical things, water and planks, rags and perhaps a ship on the distant horizon. And it includes people, competitors for space on the vessel, for whatever scant supplies of food and drink there may have been; but, also, fellow perceivers and agents who hold each other up and combine their efforts to make themselves seen. Somehow, and somewhat mysteriously, these quite distinct kinds of objects come together to produce perceptual knowledge that is enjoyed in common by all. What, then, is contributed by the world, and what by the minds, of the joint perceivers who come to know in common some perceptual characteristic of their surroundings? My guiding thought is that this question is best addressed in externalist terms. What I call *social externalism*[8] provides a framework that neither stipulates a basic form of collectivity nor conceptualizes social phenomena in the reductivist terms of states of mind of their individual constituents. If you are an externalist about knowledge, you think of it as a mental state that is factive: being in that state requires that the proposition that forms the content of your state be true.[9] Knowing, on this view, is unlike believing. While you can be in the mental state of believing that p regardless of whether p is true, you could not be in the mental state of knowing that p if the proposition were false. The mental state of knowing is individuated relative to the environment in which it is entertained. This is what gives the view its externalist credentials: it ties the knowing mind more closely to the domain about which it possesses knowledge than would otherwise be the case. The view makes not only the possibility of a subject's knowing dependent on the state of the domain it is directed at (this is the case also on the rival view that knowledge is some kind of justified true belief, suitably qualified); it makes the possibility of the subject's being in the mental state itself dependent on external factors.

I put this view to use for the question of perceptual common knowledge: the externalist about perceptual common knowledge holds that joint perceivers and knowers are in factive mental states that are individuated relative to their surroundings. The externalist explains the public character of our perceptual surroundings by appeal to the organization of the perceived environment rather than to the organization of the minds that perceive it. The advantage of externalism for a treatment of joint perception and perceptual common knowledge is that it does not force the intractable question of how individual minds have to be related to perceive jointly. The answer could only appeal to some kind of mutual dependency between perceptual or cognitive states, and the hopes for this project are, I think, scant. Externalism boldly shifts the focus of inquiry from the minds of the joint perceivers and knowers to the environment in which they operate and about which they acquire knowledge. Here, though, a core tenet of the externalist stance has to be abandoned: the powerful distinction between the individual's "internal" mental life and the "external" environment in terms of which her state of knowing is individuated can no longer be drawn in its social variant. In the familiar case of an individual's knowledge of a proposition about some aspect of the environment, its physical characteristics[10] determine the subject's factive mental state if the externalist stance is correct: the "internal"/"external" divide corresponds neatly to the divide between the subject's mental life and her (in the simplest case, nonminded) surroundings. But in the case of perceptual common knowledge, the perceiver's mental state of knowing is individuated by an environment that itself has a mental dimension. The boundary is no longer situated between mind and world, but between the socially structured environment and the perceiver's knowledge about it.

How can you give substance to the idea that the mental states of perceivers who know in common a perceptual proposition are individuated by the environment in which they operate? I begin with the consideration that joint perceptual constellations are, always and necessarily, communicative. That the people on the raft can come to know in common that there is a ship on the horizon is a consequence of a communication in which bodily interaction plays a vital role: pointing out and following gaze; touching, embracing, holding steady, pulling, and nudging toward the saving object. This capacity for what I call demonstrative communication is the topic of part 2. You can see the raft's occupants as entangled in one giant communicative exercise: each occupant is reeled into the joint effort that is expressed in the triangle rising from the dead man's legs at the rear to its culmination in the foreman's upright torso at the front. There is no sharp distinction between their demonstrative and their communicative doings; they are singling out the distant ship for the triple purpose of fixing the reference of their demonstrative thoughts ("Where is that ship? Over there? No, it's disappeared—oh, I've got it again, yes, yes—it's a ship all right!"), pointing it out to their fellow sufferers, and attracting the ship's attention. Reference fixing already is an exercise in communication on the raft, and joint perceivers always enjoy at least a minimal kind of perceptual common knowledge about the object of their shared interest. This knowledge turns out to be of a spatial kind: demonstrative communication requires that speakers be able to determine the location of the objects of their referential intentions by means of exercises in what I call *social triangulation*. Creatures who can socially triangulate treat a variety of locations in the relevant region as centers of egocentric space. The spatial organization of joint perceivers' environment explains the common character of the knowledge they enjoy about it: perceptual knowledge about objects in social space is always knowledge about objects whose locations are individuated, by each jointly perceiving subject, relative to the standpoints of all.

The spatial order of joint perceivers' environment is the topic of part 3. It gives rise to a pressing question: How can you treat spatial positions other than the one you occupy as being on a par with your own, thus making it possible to determine the location of objects by means of an exercise in social triangulation? This question has an empirical angle: there is a recent, small but growing body of evidence in support of the idea that peripersonal space—the area around the body in which you are sensitive to both perceptual and proprioceptive information—is not restricted to your own body; perceivers can be sensitive to these distinct kinds of information in areas surrounding others, particularly if these others are fellow communicators. The integration of this information is dynamic; it can be accomplished only by creatures capable of movement. Social externalism is thus naturally aligned with embodied and enactivist approaches that take action and perception to be interdependent.

This line of thought finally enables me to discuss, in part 4, what really is the guiding thread of the entire essay: the capacity to look at the environment together with others that is usually called *joint attention*. When I started working on this book, the plan was to write a straightforward philosophical treatment of that notion. But I soon found myself confronted with the problem I mentioned at the outset: joint attention is a form of perception; as such, it is standpoint dependent; since joint perceivers occupy different standpoints, it is not clear how a genuinely shared form of perception can be possible. Addressing the problem took the entire line of thought I have just sketched. So the whole book is, in a way, about joint attention, understood as a phenomenon that facilitates particularly social forms of knowing about the perceptual environment. The actual discussion of the notion can therefore be quite brief: I restrict myself to drawing out some conclusions from the argument I have been presenting and situate them in the philosophical literature. In a final step, I demonstrate the explanatory power of the account by showing how it can help with some problems in psychology and the philosophy of perception.

The argumentative strategy I deploy in *The Shared World* is what you might call "top-down." It begins with a conceptual question about a complex kind of sociocognitive phenomenon—that of perceptual common knowledge—and works its way down to an empirically informed account of the spatial structure of the environment in and about which such knowledge is possible. You might find this strategy cumbersome and potentially misleading; after all, I do not end up arguing, despite initial appearances, for a cognitivist account of joint attention. Would it not make more sense to begin, "bottom-up," with a review of the empirical evidence supporting the hypothesized notion of social space and build the philosophical case for an externalist account of joint perception and perceptual common knowledge from there? This approach might be promising if there were an exhaustive discussion in psychology of that notion, with well-established conclusions. But the debate is in its infancy, and in any case, I am not an empirical researcher. I am in the slightly awkward position of the philosopher working on a topic in which empirical evidence is invaluable but who is nevertheless conducting what at the end of the day is a conceptually motivated inquiry. A balance has to be achieved that pays due respect to the evidence while not losing sight of the theoretical aims of the investigation. No doubt that balance is delicate.[11]

If I had to summarize my project in one sentence, I might say that it pursues a very broadly construed epistemology of perception in joint environments that is supported by an empirically sensitive description of such environments. The social externalism that forms the backbone of my approach is conjoined with a version of epistemological disjunctivism: only and all experiences that present their subjects with objects in social space generate the commonly known propositions that justify perceptual claims about their objects, absolutely, to the joint perceivers; no other experiences can have this public justificatory role. It is also in line with a relational view of perceptual experience, on which pairs of joint experiences establish a direct epistemic relation between the perceivers and the object in social space. But it is important to note the limited scope of the thesis of social externalism. Not everything that is known through perception is commonly known, not every perceptual event has two subjects as constituents, and not every demonstrative reference is communicative.

Williamson (2000) argues against the idea that our minds constitute cognitive homes in which all facts lie open to view. You might think that this is obvious where knowledge about the environment is concerned: since your factive mental state of knowing that p is individuated in terms of the characteristics of your environment and since these characteristics may not be cognitively accessible to you, you can know that p without knowing that you do. However, everything in social space is accessible to its subjects. As soon as their surroundings are organized by a social spatial framework, they know in common, minimally, where things are relative to their respective locations. In this sense, social externalism provides joint perceivers with a cognitive home. It is not a very comfortable or expansive abode, though: two subjects can know in common where an object is in social space, and thus be in a position to demonstratively reason about it, without knowing where it is in allocentric space (for instance, they can determine its location by means of social triangulation even if the object of their joint experiences is presented to them in a mirror that misrepresents its location). And they can enjoy common knowledge of its location while knowing very little in common about its perceptual properties. Joint perceivers operate in an environment in which everything is open to view, but this does not mean that everything a joint perceiver is perceiving is being jointly perceived. The epistemic situation of creatures like us is rather like that of the occupants of the raft: they operate in a tightly constrained environment, their shaky vessel, on which much is in public view. They can, through demonstrative communication, extend the scope of this transparent environment so as to include, for instance, the presence of the saving ship on the horizon. But only the foreman may be able to tell, from his vantage point or perhaps simply because of his superior eyesight, the distant ship's number of sails. He thus enjoys knowledge about the jointly perceived object that he cannot perceptually share with his fellow perceivers and that he therefore cannot use to discursively justify a perceptual claim. The joint character of a perceptual constellation is not an all-or-nothing affair; it allows for degrees. And it is enjoyed, to stay true to the metaphor of the raft, on the back of the dark waves of an unknown ocean whose vast expanses may, though perceivable, forever resist reflective access. We do have a cognitive home, but it is of an unstable kind; it is constituted in communication with others and exists dubiously on the back, and at the peril, of events in an environment that may not be transparent to us at all.

At the same time, it is only by virtue of this makeshift float that we are in a position to navigate the boundless seas: the rescuing craft on which the hopes of the shipwreck's survivors rest is, after all, just another slightly bigger floating device. The acquisition of perceptual knowledge, on this picture, is always moored in what is commonly known. We may be hoping to find cognitive dry land on which we can rest safely; but all we ever reach are larger vessels, slightly more securely held in place by what we know in common and can justify to each other, about the objects at the places we inhabit.

I.2 Overview

The book has four parts: two substantial ones in the middle flanked by two shorter ones at the beginning and end. In part 1, I introduce the peculiar notion of perceptual common knowledge and the difficulties we face when thinking about it. I consider two possible approaches: one that conceives common knowledge as its subjects' perceptual beliefs to which further epistemic and environmental conditions have to be added, and one according to which the subjects' mental states of knowing in common a perceptual proposition are directly individuated by the environment in which they operate. I opt for the second view, not on the grounds of a decisive argument but because it affords a promising way to think about a range of social perceptual phenomena. I then sketch, though I cannot yet solve, two problems that a convincing account of perceptual common knowledge has to address. The first problem is the threat of a regress of levels of what each subject in a joint constellation knows. The second problem is how to square the externalist contention that you can know without knowing that you do with the consideration that common knowledge is, necessarily, out in the open.

Part 2 begins in chapter 3 with the consideration that perceptual common knowledge results from linguistic communications in which uses of demonstratives and pointing gestures play an important role, and it subscribes to a Gricean model of communication (as developed by, for example, Sperber and Wilson 1995). This chapter does not offer much in terms of original insights; its job is to assemble, in a rough-and-ready way, the framework that I need to proceed. This is partly true also for chapter 4, in which I consider Kaplan's ([1977] 1989) question of the semantic contribution of pointing gestures to demonstrative utterances and argue that this question loses much of its urgency in joint contexts. The speaker's referential intention, which is anchored in her perceptual attention, determines the reference of her use of a demonstrative expression; but the speaker's act of attending to the object she intends to demonstratively single out is already communicative in joint constellations, and the pointing gesture simply reinforces its directedness. I address the question of what makes communication about demonstratively identified objects possible and suggest that common knowledge of the object's location plays a vital role here. Crudely, we can come to know perceptual propositions about jointly perceived objects because we know where they are relative to each of our positions: we know their location in what I call *social space*. In social space, we can direct our respective foci of attention to the intended objects and discursively justify our perceptual claims about them to each other.

I then ask how to individuate locations in social space. Ordinarily, there is no big problem here: these locations are delineated by the boundaries of the objects that occupy them. However, we can perhaps think of cases in which demonstrative communication succeeds even though there is no discrete object (but only a feature, such as a color) at the location indicated by the speaker. I suggest that in such cases, it suffices for communication that there be an overlap between the locations on which speaker and hearer focus, respectively. This suggestion gives rise to a problem: how can speaker and hearer know, in the absence of a discrete object at the location of their joint focus, that they are attending to the same place? What explains communicators' common knowledge of the location of the object (or feature) of their communication is, I suggest, the nature of their experience: when they are jointly perceiving an object, they are enjoying an experience that is quite unlike that of a single subject, not even one who mistakenly believes herself to be in a joint constellation. The experience enables them to justify to each other claims about the jointly perceived object. They could not be jointly mistaken about its location, since they help constitute the joint constellation that determines the object's location. I call this view *social disjunctivism* and suggest that it explains the transparency of social space: its occupants always know in common the location of the objects of their joint perception.

This feature of joint constellations, I suggest in chapter 4, deflates the threat of a regress of infinite layers of knowledge that the subjects of perceptual common knowledge apparently have to possess. Not so: the base of this knowledge is the location of the object in social space. Because this location is determined by means of an act of triangulation relative to the standpoints of the subjects, the base contains the regress. The externalism that I opted for in part 1 turns out to be of a social kind; subjects' mental states of knowing in common a perceptual proposition about a jointly perceived object are individuated relative to an environment that they help constitute. In the closing chapter of part 2, I argue that thinking about perceptual reasoning in dialectic terms can help with a looming suspicion that the justification of a perceptual claim by appeal to experience might be circular, and I briefly suggest that this should motivate us to see dialectic perceptual justification as a sui generis phenomenon.

In part 3, I make an empirically informed case for the existence of a social spatial framework. So far I have been considering more or less exclusively the spatial ordering of joint perceivers' environment with regard to the production of perceptual, propositional, common knowledge about the objects it contains. This spatial order is of a reflective kind; it requires the capacity for conscious perspective-taking, and thus a conception of space in which positions other than one's own can be thought of as centers of perception and action. But this approach gets us only so far: the capacity for what is usually called joint attention sets in around the end of the first year of human life, well before the infant is capable of linguistic communication about jointly perceived objects. I consider the distinction between level 1 and level 2 perspective-taking (broadly, the distinction between knowing *what* another perceiver can see and *how* she sees it) and focus on the level 1 kind as particularly relevant for thinking about the notion of social space.

The idea is that level 1 perspective-taking already requires you to operate with a spatial framework in which you can treat the positions of others as origins of viewpoints. The question of what it takes for a spatial location to be assigned the role of such an origin then arises. Drawing on Evans (1982), I begin with a reflection on the importance of action for a conception of space and suggest that action space has a bodily dimension: it requires the integration of proprioceptive and perceptual information. Only thus can an individual enjoy the practical knowledge of its location that enables her to act on it.

I introduce some evidence in support of the existence of such a peripersonal spatial framework (for instance, Làdavas 2002; Di Pellegrino and Làdavas 2015) and ask how to make sense of its social variant: a spatial order in which the practical knowledge of how to act jointly on an object is gained by treating both one's own and the cooperator's location as areas at which both proprioceptive and perceptual cues are available. I introduce some recent studies in support of the idea that there is such a thing as a social spatial framework (for instance, Costantini and Sinigaglia 2011; Maister et al. 2015; Teneggi et al. 2013).

The final step in part 3 is to explain the role of social action space in the acquisition of the kind of frame of reference that makes reflective level 1 perspective-taking possible. My proposal is that indexical spatial thinking has an important role to play here. There are two ways in which you can be perceptually aware of your own location: you can know your location in external space by treating your body as a visual object like any other, and you can know your location in peripersonal space relative to the objects that offer opportunities for action. Thinking of your own location as "here" requires you to integrate those two frameworks: "here" designates a place in allocentric space at which perceptual and proprioceptive cues can be exploited for action. In social space, there is more than one location at which both kinds of information are available, so the question arises how joint agents come to distinguish between their own locations and those of their cooperators. I draw on the view that an agent's sense of control over her doings is the result of a matching of internally generated predictions about the outcome of a motor command with its actual consequence (for instance, Georgieff and Jeannerod 1998; Van den Bos and Jeannerod 2002): "here" is the location at which the agent experiences a sense of control over the movements performed at it. Once the agent has learned to think of her location as "here," and the location of her cooperator as "*there" (an origin of actions over which the agent has no control), she has acquired the kind of conception of space that makes reflective level 1 perspective-taking possible.

Parts 2 and 3 are related as follows. In part 2, I show that a range of questions arising in the context of demonstrative communication can be answered once you suppose that speakers and hearers operate with a social conception of space. In part 3, I make the empirically motivated case in its support. Some considerations in part 3 are quite speculative, but I hope that the cumulative evidence on offer, in conjunction with the conceptual arguments introduced in part 2, is sufficient to support the view that a particular spatial order underwrites our capacity for joint action and demonstrative communication.

In part 4, I build on the externalist account of perceptual common knowledge, and the idea that we can substantiate this externalism by introducing the notion of a social spatial framework, in order to come to a view about what is usually called *joint attention*. The label turns out to be, strictly speaking, a misnomer: it is better thought of in terms of individual perceivers' attention to objects presented to them in social space. I distinguish between *proximal joint perception*, in which the object of their interest is ready-to-hand; and *distal joint perception*, in which the area of social space is imaginatively extended, so as to make it possible for them to focus together on objects beyond their reach. I offer some evidence from psycholinguistics (Peeters, Hagoort, and Özyürek 2015; Peeters and Özyürek 2016) to support this distinction. In a final step, I put the account to use: I show that it can answer the developmental question of how to account for the role of social space (as introduced by Moll and Kadipasaoglu 2013) in enabling the capacity for explicit level 1 perspective-taking; I argue that it offers an alternative to the idea (defended by Apperly and Butterfill 2009 and Butterfill and Apperly 2013) that infants in their second year of life are mindreaders (albeit minimal ones); and I suggest that it can help substantiate the contention (put forward by Schellenberg 2007) that the perception of objects' spatial properties presupposes a particular kind of conception of space. If this last point is on the right track, the relevance of social space is not restricted to joint perception and action; it helps us explain how we come to perceive the world as independent of the perspectives we bring to bear on it.

1 Perceptual Common Knowledge

Introduction

For beings like us, perceptual common knowledge is as ubiquitous as it is important. You enjoy it as soon as you, an ordinary human visual perceiver, encounter the environment together with others like yourself. It has the vital function of anchoring us in what there is so that we can justify our perceptual claims to each other. Consider this passage from Sarah Perry's (2016) *The Essex Serpent*, a novel in which the population of an estuary on the English coast succumbs to the collective imagination of a mythical sea monster that is said to roam the marshes claiming human lives and that for a whole summer instills terror in those under its spell. In September, an unbearable stench wafting inland from the sea provokes a search expedition, whose members discover the putrefying carcass of an enormous sea creature at the water's edge:

> "Look," said Banks, "that's all it was, that's all it was." He plucked off his hat, and held it to his breast, looking absurdly as if he'd encountered there in the Essex dawn the Queen on her way to parliament: "Poor old thing, that's all it was, out there in the dark, lost, I daresay, damaged, cast up on the marsh and sucked back out on the tides."
>
> *And it did seem a poor old thing,* thought Will. For all its look of having detached itself from the illuminated margins of a manuscript, not the most superstitious of men could've believed this decaying fish to be a monster of myth: it was simply an animal, as they all were; and was dead, as they all would be. There they stood, reaching by silent agreement the conclusion that the mystery had not been solved so much as denied: it was impossible to believe that this blind decaying thing— cast out of its element, where its silver flank must've been lithe, beautiful—could have caused their terror. (Perry 2016, 326)

The passage illustrates the particular epistemic power of triadic perceptual constellations: it is the shared sight of the carcass that breaks the collective spell. Had Banks gone down to the shore alone and reported what he found, the effect would not have been nearly the same. A single report of a stranded dead fish would not have dissolved the collective fantasy, but the public viewing does the job: there is now no option but for everyone to acknowledge the facts, brought home not just by the sight of the animal but also, crucially, by everyone's knowledge that everyone is seeing the same thing. The scene highlights the key requirement for public reasoning: the facts have to be out in the open.

The main aim in part 1 is to get a first, tentative grip on what it takes for perceptual facts to be out in the open in the way of the Essex Serpent. It does this by asking about the mindset of individuals who know in common a perceptual proposition: Should we think of their cognitive states as beliefs that qualify as knowledge because a range of further, nonmental conditions (such as the truth and justifiability of these beliefs) are also being met? Or should we say that the joint perceivers are in factive mental states—that being in the right kind of mental state suffices for them to know in common the perceptual proposition?

In chapter 1, I introduce two possible views of thinking about perceptual common knowledge and opt for the externalist idea that such knowledge is to be accounted for in terms of its subjects' factive mental states. In chapter 2, I consider (though I do not yet have the resources to dissolve) the threat of a regress of infinite layers of knowledge that joint perceivers may be thought to need (but must forever fail) to possess.

1 Conceptions of Common Knowledge

1.1 Common Knowledge

Common knowledge is of vital importance for social interaction. Consider the traffic regulations that stipulate which side of the road to drive on. For traffic to function smoothly, each participant must know what the convention (and law) prescribes: in the United States, for instance, you must drive on the right. But knowing this is not enough: each participant must know also that every participant in traffic knows, and knows that everyone knows, which side of the road to drive on. Otherwise smooth coordination would be impossible, and it would be extremely imprudent to ever get into a car.

An early rendering of the problem of common knowledge can be found in Hume (1740): suppose two farmers know in common that each needs the other's help to harvest their crops, which mature at different times. Then it is in each farmer's interest to help the other, thus ensuring the harvest of both crops. But the farmer whose crop ripens later reasons that it will not be in the other's interest to help, having already received help herself. So she does not help with the earlier crop; the second farmer, not having received help himself, will refuse to help the first, and both crops will rot in the field. Versions of Hume's problem are at the heart of game theory: the course of action that is collectively best for each player is at odds with the course of action that maximizes the individual's utility (but is unavailable if the other player individually seeks to maximize her own utility).[1]

Another puzzle arising for the notion of common knowledge is the regress it gives rise to. Lewis (1969; and, similarly, Schiffer [1972]) analyzes common knowledge as an infinite iteration of propositions ("S knows that

H knows that S knows . . . that p'') that each subject needs to know. The difficulty for this analysis is that it appears to require that S and H know this infinite number of propositions if they are to enjoy the common knowledge that p. The problem is particularly pressing if the base of their common knowledge is perceptual. Schiffer gives the example of S and H being seated at a table, with a candle between them. Suppose S and H are each looking at the scene in front of them. Then S perceptually knows that there is a candle on the table and that H knows this; the same is true for H. S knows, furthermore, that H knows that S knows that there is a candle on the table; the same is true for H, and so on. But the perceptual constellation immediately makes available everything they need to know in order to communicate about or act on its object: they do not need to compute infinite iterations of propositions expressing what each party knows. Campbell (2002, 164–171) highlights this point by introducing a game in which two players are coordinating their attack on a target that they see on a common screen while sitting in separate booths that obscures their views of each other. They communicate via a messaging system that allows them to single out objects on the screen for collective attack and to confirm receipt of messages about which object to attack. But the system only works half of the time. Suppose that an individual attack by either player means certain defeat. Then S and H will never be in a position to attack: they never have the kind of knowledge that is required for collective attack, even if S manages to communicate to H which target he wants to attack and when, and H manages to confirm receipt of the message to S. For attack is rational only if S in turn manages to communicate to H that he has received the confirmation; and so on. No amount of sending messages to and fro will put the players in a position to rationally attack: it is always possible that the latest message has not been received, so a further confirmation of receipt always has to be sent. Yet in the ordinary case, the joint perceptual constellation immediately produces the kind of knowledge that would enable the two agents to attack.

This problem is different from Hume's: it is about the character and role of perceptual constellations in which two individuals attend to a target, so that their focus immediately enables them to know in common what target they are focusing on. My discussion in what follows is concerned exclusively with perceptual common knowledge. I approach this topic in a somewhat unusual way. The approach taken by Campbell is to ask how to account for the perceptual constellation that makes available common knowledge about its object. By contrast, I begin with the question of how to characterize the mindsets of the possessors of perceptual common knowledge.

1.2   Common Knowledge and Justified True Belief

The idea that knowledge can be characterized in terms of its subjects' (suitably qualified) beliefs has a long-standing history in epistemology.[2] It is a conjunctive analysis: it supposes that knowing that p requires a number of distinct conditions to be met. The knower has to be in the right kind of mental state (she has to have the attitude of belief toward the known proposition); the belief has to be true; and she has to have good reasons for holding the belief—she must not merely believe truly by accident. I abbreviate this kind of analysis as JTB. However intuitively compelling it may be, the approach has run into significant difficulties, triggered by Gettier's (1963) introduction of cases in which these conditions are met even though the subject cannot be said to know that p. Gettier's cases highlight the problem that a subject can be justified in holding a true belief as a matter of luck; the long-standing debate of the difficulties that beset an analysis of knowledge as JTB is inconclusive. Williamson (2000) suggests that the failure of so many attempts to reductively analyze the notion of knowing gives us reason to think the analysis may be misconceived. But not everyone thinks it is beyond salvaging (see Goldman 2009 for a recent defense). I am not interested here in the merit of this kind of analysis per se; the point is whether it can be put to use in an account of perceptual common knowledge. Consider this proposal:

CJTB: Two subjects commonly know that p just when each has a justified true belief that each of them has a justified true belief that p.

CJTB quickly runs into a version of Gettier's problem. Wilby (2010, 88) writes out the regress inherent in what Schiffer (1972) calls *mutual knowledge* thus:

A speaker (S) and an audience (A) mutually know that p provided that:
1. S knows that p.
   A knows that p.
2. S knows that A knows that p.
   A knows that S knows that p.

3. S knows that A knows that S knows that p.

   A knows that S knows that A knows that p.

   . . . etc.

   . . . etc.

   . . . etc. ad infinitum.

If you think of common knowledge in terms of CJTB, this formulation is equivalent to the following:

A speaker (S) and a hearer (H) commonly know that p provided that:

4. S truly and with justification believes that p.

   A truly and with justification believes that p.

5. S truly and with justification believes that A truly and with justification believes that p.

   A truly and with justification believes that S truly and with justification believes that p.

6. S truly and with justification believes that A truly and with justification believes that S truly and with justification believes that p.

   A truly and with justification believes that S truly and with justification believes that A truly and with justification believes that p.

   . . . etc.

   . . . etc.

   . . . etc. ad infinitum.

This account of common knowledge leads to an inconsistency in A's mental economy if she finds herself in a Gettier-type situation. Imagine a case (which I call "Hologram") in which S and A are seated at a table with a candle between them, as in Schiffer's classic scenario. But only S sees the candle on the table, while A sees a hologram of an identical-looking candle that obscures the actual candle seen by S. By some feat of technology, the hologram is not visible to S. Then A is in a Gettier-type situation: she holds a belief that is true (there is a candle on the table) and justified (her perceptual experience provides her with justification for her belief), but she does not know that there is a candle on the table because her justification for her belief is provided by the perceptual experience of the hologram. She is mistaken about the object whose perception provides her with justification for her belief; that the belief is true is a matter of luck. Then the following situation arises:

7. S believes truly and with justification that there is a candle on the table.

8. S knows that there is a candle on the table (via JTB).

9. A believes truly and with justification that there is a candle on the table.

10. A does not know that there is a candle on the table (via Gettier).

11. A believes truly and with justification that S knows that there is a candle on the table.

12. A knows that S knows that there is a candle on the table (via JTB).[3]

13. If A knows that S knows that p, then A knows that p (via the social transitivity of knowledge).

14. A knows that there is a candle on the table.

15. Therefore, A knows and does not know that there is a candle on the table (via propositions 10 and 14).

A thus entertains two inconsistent mental states. She has, so to speak, two epistemic avenues to the acquisition of the knowledge that p. She can come to know that p by inference from her knowledge that S knows that p, and she can come to know that p directly, by looking at the scene before her. But the two avenues lead to different destinations. Since A does not know that p, though she does know that S knows that p, she ends up knowing and not knowing that p.

One possible reaction to this outcome is to try to add suitable, luck-eliminating conditions to the analysis of knowledge as JTB, so as to rule out Gettier-type cases.[4] As Goldman (2009, 75) puts it, it would be "a laugher" to take the difficulty flagged up by Gettier as a conclusive argument against conjunctive analyses of knowledge. It is not clear, though, that a successful such amendment is in principle possible (Zagzebski 1994). And however amended, JTB has built into it an internalism that is unattractive for the characterization of perceptual common knowledge: its social character could then only be captured in an account of the relation between individuals' beliefs, and such an account is vulnerable to the threat posed by the regress of infinite layers of knowledge that are generated by what each joint perceiver knows (see this part's introduction and section 6.2).

The alternative is to suppose that the subjects who know a perceptual proposition in common are in factive mental states. This is the view I am adopting. My strategy is to substantiate it by showing that an externalist account of perceptual common knowledge has significant advantages: it can help solve some of the perennial problems besetting that notion, and it is useful also for thinking about the larger picture of the epistemic and pragmatic situation in which joint perceivers and common knowers find themselves. In the interest of brevity, I am not going to attempt to decisively show that no version of CJTB can be made to work. My approach is of a constructivist rather than critical bent: I try to demonstrate the merit of my strategy by showing what it can achieve, not by highlighting the problems arising for a rival view.

1.3   An Externalist Take on Perceptual Common Knowledge

Williamson (2000) proposes to treat propositional knowledge as a mental state:

KMS: Knowledge is a mental state.

The key consideration is that the state of knowing that p is not analyzable in terms of other, supposedly more basic mental states. In particular, it is not analyzable in terms of the notion of belief. At the heart of the proposal is the idea that whether you are in the mental state of knowing that p is constitutively dependent on facts about the (external) environment rather than merely on (internal) psychological facts about the subject. Knowing, like seeing but unlike believing, is factive: you can only see that p if p, and you can only be in the mental state of knowing that p if p, but you can believe that p regardless of whether p. This feature of KMS sharply distinguishes it from JTB.

Williamson's proposal, laid out and defended carefully in *Knowledge and Its Limits* (2000), has been enormously influential. It has also attracted its fair share of criticisms (for instance, Fricker 2009). My aim here is not to give a comprehensive account of the proposal or consider objections to it. I simply take the idea that knowledge is a factive mental state, to be individuated relative to the environment in which it is entertained, as my starting point. I fill in the picture somewhat as I go along, but the project is emphatically not to build a conception of perceptual common knowledge that is faithful to Williamson's account of KMS. It is not a matter of applying his account to the analysis of common knowledge but rather of building an independent view on the basis of the broad externalist take on knowledge he recommends.

KMS is attractive for the analysis of common knowledge because its externalism lets it avoid the Gettier-type problem facing CJTB. If the mental state of knowing that p is determined by the environment in which a subject operates, then two subjects' mental states of knowing that p have exactly the same conditions of satisfaction if they operate in the same environment. Suppose that some feature of the environment explains what makes two subjects' mental states of knowing that p amount to common knowledge. Then a scenario such as "Hologram," in which only one subject of a joint perceptual event can be said to know that p even though the conditions of satisfaction for their justified true beliefs are met for both, cannot arise. Of course, this move makes everything depend on whether we can say what feature of the environment accounts for the commonality of subjects' mental states of perceptually knowing that p. Fully addressing this task will take until the end of part 3. For now, I work with the unanalyzed contention that joint perceivers are each in a mental state of knowing that p, where p is a proposition that expresses a perceptual fact about a perceived object or scene, and that the nature of the environment in which each knows that p explains why they know p in common:

CKMS: Two subjects who know in common that p, where p is a proposition expressing a perceptual fact about a jointly perceived object or scene, are each in factive mental states whose conditions of satisfaction are set by the environment in which they operate.

The proposal faces an immediate problem. One implication of KMS, as proposed and elaborated by Williamson (2000), is that you can be in the mental state of knowing that p without knowing that you are: knowledge, to use Williamson's term, is not "luminous."[5] But subjects who know in common that p must always know that they know. Just this consideration leads Sperber and Wilson (1995) to argue as follows:

> By the very definition of common knowledge, people who share mutual knowledge *know* that they do. If you do not *know* that you have mutual knowledge (of some fact, with someone), then you do not have it. Mutual knowledge must be certain, or else it does not exist; and since it can never be certain it can never exist. (19–20)

As will become clear in the course of this book, there are good reasons to resist Sperber's and Wilson's skeptical conclusion. But they are undoubtedly correct in claiming that the possibility of common knowledge depends on its subjects' knowledge that they have it. This is a difficulty that an externalist account of perceptual common knowledge will have to address (see chapter 5).

Williamson's externalism is motivated by considerations that were originally put forward in the discussion of the reference of proper names and subsequently extended to mental contents. McGinn (1977) builds on Putnam's (1973) Twin Earth scenario to discuss the case of an individual who is expressing the belief that "water quenches thirst." This belief is true only if H_2O quenches thirst. Now consider the case of a parallel individual on Twin Earth, where water is XYZ. The Twin Earth individual's belief that water quenches thirst is true only if water is XYZ. This individual has never been to Earth and is not familiar with H_2O. Hence this individual does not believe that water quenches thirst. The two individuals have different beliefs; their mental states are individuated by distinct features of the environments in which they operate. These features may not be known to the individuals. On an externalist view, the individual on Earth is holding a belief about H_2O even if she entertains it prior to the discovery of the molecular structure of water.

Similarly, the features of the environment that individuate a subject's mental state of knowing might not be known to her. If knowledge were luminous, the environmental facts that individuate a subject's state of knowing would themselves have to be cognitively accessible. Suppose that the respective individuals on Earth and Twin Earth each *know* that water quenches thirst. For their knowledge to be luminous, they would also have to know, respectively, that water is H_2O and that it is XYZ. The environment must provide the subjects with knowledge of the conditions that individuate their state of knowing that p. Call such environments *transparent*:[6]

Transparency: A subject's environment is transparent relative to a known proposition p just when it provides knowledge of those of its features that individuate her mental state of knowing that p, and when this knowledge itself is consciously accessible to her.

What does it take for an environment to be transparent? The answer is not obvious. Suppose you think the environment on Earth is transparent to the contemporary inhabitant relative to the proposition that water quenches thirst. It is transparent because the inhabitant could always find out about the molecular structure of the substance she calls "water"—for instance, by consulting a chemistry textbook. She could then distinguish between thirst-quenching "water" on Earth and thirst-quenching "twater" on Twin Earth, and the knowledge that water quenches thirst would be luminous. But what if the subject is a schoolboy in a remote part of the world where chemistry textbooks are scarce? What if the subject is beholden to a cult that denies the accuracy of the scientific establishment's view of the molecular structure of water? You might or might not think that these circumstances affect the transparency of the inhabitants' environments; disagreement is possible. If transparency is relativized to particular environments (in which, perhaps, "normal" epistemic conditions obtain), there is no saying what the standards of normalcy are in the particular environment.[7] But transparency cannot simply be a matter of the idealized absolute accessibility of all facts about the environment either, since the notion then loses all practical significance. If only absolute transparency of an environment secures the luminosity of the knowledge that can be had about it, the knowledge of ordinary individuals, who are operating under cognitive and environmental constraints of various kinds, can never be luminous. The chances for luminosity look dim.

Williamson (2000) introduces the notion of a "cognitive home" in which "everything lies open to our view":

> To deny that something is hidden is not to assert that we are infallible about it. Mistakes are always possible. . . . The point is that, in our cognitive home, such mistakes are always rectifiable. (94)

Environments that are transparent provide their subjects with cognitive homes. The antiluminosity theorist denies that there are such homes, for excellent reasons, if the above remarks are anything to go by. But if common knowledge is luminous and if we possess common knowledge, the environments about which propositions can be commonly known must be cognitive homes in Williamson's sense. What needs to be shown is that there are such environments. I can only state the challenge here: addressing it is a project requiring various steps, to be undertaken in the course of this book. It is only in part 3 that I can finally provide an account of the kind of environment that makes perceptual common knowledge possible.

2 The Regressive Nature of Perceptual Common Knowledge

I already said that one main difficulty for a conception of perceptual common knowledge is the regress to which it gives rise. In triadic perceptual constellations, the perceivers acquire, at one glance, a kind of perceptual knowledge that apparently can only be spelled out in terms of an infinite sequence of $(n + 1)$ layers of what each perceiver knows. Recall Wilby's (2010) rendering of Schiffer's (1972) "mutual knowledge" analysis:

A speaker (S) and an audience (A) mutually know that p provided that:
1. S knows that p.
   A knows that p.
2. S knows that A knows that p.
   A knows that S knows that p.
3. S knows that A knows that S knows that p.
   A knows that S knows that A knows that p.
. . . etc.
. . . etc.
. . . etc. ad infinitum.

The problem here is not, in the first place, that it takes an infinite mind to compute the regress. If this were the main problem, you could argue, with Tomasello (2008, 96), that it suffices for S and A to compute the first few levels of the regress in order to commonly know that p. But as Wilby (2010, 86) points out, this proposal misconstrues the problem. The problem is that in a joint perceptual constellation, the whole triadic constellation is open to view: each subject is familiar with the whole perceptual scene. And she has to be familiar with it if she is to compute any levels of the regress at all. First, you need common knowledge of the triadic constellation; then you can work out what it is that each of its subjects knows about it.

This observation has led to the suggestion that there must be some finite property that both S and H possess and whose possession is sufficient for the inference of (n + 1) levels of hierarchic knowledge. Thus, Schiffer (1972, 31) introduces the property of "normalcy" concerning S and H's sensory faculties, intelligence, and experience. If a normal person is placed before an object with her eyes open, she will know that such an object is in front of her. A normal person knows that this is true for all normal persons and that all normal persons know this. Furthermore, all normal persons know that anyone who behaves in a certain way is normal, and all normal persons know this. Then it follows that if two normal persons are placed in a joint perceptual constellation in which each of them faces a candle on the table between them and the other person, they mutually know there is a candle on the table. As Schiffer (1972, 34) puts it, "In each case of mutual knowledge we have a finitely describable situation such that in virtue of certain general features of this situation it follows that two people have an infinite amount of knowledge about each other." The regress is contained by the appeal to rational perceivers' ordinary mental capacities and each perceiver's awareness of both perceivers' possession of these capacities.

Wilby (2010) thinks that this proposal, though it is on the right track, does not yet offer a satisfactory solution to the problem. Schiffer's (1972) proposal does not eliminate the regress; it merely renders it harmless because the iterations generated by the perceptual situation can be implicitly known by each subject even though neither explicitly entertains them. The appeal to implicit knowledge does not solve the problem because it does not explain the openness of the joint constellation that enables two subjects to act on what is jointly perceived. In order to act collectively, you need to not only recognize the implications of what you know for yourself; you also "have to be assured that the other did so too" (Wilby 2010, 94). Being so assured amounts to more than being in a position to draw the inference that mutual knowledge obtains about the presented scene. It amounts, he says, to being "aware" that this is so; the reciprocity of the perceptual scenario has to feature in the agent's conscious mental life if she is to act jointly with the other subject on what both mutually know. Wilby's solution is to relativize the unique regress-generating property to the situation at hand. Along his lines, mutual knowledge is not regressive; it is a "primitive relational property" that obtains, jointly, of S and H in the particular situation. This is an externalist move; it is not, as in Schiffer's proposal, that each subject individually has the property of normalcy that makes available infinite amounts of knowledge about each subject to each. The perceptual situation in which common knowledge is available itself hosts the property.

Wilby (2010) sees perceptual common knowledge as metaphysically quite distinct from ordinary perceptual knowledge; you cannot explain it by appeal to any particular feature of any single subject. This seems right (compare the related proposal in Campbell 2005, 2011a), and yet one cannot avoid a sense of lingering unease: just how much does the proposal accomplish? More needs to be said about what the relational property in question amounts to before we can assess the usefulness of the proposal. Wilby himself feels keenly the need to demystify mutual knowledge and proposes that one way of achieving this is by thinking about it as "a driving principle behind a child's psychological development" (Wilby 2010, 96), a developmentally early phenomenon that makes available explanations of how humans come to understand others. But it is not obvious just how the relational analysis can help here. Schauer points out in response to Wilby's suggestion:

> Since children need a sequence of communicative looks to engage in joint attention, it seems intuitive to assume that that sequence is accompanied by propositions in the form of "Amalia knows x"; and that all cognitive facilities needed for joint attention are present in every participant's own mind. (Schauer 2012)

Schauer's complaint is that Wilby's (2010) modification of Schiffer's (1972) proposal does away precisely with what makes this proposal attractive: it explains how perceptual common knowledge can be anchored in individual minds. Once you stipulate a relational property that obtains of S and A jointly, this explanation comes under threat. You then cannot, Schauer worries, explain how joint attention and common perceptual knowledge come about through a series of communicative acts that are, after all, carried out by individuals.

We can frame the problem in terms of the view I adopted in the previous chapter. Perceptual common knowledge is enjoyed by a plurality of subjects whose mental states of knowing are individuated by characteristics of their environment. This environment has two features: it is transparent relative to the commonly known proposition, and it explains the common character of the knowledge the subjects enjoy about it. How can it do this? As a first approximation, you might say that the environment has to be of a social kind: it contains not only the perceptual object but also the two perceivers. Only thus is a triadic perceptual relation, constituted by the perceivers and the object of their common knowledge, possible. The immediate problem with this suggestion is that it seems to run counter to any plausible view of perception: perceptions, and perceptual experiences, are enjoyed by individual perceivers. But if only individuals can be perceivers, it is utterly unclear how to make sense of the idea of a triadic perceptual constellation that involves two perceivers. You might try to reductively analyze the constellation in terms of an account of what each perceiver sees (and thus comes to know).[1] But that kind of account is unable to relativize the regress-generating property to the perceptual situation. Suppose that "seeing" that p implies "perceptually knowing" that p. Then if I see that you are looking at the candle, I know that you are looking at the candle. Correspondingly, if you see that I am looking at the candle, you know that I am looking at the candle. If the perceptual situation is not of a joint kind (each of us sees the other looking at the candle, but neither of us knows that the other knows that the other person is looking at the candle), there is no perceptual common knowledge. If it is of a joint kind, so that each of us knows that each of us knows that the other is looking at the candle, the regress arises. The fundamental problem remains unsolved: how can individual perceivers be constituents of a joint perceptual constellation?

To forestall undue suspense: the answer is to be found, I think, in the spatial organization of the environment in which joint perception is possible. The environment can accommodate the twin demands of transparency and commonality if the objects in it are in locations that are determined, by each perceiver, relative to the positions of both (or all). The candle is presented to me in a location that I identify relative to my own and your position, and vice versa. Then you and I each know the location of the candle, and we each know this, in socially organized space, in virtue of our common knowledge of where it is. We have then relativized the regress-generating property to the situation at hand. This, at any rate, is the proposal I shall develop.

II Demonstrative Reference and Communication

Introduction

In J. L. Carr's ([1980] 2000) novel *A Month in the Country*, a survivor of World War I, Tom Birkin, is hired to uncover a painted-over mural in a church in a Yorkshire village. Inch by inch, he cleans the painting, a Last Judgment, allowing himself to focus on only a tiny part of the vast wall until the whole artwork lies open to view. One evening, he is joined in his contemplation of the restored mural by an archaeologist, Moon, who is working on a nearby excavation site:

> I was so lost in it that I didn't hear Moon climb the ladder and yet wasn't startled finding him by me. When, after a few moments, he spoke, it was plain that he, too, had been lost in it. . . .
>
> "Look," he said. "Look at the faces. They're oddly alert. You could swear they're real people. Well, *were* real people. Those two herdsmen angels, the ones with the whips: I swear they're dancing, Amazing! Do you know, in some ways, it brings back the whole bloody business in France—particularly the winters. Those red evenings when the barrage was starting up and each man wondered if this was to be the night. . . ."
>
> . . .
>
> I didn't see it like that. No doubt I didn't want to. Oxgodby was another world: it had to be. To me, this was just medieval wall-painting, something peculiar to its time and nothing more. Well, we all see things with different eyes, and it gets you nowhere hoping that even one in a thousand will see things your way. (Carr [1980] 2000, 46–47)

"We all see things with different eyes," says Tom Birkin: but it is the same things we are seeing differently. And in order to be in a position to know that we are seeing them differently, we have to know that they are the same things in the first place.

Part 2 is concerned with our ways of acquiring perceptual common knowledge about the things we see together, albeit at times differently. You can, off the cuff, distinguish between two kinds of perceptual common knowledge. There is, first, the minimal common knowledge that is required for communication. Birkin and Moon can communicate about the scene in the mural that they experience so differently only because they know in common what it is that they are looking at. But then there is also the kind of perceptual common knowledge that can be acquired once communication is established. Perhaps Birkin had not so far paid full attention to the faces of the dancing angels in the way he is now, after Moon has pointed them out. Once we know what the object of our joint attention is, we can teach each other how to look at it. We can also justify perceptual claims about the thing: if Birkin were to doubt that the herdsmen angels had whips, Moon could simply show him where to look. Demonstratives and demonstrations play an indispensable role here: it is by instructing the other person about the location and nature of the targeted object that communicators can enlarge the stock of their perceptual knowledge about it. And it is in virtue of the joint nature of the perceptual constellation that demonstrative utterances and gestures can play this role. Compare the following two scenarios, in both of which speakers use demonstrative expressions in order to inform their hearers of a perceptual fact:

"Turner": You and I are jointly contemplating JMW Turner's seascape *Helvoetsluys*. I am wondering aloud about the significance of the curious red spot of paint on the surface of the water. You tell me that the spot is a buoy, dabbed on by Turner just before the painting was exhibited at the Royal Academy in order to provoke the public's attention and spite his arch-rival Constable. Perhaps I don't believe you at first. "This," I say, pointing at a particular location in the seascape, "is just a spot of paint!"—"No," you respond. "This is a buoy!" I look more closely and come to see that you are right and that the object at the location indicated by you really is a buoy; and I tell you so.

In this scenario, our joint attention to the painting allows you to provide me with new knowledge about it that thus becomes common knowledge between us. You use a demonstrative expression, supplemented with a pointing gesture, to get me to focus on an aspect of the perceived environment in a new way: you show me how to see it differently. The extension of our common knowledge about the jointly experienced seascape is a direct consequence of your utterance. Crucially, our common knowledge is perceptual. It isn't simply that I tell you a fact, and as a consequence of our communication, the fact becomes common knowledge between us. Rather, we know in common that the spot of paint on the water is a buoy because each of us sees that it is, and each of us knows that each of us sees that it is. In a sense, the Turner scenario is the flip side of the scenario in the Yorkshire church: I come to discover a new aspect of the jointly perceived surroundings through your demonstrative utterance; Birkin finds out that his way of seeing the mural is quite distinct from Moon's. In both cases, the protagonists share the first kind of perceptual common knowledge, but only in "Turner" does the enjoyment of it lead to an extension of what is perceptually known in common.

Now consider this scenario, broadly adapted from Campbell's "Collective Attack" (see p. 18):

"Remote Pointing": Suppose you see a range of objects arranged in the room you are in. I am in an adjacent room, which is equipped with a mechanism that allows me to highlight the objects in your room by operating spotlights mounted above them. There is one switch in my room that is labeled "the square one," another switch labeled "the round one," and so on, so I can communicate to you which object I intend to refer to. We can also talk to each other over an intercom connecting the two rooms. "This one is round," I say and operate the switch with the label "the round one." "Yes," you reply, "the object you highlighted is round."

In this scenario, also, we come to acquire common knowledge about an object by demonstratively communicating about it.[1] We come to commonly know that *this* object (indicated by my operation of the spotlight) is round, just as we come to commonly know in "Turner" that *this* object is a buoy. But only in "Turner" can you and I both perceptually verify the proposition I put to you. Because we jointly perceive the object, we can extend our stock of perceptual common knowledge about it simply by focusing on the object in the demonstrated location. By contrast, the scenario in which I identify the object by means of a mechanical pointing device does not allow us to extend our stock of common knowledge in this way. You might tell me that the round object I have identified is green, and we might thus come to commonly know that it is green. But we could not increase our stock of *perceptual* common knowledge of the thing by this kind of demonstrative reasoning.

The roles played by the pointing gestures in the two scenarios are thus quite distinct. In the first case, it is my demonstrative identification of the jointly perceived object that allows us to single it out. This identification does not draw on a description of the object's perceptual characteristics. I could simply ask you to "look at this one" while pointing at it, and as long as there was a visually identifiable object at the indicated location, we would know in common which object I intended to single out. By contrast, my mechanical demonstration in the second scenario gets off the ground only because I can rely on a description of the object's uniquely identifying perceptual characteristic: all I am doing is getting you to focus on an object that I identify as "the round one." I do not single out the object visually; I am not even seeing the thing. It takes the joint attention to the object that we enjoy in the first case to commonly know, immediately and noninferentially, that the object has the perceptual properties I am ascribing to it.

Joint perceptual constellations have a special kind of epistemic power: they provide their subjects with the kind of common knowledge about their objects that makes demonstrative communication possible, and they thereby enable them to extend their stock of perceptual common knowledge about these objects. The core question in part 2 is how they can have this power. I begin by considering in chapter 3 the semantic and communicative roles of speakers' demonstrative acts.[2] In virtue of what do their linguistic utterances refer, and what enables hearers to understand speakers' uses of a demonstrative expression? This is followed in chapter 4 by a discussion of the distinction between the sense and reference of demonstrative utterances in joint perceptual contexts. This distinction matters here because it raises the question of how we can communicate about a jointly perceived object if the thing is presented to each of us differently. In chapter 5, I investigate the spatial awareness of subjects in joint perceptual contexts and argue that these contexts are transparent to them. In chapter 6, I introduce the notion of social externalism and show how it can help with the threat of a regress besetting analyses of perceptual common knowledge. Finally, in chapter 7, I develop the suggestion that arguments containing demonstrative expressions in joint contexts play a unique justificatory role.

3   Intention and Communication

Perceptual common knowledge is typically acquired by way of linguistic communications in which subjects perform speech acts through the utterance of sentences that contain demonstrative expressions.[1] Often these utterances are accompanied by demonstrative gestures such as pointing. The environment of subjects who enjoy perceptual common knowledge hosts not only the object of communication but also the speakers and hearers themselves. This consideration turns out to be vital for the project of explaining its transparency. The first step, which I undertake in this chapter, is to come to a view about the kind of communication that produces perceptual common knowledge.

3.1   The Inferential Model of Communication

Recall the two protagonists from the opening of this chapter. Moon and Birkin do not merely happen to be looking at the same scene in the mural; they are communicating about what they see. Moon is making a linguistic utterance: "Look at the faces," he says, and perhaps he points at a particular location on the wall. He is thereby putting Birkin in the position to know where to look for the object of his demonstrative reference and what kind of thing to look for. It is no accident that Moon and Birkin, who produce propositional common knowledge by communicating about what they jointly see, are speakers and hearers as well as perceivers. Propositional common knowledge in perceptual contexts is tied to communication about what both perceive. Indeed, the very possibility of perceiving jointly, without which there can be no perceptual common knowledge, appears to depend on communication of some sort. Imagine a scenario in which two subjects are looking at the same scene and each of them sees the other looking at that scene, but in which there is no communication whatever. Imagine two strangers who, standing uncomfortably close to each other, are focusing on the same picture in a crowded gallery. Each of them is quite keenly aware of the other, and each is at pains not to let the other interfere with her viewing experience: there is no pointing, no verbalizing, no intentional gaze following, no exchange of glances. It is not credible that the two spectators should possess common knowledge about what they see. In such a scenario, each subject would be in a position to know that the other subject is looking at the same scene as she is herself. But, as has repeatedly been pointed out (for instance, Peacocke 2005, 299; Wilby 2010, 85), this is not sufficient for common knowledge. For p to be commonly known, it is necessary that each subject know that each subject knows that p. Meeting this demand requires them to communicate.

That the subjects of perceptual common knowledge are necessarily communicators has been observed and conceptualized in a variety of ways by psychologists, cognitive scientists, and philosophers.[2] But its epistemological relevance has not yet been fully understood. To make progress here, it will be necessary to come to a view on the success conditions of intentional communication about jointly perceived objects. Importantly, what is at stake is not a general account of communication but a model for cases in which speaker and hearer attend to a perceptual scene together and linguistically communicate about that scene. Even more specifically, I am (for now) interested only in communications that are carried out in the pursuit of propositional common knowledge about some perceptual feature of that scene. That is, I am, for now, not interested in the acquisition of the practical knowledge that underwrites joint activity (this is a topic for part 3). And I am not interested in speech acts other than assertions: in the relevant kind of communication, speakers are in the business of sharing perceptual knowledge with their hearers. The kinds of acts by means of which they achieve this have a characteristic form. Campbell observes:

> If I am to know which demonstrative thought you are having, there has to be some way in which it is indicated to me which thing you are thinking about. If you are expressing your thought to me, using a demonstrative term, there has to be what Kaplan (1977/1989) called the demonstration accompanying the demonstrative—a pointing gesture, some description indicating where to look, and so on. (Campbell 2005, 290)

The act by means of which a speaker communicates with the hearer in joint perceptual contexts usually has two components. It has a linguistic component: the utterance of an assertive sentence that typically contains a demonstrative expression. And it has a deictic component, such as a pointing gesture, that makes salient an aspect of the perceivers' surroundings.[3] There is a question about the semantic contribution of the pointing gestures with which speakers accompany their demonstrative utterances, which I consider in chapter 4. But whatever their semantic significance, there can be no doubt that they are communicatively crucial in joint contexts. Speakers' deictic gestures play an essential role in getting the hearer to understand what object the speaker intends to point out to her.

A good way to describe the success conditions of linguistic communication about jointly perceived scenes is in terms of Grice's "inferential" model of communication.[4] On this model, communication is, in essence, a matter of acting so as to get one's intentions recognized. The *locus classicus* of this model is Grice's:

> [S] meant something by x is (roughly) equivalent to "[S] intended the utterance of x to produce some effect in an audience by means of the recognition of this intention." (Grice 1957, 385)

Grice proposed this account as an analysis of speaker meaning, but his proposal was subsequently recognized as capturing the key element of what it means to intentionally communicate. Sperber and Wilson, whose influential "relevance theory" builds on the view that the recognition of intentions is crucial for understanding language, point out:

> The description of communication in terms of intentions and inferences is, in a way, commonsensical. We are all speakers and hearers. As speakers, we intend our hearers to recognise our intention to inform them of some state of affairs. As hearers, we try to recognise what it is that the speaker intends to inform us of. Hearers are interested in the meaning of the sentence only insofar as it provides evidence about what the speaker means. Communication is successful not when hearers recognise the linguistic meaning of an utterance, but when they infer the speaker's "meaning" from it. (Sperber and Wilson 1995, 23)

For my purposes, what the speaker intends to inform the hearer of is a perceptual fact about the jointly perceived environment. Call this intention the speaker's *informative intention*. In joint perceptual contexts, an intention to inform a hearer about a fact by means of demonstrative utterances and accompanying pointing gestures is necessarily an intention to produce perceptual knowledge in the hearer, and thereby an intention to produce perceptual common knowledge. In such contexts, when what the speaker says is true, and the hearer recognizes the speaker's intention in virtue of the speaker's utterance, the perceptual fact of which the speaker intends to inform the hearer automatically becomes common knowledge between speaker and hearer.[5]

What does it take for a hearer to recognize the speaker's informative intention? One requirement is that she must understand which object the speaker's demonstrative utterance refers to. Only then can she come to know the fact that the speaker intends to inform her of by means of his utterance. Evans (1982, 89–92) discusses Russell's view that a subject must know which object he is thinking about in order to make a judgment about that object. Whatever its merits for a general discussion of the concepts of thought and judgment, a version of it is attractive for thinking about the success conditions of intentional communication about jointly perceived objects: the speaker has to know which object his informative intention is about, and the hearer has to recognize the speaker's informative intention and thus come to know about which object the speaker intends to inform her, if they are to increase their stock of common knowledge about it. So much is implicit in the Gricean idea that communication is to do with intentions and their recognition and the adjacent consideration that intentional communication aims at the transmission of knowledge rather than merely reference. Along those lines, the transmission of perceptual knowledge about a jointly perceived object requires that the identity of the perceptual object of communication be itself commonly known. Call this the *communicative principle for joint contexts* (CP):

CP: In order for a speaker to be in a position to inform a hearer of a perceptual fact about a jointly perceived object by means of a demonstrative utterance, speaker and hearer must perceptually know in common which object the speaker is intending to refer to and communicate about.

As Evans (1982) observed, the expression "knows which" is far from precise. It provokes two questions. First, what are the individuation criteria for the object of communication? This question is a topic for the next chapter. Second, what role does speaker intention play in picking out that object? This question is the topic for the remainder of the present chapter. The demands

CP imposes on speakers are quite distinct from those it imposes on hearers, and I discuss them separately. But it is important not to exaggerate the importance of the distinction between speakers and hearers in ordinary linguistic exchanges: communicative acts are typically parts of conversations whose subjects take on both roles.

3.2   The Significance of Speaker Intentions

How do communicators come to perceptually know in common which object is singled out by the speaker's demonstrative utterance? The short answer is, by achieving the right kind of perceptual arrangement—the kind of triadic constellation that is usually called joint attention. One way to bring about this constellation is by a speaker's performance of a demonstrative act that makes salient the object of his referential intention to the hearer. A view is needed on the question of how speakers refer to the objects of their informative intentions: you need to know what determines the reference of a speaker's demonstrative utterance in order to develop an answer to the question of what it takes the hearer to know which object the speaker is intending to inform her about. Formulating such a view is the task for this section. The task here is not a comprehensive discussion of theories of demonstrative reference; it is the much more limited one of sketching a view that is useful in explaining what it takes to communicate demonstratively about a jointly perceived object.

Reimer (1992) organizes the debate about the semantics of demonstratives along the lines of three possible positions. You can either, with Kaplan (1989) and Bach (1992), think that only the speaker's intention is semantically significant. A demonstrative utterance refers to whatever the speaker intends to refer to in making it. Alternatively, you can think, with Wettstein (1984) and McGinn (1981), that demonstrative referential success is determined by contextualist cues, not by the speaker's intention in making the utterance. Finally, Kaplan (1979) and Reimer subscribe to views that assign semantic significance to both the speaker's intention and her pointing gesture. We can begin to think about the success condition of communications in joint perceptual contexts by briefly considering this debate. The speaker who succeeds in demonstratively communicating a fact about a jointly perceived object to a hearer must, along the lines of CP, know which object she is communicating about. So she must know which object she is referring to with her demonstrative utterance. What are the conditions she has to meet to enjoy this knowledge?

The Speaker's Referential Intention

I can ignore cases in which demonstrative reference to an object is achieved in the absence of a perception of the object. Perhaps demonstrative reference to an object is possible if the speaker is blindfolded.[6] Certainly it is possible that the blindfolded speaker can intend to inform the hearer about an object that she is pointing at and that she knows the hearer can see (Evans 1982, 171). But these cases are not relevant for present purposes, since speaker and hearer could not acquire perceptual common knowledge about a demonstratively identified object if they didn't jointly perceive the thing. For perceptual common knowledge to be available about an object, the speaker has to see the object. Furthermore, she must be able to point out to the hearer the object about which she intends to inform him. The object she is pointing out will be salient to her; it will be highlighted among all the things she is currently seeing.[7] What is not necessary, by contrast, is that the demonstrative thought the speaker is expressing is true. Consider a case discussed by Reimer (1992, 382–383) in which a speaker is confusing two perceptually present dogs, Spot and Fido. She says, "That is your dog, Fido," to the owner of Fido while pointing at Spot. A competent hearer will take the speaker to have referred to Spot and thus to have said something false. However, there can be no doubt that the communication has succeeded: the hearer has understood the speaker's utterance perfectly well.

This scenario, which I call "Fido," raises the question of whether it is the speaker's referential intention or her pointing gesture that determines the reference of her demonstrative act. In the kinds of cases under consideration, the speaker's pointing gesture plays a necessary role in securing communicative success. If the speaker did not perform such a gesture, the hearer could not know which dog the speaker had demonstratively identified, and he would then not be in a position to judge whether what the speaker said was true. So it can seem that the pointing gesture is not only communicatively but also semantically relevant. What cannot be right, though, is the view that the speaker's pointing gesture fixes the reference of his use of the demonstrative, since the speaker's intention to refer to the dog that he thinks is Fido then drops out of the picture completely.

And since the speaker does not know, on this account, which object he is demonstratively identifying, it then becomes impossible to explain how speakers and hearers can meet the demands of CP if what the speaker says of the demonstratum is false.

Bach (1992) proposes to accommodate the divergence between the speaker's description of the object he intends to demonstratively single out and the object he is deictically making salient to a hearer by ascribing two distinct intentions to the speaker: he has the intention to pick out the object he has in mind and the intention to refer to the object he is demonstrating. In "Fido," S has in mind Fido, but he refers, demonstratively, to Spot. Along Bach's lines, S's referential intention is part of a larger Gricean communicative intention whose fulfillment consists in its recognition by the hearer. As such, it needs to be distinguished from the speaker's intention to pick out the object he has in mind. Bach's distinction is useful for the question of communicative success because it can help explain how communication is possible in cases where the object the speaker has in mind is not the one he is making salient to the hearer. Along those lines, the demands of CP are met in "Fido" because of the hearer's recognition of the divergence between the object of the speaker's referential intention and the object he has in mind.

Siegel (2002) argues that Bach's distinction is underspecified: it draws on the notion of "public salience," but it may be that what is publicly salient is not perceptually but conversationally determined. I can ignore this kind of scenario for present purposes, since I am concerned only with the more limited case in which perceptual salience is decisive. However, Siegel also points out that the notion of public perceptual salience itself can be underspecified. This is the case in a different scenario discussed by Reimer, which I call "Keys." Suppose two sets of keys are visible on the table: the speaker's and someone else's. The speaker says, "These are my keys," and takes the set not belonging to her. Here it is not clear which set is more salient to the speaker. Siegel proposes that the speaker entertains two conflicting referential intentions: one that is anchored by a past visual link to her own keys and one that is anchored by a present tactile link to the keys not belonging to her. Since the latter is the present one, the speaker intends to refer to the keys she is taking. Siegel argues that her notion of "perceptual anchoring" makes clear predictions as to the referential intention of the speaker in cases in which the notion of public perceptual salience does not. "Keys" makes

vivid the importance of the visual component in the kind of perceptual
constellation that produces common knowledge: speaker and hearer could
not be said to stand in the kind of triadic relation that produces in them the
common knowledge of a perceptual proposition about the object if their
current perceptual link to the object were not of a visual kind. Suppose the
speaker is touching (but not seeing) the thing the hearer is seeing (but not
touching). The speaker may come to know by touch a variety of perceptual
facts about the keys (for example, whether they are hot and cold, heavy
or light), and the hearer may come to know a variety of visual facts about
the keys (for example, their shape and color). Speaker and hearer may even
come to know the same perceptual fact, such as the keys' shape, by means
of different kinds of sensory information. But the resulting knowledge is
not of the right kind, since speaker and hearer could not mutually know, in
virtue of the perceptual constellation, that they have it. As far as joint perceptual constellations go, the perceptual anchoring of a speaker's referential
intention can only be of a visual kind.[8]

Siegel does not give a full account of the notion of perceptual anchoring. She merely illustrates it with an example in which a speaker is able to
demonstratively refer to an object in virtue of his perception of it; the "in
virtue" relation is deliberately left unspecified. One way to think of this
relation is in terms of the speaker's visual attention to the object of demonstrative reference: it is because the speaker is able to highlight objects in
vision that he is able to demonstratively reason about and act on them.[9]
Campbell introduces and develops this account:

> Knowledge of the reference of a demonstrative is provided by conscious atten-
> tion to the object. And conscious attention to the object is what causes and
> justifies the use of information-processing routines in acting on the demon-
> strative thoughts about the thing, and it is what causes and justifies the use
> of information-processing routines in verifying propositions about the thing.
> (Campbell 2002, 28)

This approach is useful for specifying the role of visual perception in anchoring the use of a demonstrative in joint contexts because it substantiates the
functional role of experiential highlighting; it connects it to demonstrative
reasoning, and thus to the capacity to form referential intentions, in a way
that can be exploited by a hearer. Campbell accounts for this role of conscious attention by an appeal to vision science. This argument is not the
focus of my interest, though I briefly consider it in section 12.3. All I am

doing here is filling in Siegel's notion of perceptual anchoring insofar as it applies to joint perceptual constellations, in terms of Campbell's proposal, notwithstanding the very different outlooks on the nature of visual perception of these two philosophers.[10] The resulting view is that in the relevant cases, a speaker's current visual attention determines the object of her referential intention, and her referential intention determines the reference of her use of a demonstrative expression. On this view, perceptual attention comes first: it individuates the referent of the speaker's use of a demonstrative. And it is the hearer's recognition of the speaker's referential intention, which is brought about by the hearer's attention to the object that the speaker is demonstratively singling out, that produces the common knowledge needed to satisfy the demands of CP.

This view is, of course, very broad. But it is still concise enough to give me a useful starting point for the investigation of joint perceptual phenomena. I shall specify the view further as I go along.

The Hearer's Recognition of the Speaker's Referential Intention

In an ordinary demonstrative act, the speaker combines the utterance of a sentence that has the expression "this F" as its subject term with a pointing gesture. This gives the hearer three distinct cues in her attempt to determine which the object is of the speaker's referential intention. She can look for an F; if the predicate term of the sentence uttered by the speaker conveys a description of the object, she can look for an object fitting that description; and she can find out where to look for the object by following something like the procedure described by McGinn (1981, 163), in a contextualist vein, as a "rule of reference" for demonstratives. The hearer extends the axis that runs from the speaker's wrist to the point of his index finger until it meets a particular object (or an opaque surface pertaining to an object). She then recognizes this object as the one the speaker intends to demonstratively identify. Call this the hearer's *search procedure*:

Search procedure: H determines the referent of S's demonstrative utterance "this F" by following the axis that runs from S's wrist to the tip of his pointing finger until it meets the first F.

The axis specified by McGinn is illustrative. You can think of scenarios in which it is constituted in different ways (by the speaker's outstretched arm, for instance, or turn of his head). The important point is that the search procedure enables H to know which object S is intending to inform her about. It can do this because the speaker's deictic gesture allows her to single out the object of his referential intention. If *F* is a singular pronoun (as in "this one"), the object that S intends to refer to is simply the first thing with an opaque surface along the extended axis of S's outstretched finger. If *F* is a general term, H knows which kind of object to look for in the designated location. But it is not necessary that both conditions be met. In certain cases, communication can succeed even if there is no *F* in the demonstrated location. Suppose S points at a colorful moth and says to H, "This butterfly is pretty." H is likely to infer that S is intending to refer to the moth, which he is mistaking for a butterfly. Similarly, the location of *F* can diverge from the one determined by H's application of the search procedure. If the moth is slightly to the left of where S is pointing, H is likely to conclude that the speaker's gesture is imprecise and will take him, charitably, to refer to the animal. If there is no butterfly and there is no similar-looking object at or near the designated location, H will not know which object S is attempting to designate, and the communication will have failed.

It turns out, then, that not all of the cues made available to the hearer by the speaker's demonstrative act have to be accurate if the speaker's attempt at demonstrative communication is to succeed. The object of his intended reference need not be at the precise location indicated by his pointing gesture, and the object need not be of the kind specified by the singular term he uses or the description he offers. But the location indicated by the speaker is the hearer's primary cue in her attempt to determine the object of the speaker's intended reference: if she does not know where to look, demonstrative communication cannot get off the ground. By contrast, it can succeed if the speaker does not specify a particular kind of object in his demonstrative utterance, or if what he says of the object is false. As long as the hearer knows where to look, demonstrative communication is possible even if the descriptive cues offered by the speaker fail to specify the kind of item to be picked out by his demonstrative utterance.

4   Sense, Reference, and Communication

4.1   Sense and Communication

You can approach the question of the possibility of demonstrative communication with a reflection on the distinction between sense and reference. The notion of sense has its roots in Frege's ([1892] 1984) question of how identity statements can be informative. How can statements such as "The Morning Star is the Evening Star" convey new knowledge even though the two referring terms contained in the sentence pick out the same object? Frege's answer was that they have distinct senses. They present the same individual in distinct ways; the individual uniquely satisfies distinct conditions. The challenge for an account of communication in joint contexts is to square the divergence in the senses that speakers associate with a demonstrative expression with the possibility of communicating about an object by using that expression. How can we demonstratively communicate about an object if each of us experiences the thing differently? It appears that the demands imposed by CP—that successful communication requires the speaker's and hearer's common knowledge of which object they are communicating about—are so severe that the possibility of demonstrative communication comes under threat.

Heck (1995, 2002) considers the question of sense in communications involving singular terms. He discusses, and rejects, what he calls the "hybrid view" of Frege's distinction between sense and reference. This view combines an intensional account of belief with an extensional account of proper names. What individuates a belief is facts about the speaker's psychology: the conditions of satisfaction for the belief that p are of a mental (intensional) kind; whether p is true has no bearing on your mental state of believing that *p*. However, the reference of names is determined by a causal chain that links a use of the name to its original bearer (Kripke 1980): "Aristotle" refers to the person who was baptized Aristotle, regardless of what a community of users takes the name to refer to. The consequence of the hybrid view is that what gets transmitted in communication about the referents of names is reference, not knowledge. Referential success, on the hybrid view, is independent of the speaker's knowledge of which object is being picked out by his use of a singular term; since all uses of the same singular term carry the same reference, speakers can communicate, and transmit information, about the referent of the term they use in their communication without knowing that they do.

Heck argues that the aim of communication, in ordinary cases, is the transmission of knowledge about the object of reference and not merely referential success. Such knowledge requires "cognitive and epistemological" relations between beliefs about the referent that successful communication transmits between speakers. In order to preserve these relations, speakers cannot merely be referring to the same object when successfully communicating; they must also associate the terms they use with the right kinds of "cognitive significances."[1] What is required for understanding is "not preservation of reference, but *knowledge* of reference" (Heck 1995, 98). This is what it takes for people "to engage one another rationally; it makes it possible for thinkers to bring their beliefs to bear upon the cognitive lives of others and to allow their own cognitive lives to be influenced by those of others" (Heck 2002, 16). One way to do justice to this consideration is to suppose that the possibility of communication about a particular object depends on the sameness of the senses speakers associate with the singular terms they use to refer to that object. But this condition is too strong: two speakers can communicate using singular terms even if they think of their referents in different ways. Of course, there are limits here, and the question is how to account for the possibility of divergence in the cognitive significances speakers associate with singular terms while maintaining that the aim of communications involving such terms is the transmission of knowledge. Heck suggests that they have to be appropriately related but recommends resisting the temptation to search for a unifiying account of that relation: to do so would be to "define something shared into existence" (Heck 2002, 31).

Heck's insistence that the aim of communication is the transmission of knowledge is in line with the account of demonstrative communication developed in the previous section. In joint contexts, the passing of information from speaker to hearer necessarily results in their common knowledge of this information. And it could not be that you successfully communicate in joint contexts without enjoying the kind of knowledge at stake in CP. But Heck's somewhat pessimistic conclusion appears to run counter to the account of communication I have been developing: the joint constellation seems to be guaranteeing communicators' common knowledge of the speaker's intended object of reference. It is just the kind of "something shared" whose existence he denies. So I need to explain what it is that generates the minimal common knowledge that satisfies the demands of CP. How can it be that joint perceivers, when demonstratively communicating about an object, necessarily know which object they are communicating about?

Dickie and Rattan (2010) take Heck's papers as the starting point from which they develop a view on the nature of communication-facilitating senses associated with singular terms. They agree with Heck that a promising view of communication must take it to aim at the transmission of knowledge. But they do not share his skeptical conclusion. One of their considerations is that solving the problem of communication requires a notion of sense that can accommodate both "multiplying" and "consolidating" explanations. A multiplying explanation enables a subject to acquire knowledge about the referent of the co-referring singular terms contained in the premises of the argument that provides the subject with this knowledge by drawing on the different senses of these terms. In such cases, effort is required to work out that these terms have the same referent. For instance, it may be necessary to supply an identity statement about the co-reference of the names contained in the argument to make the argument valid. Consider:

P1: Robert Galbraith wrote *The Cuckoo's Calling*.

P2: Robert Galbraith is J. K. Rowling.

C: J. K. Rowling wrote *The Cuckoo's Calling*.

Here the conclusion follows from P1 only if you add P2. Without this further premise, the argument is not valid, and it cannot enlarge the stock of knowledge of the individual who considers it.

A consolidating explanation, by contrast, makes it possible to extend one's knowledge without requiring the premise that the singular terms contained in it have the same referent. A full understanding of these terms already provides the subject with the knowledge that they have the same referent. Thus, consolidating explanations make new knowledge available as soon as one fully understands the singular terms they contain. But to account for this possibility, Dickie and Rattan say, the Fregean notion of sense has to be discarded. That notion is intrapersonal and synchronic: Fregean senses are individuated in terms of their cognitive significances for individual subjects at particular times. But in certain situations, two subjects can immediately extend their knowledge about an object by considering arguments whose premises contain singular terms that co-refer to the object, despite associating them with different cognitive significances.

Dickie and Rattan (2010) suggest that two singular terms, used by certain subjects at certain times with certain modes of presentation (all of which can be distinct), have the same sense just when the "engagement-relevant factors in the situation of use generate the possibility of the immediate extension of knowledge." Vitally for present purposes, one such factor is two subjects' joint attention to an object. To illustrate their point, Dickie and Rattan (2010, 147) introduce a scenario in which two individuals are using a demonstrative to refer to a jointly perceived object. The first subject says, "That is F [at t_1]." The second subject says, "That is G [at t_1]." Then both subjects are warranted in concluding, "Something is both F [at t_1] and G [at t_1]." This is a case, as in "Turner," in which the two subjects gain knowledge from each other immediately, without having to establish that they are referring to the same object; the perceptual constellation takes care of that. Here, then, is a situation in which the subjects can rationally engage with each other's demonstrative claims, and it is hence a situation in which the two subjects' uses of *that* share a sense. It is this shared sense that explains how an immediate extension of the subjects' knowledge about the jointly perceived object is possible. The question is in virtue of what feature of the joint constellation the demonstrative expression can have this communicative sense. Dickie and Rattan are no doubt correct in thinking of such constellations as providing the demonstratives used to pick out objects in them with communicative senses. But how?

4.2 Demonstrations

This question makes it necessary to consider the role of pointing gestures in achieving communication: it is because the speaker's gesture allows the hearer to look for the object of his demonstrative intention in the indicated location that his demonstrative utterance can have a communicative sense. Kaplan ([1977] 1989) introduces the notion of true demonstratives, expressions such as *this* or *that*, that require complements such as pointing gestures to uniquely determine particular individuals in given contexts. On the Fregean view, as construed by Kaplan (516), demonstrations have senses, and demonstrative expressions are something like placeholders for the associated demonstrations. It follows that demonstratives themselves have senses, and the sense of a demonstrative is a constituent in the proposition expressed by a sentence that contains the demonstrative. This, Kaplan argues, gives rise to a problem, which he illustrates with a scenario in which a speaker points at someone named Paul and says,

He now lives in Princeton, New Jersey.

The expressed proposition is true only if Paul currently lives in Princeton and false if he does not. Kaplan asks us to suppose that Paul and Charles each had disguised themselves as the other. Then it would look to the speaker as if Paul were Charles, and vice versa. If Paul looks like Charles, then Charles becomes the referent of the indexical expression "He," and since Charles does not live in Princeton the proposition expressed by the utterance comes out false even if Paul lives in Princeton. This scenario shows, Kaplan argues, that the demonstrated object, rather than the sense of the demonstrative used to single it out, is a constituent in the expressed proposition. Demonstratives refer directly: as Kaplan says in "Afterthoughts" (1989), "The relation between the linguistic expression and the referent is not mediated by the corresponding propositional component, the content or what-is-said" (568); the referential term does not "first pass through the proposition" (569). A demonstration then does not introduce a descriptive element into the content of the utterance: "It determines and directs attention to what is being said, but the manner in which it does so is not strictly *part* of what is asserted" (Kaplan 581).

But Fregean senses nevertheless have an important role to play in Kaplan's account. He endorses the view that demonstrations accompanying utterances of true demonstratives constitute modes of presenting the same object in standpoint-specific ways to different speakers (Kaplan [1977] 1989, 514):

> The same individual could be demonstrated by demonstrations so different in manner of presentation that it would be informative to a competent auditor-observer to be told that the demonstrata were one. For example, it might be informative for me to tell you that
>
>> That (pointing to Venus in the morning sky) is identical with that (pointing to Venus in the evening sky).

On this view, the demonstration presents the object so as to enable occupants of different standpoints to extend their knowledge about it. To do this, they have to realize that the referent of their demonstrative utterances is the same in each case. The question is how demonstrations accomplish this: how can a single demonstration enable a pair of speakers and hearers to extend their common knowledge about the demonstrated object?

One option Kaplan considers is that the speaker's demonstrative gesture contains two demonstrations, one from the perspective of the speaker and one from the perspective of the hearer. Another option he introduces is to think of one demonstration as having two audience-specific senses:

> There are some relevant respects in which descriptions and demonstrations are disanalogous . . . to different audiences (for example, the speaker, those sitting in front of the demonstration platform, and those sitting behind the demonstration platform), the same demonstration may have different senses. Or perhaps we should say that a single performance may involve distinct demonstrations from the perspective of distinct audiences. (Kaplan [1977] 1989, 515)

But the problem both of these proposals face is the same as the one discussed in the previous section: once you suppose that a referring expression singles out an object by way of distinct audience-specific senses (or, in this case, by way of distinct accompanying demonstrations that are individuated in terms of their audience-specific senses), it is difficult to explain what enables these audiences to know that their referring expressions, or demonstrations, pick out the same object. Once again, the possibility of communication comes under threat.

Progress can be made by considering the function of demonstrations. In his discussion of Kaplan's treatment, Campbell draws a distinction between their attention-fixing and communicative uses and criticizes Kaplan for not clearly distinguishing between the two:

There is an oscillation in Kaplan's account of demonstratives between viewing "demonstrations"—the (in general, non-linguistic) complements of a use of a demonstrative term such as "this" or "that"—as instruments of communication, and viewing a demonstration as the way in which the individual thinker achieves a perceptual fix on the object. When we are thinking of demonstration as an instrument of communication, it is simply the method by which, by hook or by crook, you get your audience to attend to the right object. One method would be to grasp your hearer's head and turn it firmly towards the object, meanwhile waggling the object itself. On that kind of understanding of the role of the demonstration, it really is a ladder you climb to secure understanding, but you throw it away at the conclusion. (Campbell 2002, 105)

It is the attention-fixing use that is semantically relevant in Campbell's view and that, he argues, Kaplan should be concerned with when thinking about Frege's question of how what Campbell calls the "trading on the identity" of the referents of demonstrative expressions can be informative. You trade informatively on the identity of the referents of two demonstrative terms if the different senses associated with those terms extend your knowledge about the object. The remainder of this chapter revolves around the question of how we should think of the relation between communicative and reference-fixing demonstrations and its implications for the question of interpersonal sense.

4.3   Referential and Communicative Uses of Demonstrations

Campbell's insistence on a careful differentiation between the semantic and demonstrative uses of demonstrations is supported by the considerations put forward in chapter 3: communication is achieved by the hearer's recognition of the speaker's informative intention, of which his referential intention is a part. In one way, this model privileges the semantic over the communicative role of demonstrations: without a referential intention, communication (of the Gricean kind) does not get off the ground. Furthermore, the idea that the referential intention expressed by the speaker's use of a demonstrative can be perceptually anchored, and that we can think of this anchoring in terms of the speaker's visual attention to the object of his referential intention, privileges the speaker's referential over his communicative use of demonstrations: a speaker's communicative use of a demonstration is his means to get the hearer to understand the reference of his use of the demonstrative; for this to be possible, the reference has to be fixed already.

However, we saw that Bach (1992) conceives of a speaker's referential intention as part of a larger communicative intention. And there is an important further reason for thinking that Kaplan's oscillation between the referential and communicative uses of demonstrations is not accidental and that in joint contexts, these uses are more tightly intertwined than Campbell's stark distinction allows. Begin by considering a scenario he introduces, in which three characters are watching a play:

> Suppose we consider a case in which you are sitting on my left, Bill is sitting on my right, and there are some actors on the stage. You whisper in my left ear, "That actor (the one wearing a hat) is about to faint," while Bill whispers in my right ear, "I met that actor (the one playing King Lear) once." Can I immediately trade on identity, to conclude that, if what I have just been told is right, Bill has met someone who is about to faint? (Campbell 2002, 106)

There is no good reason to deny that trading on identity is in fact possible in this scenario (which I call "Theater"). This is so, as Campbell (2002) points out, despite a difference in the demonstrations that accompany the speakers' utterances. What explains the legitimacy of the inference is, in his view, the distinction between attention-fixing and communicative uses of demonstrations: the speakers' distinct communicative demonstrations enable the subject to focus on the object in the same way in both cases, and it is the subject's focus that allows him to legitimately trade on the actors' identity. What makes this explanation available is Campbell's sharp distinction between reference-fixing and communicative demonstrations. It is because the perceiver attends to the object in the same way, despite the speakers' distinct demonstrations, that he can know that their demonstrations are aimed at the same object.

On this view, the joint constellation has no particular role to play in the subject's extension of his knowledge about the demonstrated object. To see this, compare "Theater" and "Remote Pointing." There, a speaker gets a hearer to achieve a visual fix on an object that is visible to the hearer but not the speaker by operating a mechanism in her room that highlights the object in his. What enables the speaker to select the intended object is a descriptive label that is attached to the mechanism: if the speaker intends to get the hearer to focus on the round object, she operates the mechanism labeled "the round one." As in "Theater," the hearer/perceiver is able to extend his knowledge about the demonstrated object because of his visual fix on it; seeing that the object is highlighted allows him to know that the thing is the object of the speaker's intended reference. In contrast to Campbell's example, though, the speaker does not see the object. She singles it out descriptively, by means of the label attached to the switch operating the spotlight above the object. The speaker's demonstration has descriptive content, and it is this content that governs the hearer's selection of the object. The speaker's attention to the object is, if you want, optional; it has no epistemic role to play that could not also be played by a suitable description.

Just the same point applies in "Theater": the speakers' pointing gestures could be replaced by the descriptions under which they pick out the actor on the stage ("the one wearing a hat" and "the one playing King Lear"). The speakers' demonstrations supply quasi-descriptive content, and it is this content that governs the hearer's selection of the object of reference. That is why the joint perceptual constellation has no unique cognitive role in the hearer's selection on Campbell's (2002) approach. As soon as you endorse the view that speakers' demonstrations in joint perceptual contexts merely play an assisting role in the hearer's selection of the object of reference, you have no room to accommodate any special role such contexts may play in extending the subjects' knowledge about the demonstrated object.

But there is a special role for these contexts. Remember "Turner" from the introduction to part 2. The scenario makes available this argument:

P1: "This is a spot of paint" (said by me).

P2: "This is a buoy" (said by you).

C: Something is both a spot of paint and a buoy (known in common by us both).

The argument is consolidating in Dickie and Rattan's (2010) sense. We come to know, simply in virtue of the joint perceptual constellation, that our demonstrative expressions have the same referent. But we end up knowing more than that: we come to know, again in virtue of our respective perceptual experiences, that the premises of the argument are true and that the argument is sound. We have increased our stock of perceptual common knowledge about the object by means of our joint contemplation of it. This increase of our knowledge has been facilitated by the distinct ways in which the object is presented to each of us, but it came about because we both knew which object we were communicating about. It came about because our respective uses of the demonstrative expression had a communicative sense.

If you begin with Campbell's (2002) view that it is the individual perceiver's focus on the object that explains the extension of her knowledge about the jointly perceived object, you cannot account for a case like "Turner." You cannot explain how the perception of an object that is presented to each perceiver differently can lead to the extension of the perceivers' perceptual common knowledge simply in virtue of the perceptual constellation. You could not explain "Turner" in terms of "Remote Pointing," as is possible for "Theater." I do not come to know that the jointly perceived object is a buoy because of a description you offer; I come to know this because your demonstrative utterance teaches me to see it as you do. The perceivers in "Turner" can come to know that the argument considered in their exchange is sound simply by looking jointly at the picture.

This epistemic power of joint perceptual constellations cannot be explained on an account that treats the referential and communicative uses of demonstrations in strict separation. The point may not be immediately apparent if you take the speaker's perspective as your starting point; then it really can seem undeniable that reference-fixing demonstrations are logically prior to their communicative counterparts. But you can also approach the matter from the perspective of the hearer, whose job it is not to identify an object demonstratively but to recognize the speaker's referential intention. Evans recommends such a move when he suggests that we begin an account of demonstrative identification with the question of what it takes to understand, rather than make, a demonstrative reference:

> If we focused upon the notion of *making* a demonstrative reference, . . . we should not even be able to discern any essential connection between demonstrative identification and information-links. But if we focus rather on what is involved in *understanding* a demonstrative reference, then that connection—which seems pretty much at the heart of any interesting notion of demonstrative identification—can be preserved. (Evans 1982, 171)

What motivates this view is Evans's consideration that you can succeed in demonstratively identifying an object even though you are not perceptually linked to it. You can, in his example, demonstratively identify the person in front of you by means of an indexical expression such as "that man" even if you are blindfolded. But a blindfolded hearer could not understand your demonstrative utterance; she would simply not know which man you are intending to demonstratively identify.

Evans does not think that the ability to communicate to others which object you are intending to identify should be credited with semantic significance (Evans 1982, 171). His point is that considering the notion of understanding, rather than making, a demonstrative utterance highlights the importance of information links (such as perception) in demonstrative identification. And understanding is paramount also for a kind of epistemic function that is quite distinct from the notion of the transmission of information Evans is pursuing. It is vital for the creation of perceptual common knowledge, which cannot be generated in the absence of a hearer's recognition of a speaker's demonstrative referential intention. The view I am recommending draws a fundamental epistemological distinction between the environments populated by individual perceivers and those in which joint perceivers operate. Individual perceivers operate in environments in which attention to an object produces perceptual knowledge about it. They can, of course, communicate with others in order to pass on this knowledge. But the epistemic constellation changes quite dramatically when the hearer enters the scene. In joint environments, perceivers' attention to an object produces perceptual *common* knowledge, and the speaker's reference-fixing use of a demonstration is already a communicative use. It remains true that there is a referential intention entertained by the speaker that the hearer needs to recognize in order to understand which object the speaker is intending to demonstratively identify. But it is a mistake to suppose that the epistemic function of joint environments is restricted to the kind at work in "Theater": if the communicative use of the demonstration is secondary to the speaker's referential use, in the sense that the referential use is of just the same kind regardless of whether the speaker is operating in a joint context, we cannot explain the particular epistemic role of joint environments and the ways in which they enable us to justify perceptual claims. The joint context is not an add-on to the speaker's perceptual environment in which his demonstrative capacities remain unchanged. It fundamentally alters the way in which she demonstratively identifies objects: she identifies them so as to make demonstrative communication possible. Only thus is it possible to explain what distinguishes joint cases from "Remote Pointing."

Imagine a case in which an individual's contemplation of an object turns into a joint constellation. Suppose I am looking at the Turner seascape and the buoy in it by myself, and you subsequently join me. My first, reference-fixing demonstration is undertaken in a nonjoint context. When you join me, I use a demonstration communicatively in order to get you to look at the buoy. Campbell's (2002) picture suggests that my reference-fixing demonstration remains completely unaltered throughout this process. Consider, though, what it takes me to get you to attend to the buoy. I do not keep my gaze rigidly set on its location in the seascape while gesturing vaguely at it in the scant hope you will be attracted enough to find out what it is I am focusing on. The process is much more intricate than that: I alter my gaze between you and the object; I find out your exact location and tailor my pointing gestures accordingly. In so doing, I locate the object in a fundamentally different way than I did originally. I locate it in a spatial format that allows an exercise in triangulation whose starting points are your location and mine. I do this for the double purpose of engaging you and adapting my pointing gesture to the spatial arrangement at hand. It remains true that I have to attentively single out the object in order to form a referential intention about it, but the way in which I attend to the object in a joint context is quite different than it is in an instance of individual attention. I now locate it in a social spatial framework in which I treat your and my locations as origins of perception. In such a framework, the reference-fixing use of a demonstration already is a communicative use. Reference-fixing activity (looking, squinting, leaning forward) already is a communicative activity. And only in such a framework can the full epistemic power of joint constellations be brought to bear.[2]

Kaplan is not explicitly concerned with joint constellations. But the examples he uses are of a communicative, joint kind: he (and, similarly, Bach 1992) is interested in contexts in which the speaker's pointing gesture plays a role in getting the hearer to understand the speaker's referential expression, though he is inquiring into their semantic contribution in these contexts. You can give substance to his view that pointing gestures make an informal, nondescriptive contribution to uses of demonstrative expressions by appeal to the idea that they play out in joint contexts. Consider again the quote from Kaplan I introduced earlier:

It [the pointing gesture] determines and directs attention to what is being said, but the manner in which it does so is not strictly *part* of what is asserted. (Kaplan 1989, 581)

Think of the pointing gesture as occurring in a communicative context. Then it is used by the speaker to achieve *joint* attention to the object. The capacity to pick out a particular object by attending to it remains with the speaker, but the attention that anchors his referential intention perceptually is of the kind that is aimed at the production of common perceptual knowledge. The pointing gesture is not an add-on to his reference-fixing attention but a reinforcement, an underscoring of the directedness of what already is a communicative activity. It does not itself have semantic import, but it helps bring about the joint constellation in which perceptual common knowledge is produced by means of the hearer's understanding of the speaker's hearer-directed utterance. This idea will be developed further as I continue.

5   Spatial Awareness and Perceptual Common Knowledge

In this chapter, I suggest that the notion of social space can be put to use for an account of communicative sense. Although there are good reasons for thinking that location does not by itself individuate a demonstratum, location in social space can explain how demonstrative communication, and the creation of perceptual common knowledge, is possible about objects that are presented to their perceivers under distinct presentations. I first make the case for location in social space as a communication-enabling factor and then argue in support of the transparency of environments in which common knowledge of the object's location is available.

5.1   Spatial Awareness of Objects in Joint Constellations

On the picture I have been developing, a hearer's recognition of the speaker's referential intention in joint contexts immediately produces in them a minimal kind of perceptual common knowledge. As soon as the hearer recognizes the speaker's demonstrative intention, they know in common which object they are communicating about, and this is where their linguistic communication begins. The demonstrations with which speakers supplement their utterances play a crucial role here: they have interpersonal senses that make communication about jointly perceived objects possible.

What, then, is it about a speaker's pointing gesture that enables a hearer to understand which object he intends to single out? As I noted earlier, Kaplan ([1977] 1989) has no fully developed theory of demonstrations: he considers both the possibility that one gesture contains two distinct, audience-specific demonstrations and that one demonstration has two audience-specific senses. But neither of these views is promising with regard to the question of their communicative senses, since the communication-enabling factor must be a feature of demonstrations that are the same for all speakers.

One obviously important communication-enabling factor is the demonstrated object's location. Kaplan ([1977] 1989, 527) introduces Michael Bennett's proposal to think of the demonstratum as the object at the place indicated by the speaker's demonstration. On this view, the speaker's demonstrative utterance needs to be complemented with a noun phrase that describes the demonstrated location:

that [pointing at a person]

becomes:

dthat [the person who is there [pointing at a place]] (quoted after Campbell (2002, 107)).[1]

The proposal, though intriguing, is not without its difficulties.[2] Perhaps most importantly, it provokes the question of how to think of a location's spatial boundaries.[3] Suppose (the example is taken from King 2014, 221) I point precisely at a person while saying, "This person is F." I am then not only pointing at the person but also at objects on the person, such as her shirt or a shirt button, and constituent parts of the person, such as her head, torso, or fingernails. The pointing gesture alone does not secure the hearer's knowledge of the speaker's intended reference. It is also not obvious how the proposal copes with cases in which a speaker intends to refer to a different object from the one he is (accidentally) pointing at (Siegel 2002, 17) or cases in which the speaker's gesture is vague (Reimer 1992, 380). These problems all have to do with the communicative dimension of pointing gestures: they all raise questions about the cognitive significance of the spatial cue afforded by the speaker's pointing gesture. They seem troublesome, but they can be solved once we have in place a view on the role of spatial awareness in joint perceptual constellations.

The first step is to bear in mind that demonstrations in the cases under consideration are not freestanding communicative devices. They complement speech acts in which the speaker specifies the kind of object she intends to demonstratively identify. Recognizing the speaker's intention thus requires, ordinarily, that the hearer discern an object of the right kind in or near the indicated location. The hearer plays an active role in the communicative event: he is an interpreter rather than just a recipient of the speaker's utterance and may charitably take her to intend to refer to an object different from the one she is pointing at. In this way, the hearer can rectify the speaker's mistaken (or, similarly, vague) pointing gestures and secure communicative success. And his interpretive competence secures success also in cases in which the location indicated by the speaker is shared by a plurality of objects. If the axis constituted by the speaker's outstretched arm precisely meets the button on a person's shirt and the speaker says, "This person looks happy," the competent hearer will have no problem recognizing the speaker's referential intention.

It is, of course, possible to construe scenarios in which no appeal to a hearer's interpretive competence guarantees communicative success. Suppose the speaker says, "This one looks nice," and points at a button on a shirt worn by a person: unless further contextual cues are available, the hearer is not in a position to know which is the object of the speaker's attention. By the lights of CP, the conditions of demonstrative communication are not met. But it seems overly rigid to conclude that the communication is therefore an outright failure. The communication would fail outright if the speaker were to wave wildly at the open skies and say, perhaps, "This button is missing": the hearer would have no idea how to begin to interpret the speaker's utterance. As long as the speaker's demonstration provides the hearer with some idea of the location of the object of the speaker's referential intention (and the speaker's assertion of the existence of a particular kind of object at the indicated location is not patently absurd), the communicative lines are kept open, so to speak. Location is an indispensable search parameter in demonstrative communication; common knowledge of the location of the object of the speaker's referential intention secures communicative success. If several objects overlap at one location, the communication succeeds just when the speaker's utterance enables the hearer to determine the boundaries of the location of the object of the speaker's referential intention. This suggests the following modification of CP:

CP/1: In order for a speaker to be in a position to inform a hearer of a perceptual fact about a jointly perceived object by means of a demonstrative utterance, speaker and hearer must perceptually know in common the bounded location of the object the speaker is intending to refer to and communicate about.[4]

CP/1 expands on Bennett's proposal so as to account for the notion of communicative sense: speakers and hearers can communicate about perceptual objects with standpoint-dependent modes of presentation if they can single them out in terms of their bounded spatial locations. But you may think that demonstrative communication is possible about perceivable features at locations that do not have well-defined boundaries. The next section investigates this possibility.

5.2   Spatial Awareness of Features in Joint Constellations

Consider this (admittedly more than slightly recherché) scenario:

"Blue Room": You and I are in an otherwise empty, sphere-shaped room that is painted entirely in the same shade of blue. We do not touch any part of the spherical wall; rather, we are suspended midroom by an invisible mechanism. This, with the aid of clever lighting, has the effect of making it impossible for us to discern distances; we cannot tell how far away we are from the sphere's wall and how large the room is by, for example, considering the shadows of our bodies that are produced by the lighting of the room. The visual experience is simply of an indiscriminate expanse of blue all around, with you and I as the only visual objects in it. You stretch out your arm into the blue expanse and say, "This is blue."

Is demonstrative communication possible about the blueness surrounding speaker and hearer? My strong intuition is that it is.[5] The speaker's utterance puts the hearer in a position to assess her claim; the speaker can justify her claim by appeal to the surroundings' perceptual characteristics. But the communication in "Blue Room" does not meet the demands of CP/1: the blueness that the speaker intends to refer to has no spatial boundaries. It appears to be possible for a speaker to demonstratively refer to a feature at a location and for the hearer to recognize her intention to refer to the feature at the indicated location, in the absence of a discrete object at that location (and thus of a boundary singling out the location).

The idea that locations can be the focus of attention is not new. Although recent work in attention research is concerned with the role of discrete objects in guiding visual attention,[6] the view that attention operates on locations is supported by evidence from early spatial cueing studies, such as that of Posner, Snyder, and Davidson (1980). They showed that a cue to a location at which a target is subsequently going to appear speeds up the response to that target; conversely, it slows the response if the target appears elsewhere. This is explained in terms of the perceiver's attention to the indicated location prior to the appearance of the target. This evidence suggests that visual attention can be directed at spatially extended locations rather than discrete objects. It gives us a reason to take "Blue Room" seriously.

If the subjects in "Blue Room" manage to communicate, the question arises how to individuate the referent of the speaker's demonstrative intention. If the speaker's referential intention is perceptually anchored, his intention cannot be to refer to the entire room, since the entire room cannot be the object of his perceptual attention (for one thing, he cannot see behind his back). But neither is it unproblematic to suppose that the speaker's intention is to refer to a precisely defined area (say, a circle with a diameter of ten inches whose center is located exactly three feet along the axis constituted by his outstretched arm), since he is not in a position to single out this area in vision: he could not discriminate between the target of his focus and its surroundings. The most plausible view is that the speaker's attention in "Blue Room" is directed at the area broadly indicated by her pointing gesture; it is the area surrounding the axis indicated by her outstretched arm, and it has no well-defined boundary.

What does it take for the hearer to recognize the speaker's referential intention if its target is a feature at a location that has no perceivable boundaries? Hearers search for targets in the locations indicated by the speakers by attending to the broad regions indicated by their pointing gestures. Since, in "Blue Room," this region has no more of a definite boundary than the one whose blueness the speaker intends to refer to, the success of demonstrative communication in "Blue Room" cannot depend on an exact match of the locations that are being attended to by speaker and hearer, respectively. But if they are communicating, they must be attending to the same object or feature at the same location (and, by CP, know that they are); otherwise the hearer could not be in a position to assess the truth of what the speaker has said; the speaker could not justify his perceptual claim to the hearer, and speaker and hearer could not extend their common knowledge about the referent by appeal to the joint constellation. The best we can do here, as far as I can see, is to appeal to the triadic character of the constellation and say that the location of the feature about which the perceivers enjoy common knowledge is the area around the meeting point of the axes constituted by their directions of gaze. The scope of this area must be left unspecified.

The consideration that demonstrative communication is sometimes possible about features at locations without clear boundaries appears to undermine the transparency of environments that house joint constellations. If the location of a feature that is the target of a speaker's demonstrative intention has no well-defined boundaries, we appear to lose track of the condition that has to be met if communication about this feature is to succeed. This conclusion would spell seriously bad news for the overall line of argument developed so far. If the environments of demonstrative communicators are not transparent, the hearer does not always know which object (or feature) the speaker intends to demonstratively identify. Then the communicators do not always know which object they are communicating about, and in that case, they cannot know in common which object they are communicating about. But then they are not always in a position to knowingly transmit knowledge about the objects they jointly perceive through their demonstrative utterances; and then the whole idea that demonstrative communication is chiefly concerned with the transmission of common knowledge, which is distinguished from information by its conscious presence in the minds of the communicators, comes under threat. One move you could make at this juncture is to abandon the idea that two perceivers know a perceptual proposition in common just when they are in mental states whose conditions of satisfaction are entirely determined by the environment they operate in (quite what the nature of this environment is hasn't been spelled out yet). But then you have to find a solution to the problems besetting CJTB set out in section 1.2, and I suspect the prospects are dim. Another move you can make is to accept that Sperber and Wilson (1995) are right after all: since it cannot be shown that there are perceptual constellations that necessarily lead to common knowledge and since common knowledge is necessarily luminous, there can be no such thing. Once again, the whole idea that demonstrative communication has to be seen as embedded in cognitive relations and as concerned with the transmission of cognitive values then has to be abandoned.

5.3   The Transparency of Joint Constellations

In this section, I provide a first reason in support of the view that joint perceivers operate with a distinct kind of spatial framework and that this framework guarantees transparency. Suppose you follow Kaplan's anti-Fregeanism about demonstratives: you agree that demonstratives refer directly, without the mediation of Fregean senses. Then the pressing question arises as to what determines the reference of a use of a demonstrative. Campbell (2002) thinks that experience plays a vital role here: it is because experience directly relates the perceiver to the object that he can form a demonstrative thought and acquire perceptual knowledge about it. But this move alone does not solve the problem that motivates Kaplan's subscription to a direct view of demonstrative reference. The problem begins with the apparent possibility of demonstratively picking out objects in a way that allows you to think about them independently of their mode of presentation. If so, it cannot be the object's standpoint-dependent mode of presentation that determines the reference of the use of the demonstrative employed to single it out. It is then not open to the subscriber of a direct account of demonstrative reference to suppose that the phenomenal characteristics of an object of experience determine the demonstratum.

One way to address the problem is to appeal to the role of location in fixing demonstrative reference. Campbell (2002, 107) points out that speakers can visually single out (and thus, on his view, demonstratively identify) objects about whose location in objective space they are mistaken. He argues that despite the possibility of a speaker's illusion about a demonstrated object's actual location, there is nevertheless a kind of infallibility to the object's location as it is experienced by the speaker:

> I say that location shows up in which judgements involving the demonstrative are immune to error through misidentification. This does not mean that the demonstrative identification is identifying the object descriptively, as "whatever is now at place p", for example. You can visually identify an object even though you are subject to an illusion about its location, if the light is being bent, if you are viewing it through an unsuspected mirror or prism, for instance. But in vision you are identifying which object you are calling up the file on by the location you see it to have. So vision cannot have got it right about the existence of an object at that place, but called up the wrong file for the object that is at that place. (Campbell 2006, 250)

Along those lines, there is a fundamental difference between an object's experienced location and its experienced phenomenal characteristics: you cannot visually identify an object in terms of its experienced characteristics if they misrepresent the thing's phenomenal properties (as, for instance, in the case of illusions). But the parallel observation does not hold for the object's experienced location. Even if the object is presented to you as being in a location it does not in fact occupy, you can use its experienced location to demonstratively single it out. The object and its experienced location cannot come apart in the way the object and its experienced properties can. This consideration supports the idea that experienced location plays a crucial role in the demonstrative identification of an object: it is because you necessarily know where the object is that you can identify it without recourse to descriptive content. And it is thus that you can demonstratively reason and acquire knowledge about it.

A parallel case can be made for the presentation of objects in social space. Just as an object's experienced location plays a vital role in demonstrative reasoning, so its location in social space is indispensable for the acquisition of perceptual common knowledge about it. Consider the following scenario:

"Shop Window": Suppose you and I are choosing between several sweaters on display in a store window. They are all quite similar in cut and color so they cannot be readily discriminated descriptively. I say, "That's the one I want," and point at one of the sweaters. Suppose there is a video camera filming the scene, and the video is projected in real time onto a screen above the display. You look at the screen and see me pointing at a particular sweater. Now you know which one I have chosen. You have no difficulty in obtaining this knowledge even though you could not know, on the basis of your perception of the sweater's video image, its actual spatial location.

What remains unchanged in "Shop Window" is the relative positions of you, me, and the indicated sweater in relation to each other, and this suffices for you to find out which one I am considering. Suppose I am not quite sure whether you have understood which one I want and ask you to indicate it. It does not matter whether I consult the actual scene or the video to find out whether we are demonstratively identifying the same thing. It suffices that my perception allows me to locate the object relative to your spatial position regardless of the actual place you and the object of your demonstrative reference occupy. Joint constellations tolerate divergences between the demonstrated object's actual and experienced locations as long as their subjects' experiences allow them to get right the spatial relation between its constituents. The joint perceivers thus enjoy a certain infallibility about the experienced location of the object; they could not have gotten its experienced location wrong, relative to each other's spatial positions, even though they may be mistaken about its location in objective space.

This is a claim you might find puzzling. Surely the perceivers can err in their efforts, so that the hearer ends up singling out the wrong object? The short answer (to be elaborated on in the next section) is that while this is, of course, true for each individual perceiver, it does not hold for them jointly: they could not be attending to the thing together if the hearer had not identified the object of the speaker's referential intention in social space. This observation gives us a first reason to think that there really is a social spatial framework: no other frame of reference could explain the possibility of public demonstrative reasoning and the acquisition of common knowledge it facilitates about its objects. And it illustrates the transparency of environments that are ordered by such frameworks: in environments that house joint constellations, the subjects always know where the object is relative to their respective positions. They know this because the location of the thing is defined relative to their respective positions. They can work out its location regardless of whether they know its location in objective space. If they fail to determine the target's position, they cannot be jointly attending to the object, and they are not operating in social space. In this way, environments that are ordered by social spatial frameworks are transparent to their subjects and thus provide them with cognitive homes: in such environments, the subjects always enjoy, minimally, the common knowledge of the communicative object's location relative to their respective positions.

5.4 Social Disjunctivism

When a hearer recognizes the speaker's intention to demonstratively refer to a perceptual object, speaker and hearer know in common the location of the object. They are then in a position to noninferentially increase their stock of common knowledge about the thing. They can do this, as in "Theater," because they can inform each other of nonperceptual facts about the jointly perceived object or, as in "Turner," because they are able to convey to each other different ways of seeing it. In either case, they do not rely on a premise that the thing singled out by one demonstrative expression is the same thing as the one singled out by another: they can simply see that it is, in virtue of the triadic constellation they help constitute (see chapter 4). In "Turner"-type cases, the constellation can be invoked for justificatory purposes. If you ask me why I say that the demonstrated object is a buoy or that the region is blue, it can be a good response to invite you to have a closer look.

How should we explain this justificatory power of joint constellations? It will be instructive to briefly consider the parallel debate with regard to ordinary perceptual experience. McDowell (for instance, 1994, 2008) defends an epistemological kind of disjunctivism,[7] according to which experiences that produce perceptual knowledge and that can be invoked to justify perceptual claims relate the perceiver to the experienced object in a unique way; they have nothing in common with subjectively indistinguishable experiences, such as hallucinations, that do not produce such knowledge. On this view, only veridical experiences can justify claims about the perceptual properties of the objects they present. If you are hallucinating, your experience does not justify your claim; after all, you are not seeing things as they are. The correct view, according to McDowell, is that *either* the experience presents its object as it is, in which case it justifies claims about its perceptual features absolutely, *or* it does not, in which case it does not justify such claims at all.

The supporter of the rival common-factor view (for instance, Wright 2008) thinks that all experience justifies perceptual claims "defeasibly": since the subject may not be in a position to distinguish between a veridical experience and its nonveridical counterpart, any experience with the right kind of content can justify a perceptual claim, subject to further evidence relevant for assessing the truth of such claims. The justificatory burden, as it were, is shifted onto the larger epistemic context in which the justifying takes place. This move has the advantage of avoiding the need to appeal to facts about experience that may be beyond the justifying subject's ken, but the price to pay is that the link between the justificatory power of particular experiences and their accuracy is severed entirely. The choice between these two views brings with it a commitment to distinct ways of individuating experience: the common factor theorist individuates types of experiences in terms of their contents; the disjunctivist individuates particular experiences in terms of their relation to the environment.

Which approach is better suited for thinking about the nature of joint experiences? The discussion turns on the apparent possibility that veridical experiences and their nonveridical counterparts can be indistinguishable to the perceiver.[8] A promising first move thus is to consider whether a parallel possibility obtains in the joint case: whether a veridical joint experience can be indistinguishable from its nonveridical counterpart. And the tempting reaction is that such mistakes are, of course, possible. I can suffer an apparently joint experience that is not joint at all (it misrepresents you as being jointly attending to an object with me, while really you are not), and I can suffer an apparently joint experience that is not veridical (I can hallucinate the entire scene in "Turner," buoy and all).

But I think this move should be resisted. There simply is no parallel distinction to be drawn between veridical experiences and their joint counterparts. The reason can be made vivid by means of a pair of simple graphs:

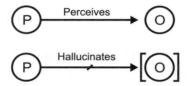

In the case of an individual experience, the discussion turns on the question of how to accommodate the distinction between the ordinary case and one in which the line between perceiver (P) and object (O) is broken, even though the experience suggests to the perceiver that it is intact. But in the case of a pair of joint experiences, there is no comparable line connecting the joint perceivers and the perceptual object:

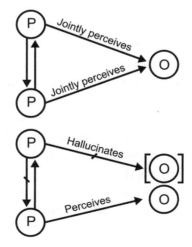

The joint constellation obtains in virtue of there being three constituents: remove one and the whole constellation falls apart. The tempting mistake is to fashion the debate about the nature of joint experiences on a model that supposes you can remove the perceptual connection with the object while maintaining the joint character of the constellation. But this is not possible: take the perceptual connection to the object away and there are only individual perceivers, or hallucinators, left. Joint illusions or joint hallucinations are simply not conceivable: they can only be suffered by individuals. The fault line does not run between joint perceivers and joint hallucinators; it runs between joint perceivers and individuals hallucinating a joint constellation, or individuals who see others perceive an object and misconstrue the constellation as joint. Since joint constellations are, necessarily, triadic, the experiences presenting them are necessarily of the objects they present. You could not have a pair of joint experiences that did not present the same object to the perceivers. As soon as the perceptual constellation is not triadic, the experiences that present the object are not joint; they are then not only entertained by individuals (this is always true on the view I have been developing), but they do not make available to their subjects the perceptual common knowledge that allows them to communicate (and thus extend their stock of common knowledge) about the thing. Whenever we perceive jointly, our experiences are of the object they present; whenever our experiences misrepresent their objects (as is the case in hallucinations), they cannot be joint.

I call *social disjunctivism* the view that there is a fundamental epistemological distinction between experiences that enable us to know in common propositions by means of which we can publicly justify our perceptual claims and those that do not. Only joint experiences provide such common knowledge, only joint experiences allow for public perceptual justification, and only joint experiences take place in transparent environments. The subjects of pairs of joint experiences really do stand in an epistemic relation to their surroundings that is fundamentally distinct from that of a subject whose experience suggests to her a nonexistent triadic constellation. The attraction of epistemological disjunctivism comes out fully in its social variant: it isn't just that the participant in a triadic constellation is necessarily standing in an epistemic relation to her surroundings that the subject of a nonveridical perceptual experience does not enjoy; she is presented with her surroundings in a spatial format that enables her to publicly justify her perceptual beliefs in a way she could not if she were not a constituent of a triadic constellation. The distinction between joint experiences and their nonjoint counterparts goes deeper than that between veridical perceptual experiences and their nonveridical counterparts; the divide is not just between different kinds of perceptual constellations but between different spatial orders and the resulting differences in modes of justification (public versus private) and kinds of perceptual knowledge (common versus individual). The subject of an experience that inaccurately presents a perceptual constellation as joint is not only mistaken in (some of) the perceptual beliefs produced by her experience. She is mistaken about the kind of justification available to her: she falsely believes that she can demonstratively single out the object so as to produce public evidence for her perceptual claim. As far as joint experiences go, the common-factor theorist's recommendation does not have any grip. There can be no question as to whether an experience that mispresents a joint constellation makes available defeasible public evidence for the subject's perceptual claims: nonjoint experiences cannot present public perceptual evidence because their subjects do not operate in a social spatial framework and the addressee of the justification (if any) does not have a jointly perceived object to consider.

What about illusory experiences that are suffered by both perceivers of a commonly perceived object? Illusions are generally more difficult to handle on a disjunctivist account than hallucinations: since an illusory experience presents the object it appears to be presenting, the disjunctivist cannot simply appeal to a broken information link between perceiver and perceptual object in her insistence on the absolute epistemological (and possibly metaphysical) distinction between the "good" case of veridical experience and the "bad" case of its falsidical counterpart.[9] And you may think that a parallel problem arises for the joint case. Suppose we are jointly attending to two lines whose arrangement gives rise to the Müller-Lyer illusion. Then we know in common where the object of our attention is located in social space, and each of us believes, mistakenly, that we know in common that one of the two perceived lines is longer than the other. This possibility does not threaten the social disjunctivist's case: what is known in common is just that one line looks longer than the other; the thus produced false belief that one line is longer than the other is entertained by each perceiver individually. Social disjunctivism is not committed to the view that experiences enjoyed by joint perceivers produce nothing but common knowledge in their subjects; it is committed merely to the weaker claim that all perceptual common knowledge is produced by joint experiences, and that only joint experiences justify claims to perceptual common knowledge. In the case of the jointly perceived arrangement of lines that give rise to the Müller-Lyer illusion, the subjects' experiences justify the claim that one line looks longer than the other; they do not justify each subject's false belief that it is.

In "Blue Room," I highlighted a difficulty with the attempt to define necessary and sufficient conditions of transparency for environments in which joint perceivers operate. We can now see more clearly why such attempts are doomed: ordinary perceivers' surroundings do not have built into them conditions that, when met, transform them into transparent social environments. If you start with the case of individual perceivers attempting to demonstratively communicate, you have assimilated the joint constellation to the ordinary relation between the individual perceiver and the environment in which the perception takes place. Social disjunctivism resists that move. We should, rather, begin with the consideration that joint perceivers always know in common which object they are communicating about, and on that basis can extend their perceptual common knowledge about the objects of their joint perceptions and discursively justify claims about their perceptual properties. On those grounds we should take the joint constellation as primitive.

6 CKMS, Social Externalism, and the Threat of Regress

At the end of part 1, I said that an externalist conception of perceptual common knowledge could explain the openness of joint constellations and thus deflate the threat of a regress of iterations of collective knowers' mental states. I hinted at the idea that the spatial ordering of joint perceivers' environment was what we had to appeal to in the attempt to explain why the regress inherent in perceptual common knowledge was not vicious. But I did not then have the resources to spell out the argument. This is now the task. Before I can address it, however, I need to make explicit an important distinction between two kinds of perceptual common knowledge that has been in the background of the discussion so far.

6.1 Kinds of Perceptual Common Knowledge

Consider the following three scenarios:

"Rubicon": You know that Caesar crossed the Rubicon because you read it in the *Encyclopedia Britannica* (which, as everyone knows, never fails). You tell me that you read in the *Encyclopedia* that Caesar crossed the Rubicon. Now it is common knowledge between us that Caesar crossed the Rubicon: each of us knows that p, each of us knows that the other knows that p, and so on.

The second scenario is already familiar:

"Turner": You and I are in the gallery in Tokyo that houses Turner's *Helvoet-sluys*. We read in the catalog that Turner painted a buoy into his painting to spite Constable, which inspires us to search for the buoy in the painting. "This," I say, pointing at a particular location in the seascape, "is the buoy."

You initially disagree: "This," you say and point accordingly, "is just a blob of paint." But then you look more closely and come to see that I am right and that the object I indicated really is a buoy. So you assent to my claim. It is now common knowledge between us that the blob of paint you demonstratively identified is a buoy.

And:

"Grand Canyon": Suppose you and I are standing on the South Rim of the Grand Canyon, looking together at the canyon wall in search of our friends who have spent the night at the bottom of the canyon and are now hiking back up (we might have to use quite powerful binoculars). I have spotted an object that I suspect are our friends and am trying to get you to focus on it. "This," I say, pointing at the object, "is where they are." You follow my pointing gesture and thus come to recognize the object I am highlighting. Now we know in common where I say our friends are.

In all three scenarios, the two subjects enjoy common knowledge of some kind. But there are significant differences between the kinds of knowledge entertained by them. There is an obvious difference between, first, "Rubicon" and, second, "Turner" and "Grand Canyon." In the first case, there is a transfer of knowledge from speaker to hearer that results in that knowledge being enjoyed in common: you tell me a fact, thereby getting me to know the fact, and your telling me ensures that the fact is known not only by each of us but that we know it in common. In both other cases, the common knowledge we enjoy is of a perceptual nature. We possess it in virtue of the triadic constellation that comes into being through our demonstrative communication. Until now, I have not drawn a clear distinction between these two kinds of cases; I have treated them as if they were epistemic equals. But there is an important difference between them, and being clear about it is vital for an adequate treatment of the regress inherent in common knowledge.

Begin by briefly considering "Rubicon." The kind of common knowledge produced in this scenario is not particularly problematic. It does not trigger the threatening regress described in part 1. There is no collective base, such as a joint perceptual constellation, that would enable each of us to come to know at a glance that we commonly know that p. The knowledge base in "Rubicon" is the *Encyclopedia Britannica*: if I am to justify my claim to you that Caesar crossed the Rubicon, the best I can do is to refer you to it. In my justification, nothing hinges on the perceptual openness of that base: my justificatory move is no weaker if you have to go to the library to check on my claim. In this constellation, the triadic nature of our common knowledge is structured "bottom-up": you can, without lack of justificatory power, cut off the regress at any of its iterations because there is no collective base that an infinite iteration of levels of knowledge attempts (but must forever fail) to capture.

Things are starkly distinct in "Grand Canyon": here it matters crucially that we jointly see the scene about one of whose objects we communicate. If there were a divider between you and me, making each of us ignorant of the other's focus of attention, we could not demonstratively communicate about the object of my referential intention. For this to be possible, each of us has to be part of the other's perceived environment: the ability to treat both one's own and the other's position as centers of perception and action is what enables us to locate the object in social space and thus to know in common where it is. This feature of joint constellations makes it necessary to take our joint experiences of the scene as primitive: what each of us knows perceptually about the scene is to be explained in terms of a spatial arrangement in which the location of things is determined relative to each of our respective standpoints. The perceptual common knowledge we enjoy in "Grand Canyon" is, in this sense, "top-down": you could not capture the common character of our respective mental states of knowing in terms of an iteration of what each of us knows about what each of us knows.

Things are different yet in "Turner." The common knowledge we enjoy on our gallery visit is squarely perceptual in nature: we come to know in common that the spot of paint is a buoy because I can point out to you which object we are communicating about. But what we are considering here is not the question of the referent of the speaker's demonstrative intention. We are considering, and coming to know in common, a property of the designated object. And each of us can know individually the proposition ascribing this property to the referent. If, during a chat in our sitting room, I tell you that the famous dab of paint in Turner's famous seascape is a buoy, you can always book a flight to Tokyo and have a look at the painting. The truth of my perceptual claim does not depend on our joint attention to its object, and my justification of my claim by appeal to the perceptual properties of the thing does not have to play out in a joint context in order to support it.

Consider how I can justify to you a perceptual claim about a jointly perceived object (the next chapter provides a more detailed treatment). If you ask me why I said that a certain demonstratively identified dab of paint was a buoy, I can appeal to the way the object is presented in experience: I can point it out to you and say that the demonstratively identified thing looks like a buoy. But note that what I am pointing out can only be the object, not its properties: the pointing gesture highlights the occupant of a particular location.[1] It is in virtue of the linguistic context of the pointing gesture that you can attend to the properties of the thus individuated object. If there is no such context, all my pointing gesture can accomplish is to get you to focus on the object occupying a particular location. What establishes the jointness of the perceptual scenario is that we are looking together at an object in a demonstratively identified location, not that each of us is experiencing its features. Scrutinizing the perceptual characteristics of an object, so that you come to find out whether what I have said is true, is something you can only undertake yourself. This point is brought home by the fact that we can look together at a demonstratively identified object and consider claims about its perceptual properties even if these properties are standpoint-dependent.

Along those lines, we need to distinguish between two types of perceptual common knowledge. There is, first, the kind enjoyed by the subjects in 'Grand Canyon." The proposition that is known here could *only* be commonly known: the hearer could not know by herself that *this* (demonstrated thing) was the object of the communicative speaker's referential intention. As soon as the hearer has recognized the speaker's demonstrative intention, it is common knowledge between them that this is the object they are communicating about. Here, the knowledge base is irreducibly collective: it is the triadic perceptual constellation that gives rise to this knowledge, and it could only be this constellation. I call this kind of perceptual common knowledge *primary*.

Then there is the perceptual common knowledge enjoyed by us in "Turner." This kind of knowledge is quite different; even though it is, in this scenario, had in virtue of a joint perceptual constellation, it need not be. If you and I were each looking at the Turner painting, with a divider between us that blocks my sight of you and yours of me, we could still come to know in common that the dab of paint on the water is a buoy, provided you have a means of getting me to know, through a suitable description, which dab of paint you are talking about. I could come to know that the dab is a buoy by looking at it by myself; you could, if I challenged your assertion, simply invite me to have another look by myself. The justificatory power of the experience is entirely derived from the perceptual characteristics of the object of your and my experiences. Nothing hinges epistemically on the joint character of these experiences. Their jointness really carries over from the spatial organization of the environment that the experiences present. Perceptual common knowledge of the "Turner" kind is in this sense secondary.

6.2   The Regress Contained

In part 1, I considered Wilby's (2010) proposal to account for the epistemically open character of joint perceptual constellations by, as he puts it, relativizing the regress-generating property to the situation in which it appears. Schauer (2012) worries that the proposal fails to explain how perceptual common knowledge could be enjoyed by individual, finite minds. I can now substantiate Wilby's (and, similarly, Campbell's 2005) proposal by drawing on the distinction between primary and secondary perceptual common knowledge. I can do this in a way that accommodates Schauer's concern.

The kind of perceptual common knowledge that is threatened by infinite iterations of what each of its subjects knows is primary. The base of primary perceptual common knowledge is social; it consists in a triadic spatial constellation that the perceivers help constitute. By contrast, the base of secondary perceptual common knowledge is the ordinary physical object, some of whose perceptual characteristics are ascribed to it in the commonly known proposition. The threatening regress arises for the primary kind because the subjects' perceptual relations themselves are part of what is known.

As noted earlier, the general intuition, articulated in different ways by Campbell (2005) and Wilby (2010), is that the triadic perceptual constellation that forms the base of its subjects' common knowledge itself has to explain why they can come to know in common perceptual propositions about the jointly perceived object simply by jointly attending to it. The proposal can seem mysterious as long as nothing further is said: just what are we to make of the notion of a triadic perceptual constellation, given that all perception is informed by the information available from the perceiver's standpoint? I am now able to solve the mystery. Primary perceptual common knowledge is of objects in social space; more precisely, it is of the location of the jointly perceived object, determined relative to the positions of speaker and hearer. This location is determined, by each perceiver, through an act of social triangulation: by means of an exercise that takes each of their positions as centers of perception.

CKMS is propositional. Hence the question arises what the proposition is that joint perceivers know in common. So far, I have been informally saying that the subjects of primary CKMS know in common "where the object is" or that they know in common "the location of the object of the speaker's referential intention in social space." But these informal ways of speaking do not make precise the proposition that is commonly known; in fact, they can misleadingly suggest that the knowledge in question is not propositional (that it is a "knowledge of" rather than a "knowledge that").[2]

Since the wanted proposition expresses the location of the communicative object in social space, it cannot be descriptive. It cannot, for instance, pick out a location on a map (a street address, say, or a set of spatial coordinates) or define the location relative to other objects in the vicinity. This includes the description of the location of the object relative to the positions of speaker and hearer in allocentric space. For instance, if the object of our demonstrative communication is three feet ahead of and placed exactly between us, I might describe its location (call this location L) as follows:

L is the vertex angle of an isosceles triangle whose base angles are constituted by your and my respective positions and whose altitude is three feet.

This description does justice to one important feature of social space: it defines the object's location relative to two other locations, irrespective of where they are in allocentric space. But it nevertheless fails to capture the specific social character of the framework: the base angles might be occupied by any physical object at all. All the description accomplishes is to define the object's location relative to other objects in its vicinity. If this proposition is commonly known to two subjects, they are in a position to justify their claims about the object's location by indicating it on a map, but they could not increase their stock of secondary perceptual common knowledge by inviting each other to look at the thing. The constellation would have a very different, and much weaker, epistemic role.

Speakers and hearers communicate about jointly perceived objects by pointing them out to each other: by using demonstrative expressions that they supplement with pointing gestures (see the discussion in chapter 4). The proposition known by the subjects of a joint perceptual constellation must contain a demonstrative expression that designates the location of the object in social space. Call this expression "*that." It designates the location of the object of the speaker's referential intention, as determined relative to the positions of speaker and hearer. If I, as a speaker, intend to demonstratively communicate about a perceptual object with you, I deploy my pointing gesture so as to make salient the object to you (see section 4.3). If I, as a hearer, attempt to recognize your referential intention, I follow your pointing gesture so as to discern what object you are making salient to me. Both operations require the deployment of a social spatial framework.

The proposition that is commonly known by the subjects of primary perceptual common knowledge can now be thought of as follows:

P(*L)   *That is the location of the object of the speaker's referential intention.

Demonstrative communicators identify the object at *that location by means of an exercise in social triangulation. When they so identify it, they each know where the object of their demonstrative communication is in social space. And they then know P(*L) in common: this is guaranteed by the social nature of the spatial framework with which they operate. They either know in common where the object is in social space or they do not know it at all (see section 5.4). In this way, the spatial order of the environment individuates each perceiver's factive mental state of knowing the location of the object in social space, and it guarantees that the proposition expressing the location of the object in social space is commonly known.

It is now clear why joint perceivers do not need to generate $(n + 1)$ iterations of what each of them knows in order to obtain primary perceptual common knowledge: what each individual knows (the object's location in social space) is determined by what they know in common. For you to individually know the reference of a token of *that, you and your fellow perceiver already have to know it in common. Your individual spatial knowledge is the consequence of your being part of a joint constellation, not the other way around. The joint constellation contains the regress.

For secondary perceptual common knowledge, the situation is somewhat different. The base of this knowledge consists in the perceptual features of the object that is being jointly perceived. These features are mind-independent, in the sense that they are not constituted by the joint perception. The blob of paint in "Turner," for example, represents a buoy even if neither of us knows that it does. Still, they can be perceptually known in common, and claims about the perceptual properties of jointly perceived objects can be discursively justified by appeal to their jointly accessible perceptual features. On the view I have been developing, this kind of perceptual knowledge is to be explained in terms of its subjects' possession of the primary common knowledge of the bearer of the properties' location in social space: it is because they can point it out to each other that they can know in common its perceptual properties. Secondary perceptual common knowledge can be available only in virtue of the subjects' primary common knowledge of the object's location. There is no threat of regress inherent in this form of common knowledge; the threat carries over from the primary kind. Once you diffuse the threat for primary perceptual common knowledge, you have already dissolved it for the secondary kind.

7 Justification and Evidence

In this chapter, I consider the notions of perceptual evidence and justification in joint constellations. Much of our perceptual reasoning plays out in the public domain; we point out things to each other, draw each other's attention to their features, and thus come to enlarge the stock of what we know in common about our environment. Thus put, there is an obvious role for perceptual evidence in joint contexts: it produces common knowledge in the perceivers. By the same token, you may think that justification in such contexts has a unique epistemic function: it backs up what we know in common, giving us a more secure footing in our shared world.

However, you could deny that there is a particular role for what Williamson (2005) calls "dialectical" justifications in perceptual reasoning. You could suppose that it is both true and irrelevant that much of our justificatory practice, including perceptual justification, plays out in the public domain. On what I call the *brute view*, public justification proceeds as follows. You work out what your evidence is for holding whatever claim you intend to justify; then you cite this evidence in the presence of a hearer. And that is it: whether your utterance is made in soliloquy or whether it is directed at an audience that sees the same thing as you do simply does not matter. After all, the quality of your reasoning does not change depending on whether you express it; good evidence remains good evidence regardless of whether it is invoked, and unconvincing evidence does not improve because you offer it to an easily duped audience.

Perhaps unsurprisingly, I suggest that the brute view does not offer an attractive account of the twin notions of evidence and justification in public demonstrative reasoning. I begin with some general remarks about the role of evidence in the justification of perceptual claims. Then I introduce the worry that perceptual reasoning might be circular. I show that the worry can be dispelled for public demonstrative reasoning and briefly suggest that this should motivate us to see dialectic perceptual justification as a sui generis phenomenon.

7.1   Circularity in Perceptual Reasoning

Consider how you can justify a perceptual claim about an object. The most direct way to achieve this is by an appeal to the way the thing is presented to you in experience. "I am saying that this thing is square, because it looks square," you might say. Then your experience of the object has provided you with evidence in support of your perceptual claim. There are two views you can take about the nature of this evidence: you can either think that the experience directly justifies the claim or that it justifies it indirectly, via a proposition expressed by the sentence by way of whose utterance you are making the claim. Indirect accounts of evidence typically take the justifier of a perceptual claim to be a belief. By contrast, Williamson (2000) argues that knowledge, not belief, is a subject's evidence: the totality of someone's evidence is constituted by the totality of what she knows. This view flows from his externalist account of knowledge, on which knowledge is a more basic mental state than belief.

Regardless of how you think of an individual's evidence for a perceptual claim, it is possible to feel uneasy about the justificatory power of the evidence marshaled in an argument that appeals to the perceived object's looks. Consider this passage that Pylyshyn attributes to Fodor (2007):

> The doctrine [that one's justification of a perceptual claim that P, is typically its seeming to one that P], though venerable, strikes me as confused; in particular, as confusing offering a justification for a perceptual claim with offering a justification for making that claim. Compare: my sincerely believing that P generally justifies my claiming that P; but it's not a reason to believe P is true (or, anyhow, it's not much of one. Surely it can't be *my* reason for believing that P is true). Why suppose that the epistemology of perception differs, in this respect, from the epistemology of other sorts of belief fixation. (Pylyshyn 2007, 124)[1]

Pylyshyn's (and possibly Fodor's) worry is this: why should we think that experience justifies a demonstrative belief about its object? After all, we don't think that naming the source of a belief justifies the belief in other domains. Suppose you hold that Ayn Rand was the greatest philosopher of the twentieth century. You say you hold this belief because your investment banker has told you so. Have you given the hearer a reason to think that your belief is true? You have perhaps explained why you hold your belief. But whether you have adequately justified it will depend on further considerations, most importantly to do with the banker's philosophical competence. Pylyshyn thinks that justificatory appeal to perceptual experience constitutes a problem of exactly the same kind: appeal to your experience explains your claiming that the demonstratively identified object is P, but it doesn't, other things being equal, justify the belief itself. Experience does not provide the subject with a warrant for her perception-based belief. All it can really provide is an explanation of the subject's holding the belief.

Brueckner flags a related problem for Williamson's idea that our total evidence is constituted by everything we know:

> Suppose that I am justified in believing that my cup is red and that my evidence is e. Then I am justified that my cup is red in virtue of, or because of, my belief of my evidential justifier—namely, e. If e = C (the proposition that my cup is red), then I am justified in believing that my cup is red in virtue of, or because of, my belief that my cup is red. *That* is the problem for Williamson's overall view. (Brueckner 2009, 8)

On Williamson's view, if a perceiver has propositional knowledge about an object's perceptual properties, her evidence for her claim about these properties consists in the proposition that ascribes these properties to the object. If, by contrast, the perceiver is suffering from an illusion, her evidence consists in the proposition that the object appears to be as experienced (Williamson 2000, 198). This has the consequence that, in the "good" case of a veridical perceptual experience, the knowledge that the perceived object is P (where P is a perceptual property) justifies itself. The apparent problem is one of circularity. And the threat of circularity is also at the heart of Pylyshyn's (2007) worry. Here, the apparent difficulty is that justification of a perceptual belief by appeal to the way an object is presented in experience does not produce a reason to think the belief is true. In both cases, the underlying concern is that the justificatory appeal to experience, or to the proposition ascribing the experienced property to the perceptual object, seems to fail to live up to a key requirement that good evidence has to meet: the evidence that justifies a perceptual belief (or knowledge) cannot be the believed (or known) proposition itself; good evidence supplies an independent reason in support of the belief (or knowledge) that is to be justified.

The problem is not unique to accounts that conceive of perceptual justification in indirect terms. In a discussion of doxastic justification, Markie (2005) introduces the *rational support principle*:

> RSP: S's belief that p is defeasibly justified for S by virtue of being based on a mental state, M, only if M has a propositional content that is an appropriate reason in support of p. (Markie 2005, 349)

RSP requires, Markie says, that "a perception justifies a belief only if its content can serve as a premise in a noncircular argument for the belief's content" (Markie 2005, 365). If a perception is to justify a belief, along those lines, its content cannot be the same as the content of the belief it is meant to justify, since otherwise the argument is circular and RSP is violated. Huemer (2001) and Brewer (1999) attempt to solve the problem; Markie argues that these attempts are unsuccessful.

7.2 Public Perceptual Reasoning

The views mentioned in the previous section are not concerned with the twin notions of evidence and justification in public perceptual reasoning. They do not consider who the addressee of the justifying speech act is: Is it the speaker himself, in which case the justifying role of the evidence marshaled in support of the perceptual claim is playing out intrapersonally? Or is the addressee a hearer who is distinct from the speaker, in which case the justifying role of the evidence is interpersonal, communicative, and public? You might think that this difference is relevant to the discussion: my perceptual experience may not constitute independent evidence in support of my perceptual claim *for me*, but that is not to say that it cannot provide new evidence for you, the hearer. The problem of circularity may simply be a consequence of the tacit adoption of an intrapersonal model of justification.

The interesting case is not one in which the sole perceiver of an object about whose properties she is making (and justifying) a claim is communicating with a hearer who cannot herself see the thing. This is the kind of case illustrated in "Remote Pointing." It is not interesting for my purposes because from the hearer's perspective, the speaker's evidence can only be testimonial: since the other party does not have perceptual access to the object, she simply has to take the speaker's word for it. The relevant case is, rather, one in which speaker and hearer have joint perceptual access to the object, as in "Turner." Here the speaker's perceptual evidence in support of his claim about the jointly perceived object is perceptually accessible to the hearer also. In this case, the speaker's justification of his claim turns out not to be circular.

Begin by ruling out cases in which a speaker's perceptual evidence in support of a claim about a jointly perceived object is not available to the hearer. This is the case for claims about objects' standpoint-dependent perceptual properties. If you and I jointly contemplate an apple placed between us that is red on your side and yellow on mine, I cannot perceptually access the evidence that you marshal in support of your claim that the apple is red, as seen from your standpoint. I can only take your evidence on testimony. The relevant cases are those in which the perceptual property at stake is standpoint-independent, such as the object's shape; or in which it is, in any case, accessible from the standpoints of speaker and hearer. To come to a view about the relation between perceptual claim and justifying perceptual evidence in such cases, it is crucial to bear in mind the distinction between primary and secondary perceptual common knowledge introduced in the previous section.[2] To recall, primary perceptual common knowledge is of the object's bounded (or overlapping) location in social space. It is the knowledge that the object (or feature) is at *that location. Secondary perceptual common knowledge is about the perceptual properties of the jointly perceived object. All secondary such knowledge requires that the perceivers know in common P(*L); otherwise, the conditions of joint perception are not met, and no perceptual common knowledge about the object is available at all.

Primary perceptual common knowledge does not allow for perceptual justification. There is no perceptual evidence I could marshal in support of my assertion that *this* (demonstratively identified) thing is the object of my referential intention. My attention to the thing anchors my demonstrative intention. If you are unsure which the object of my intention is, I can attempt to be more precise in pointing it out, or I can qualify the term following the demonstrative in my utterance; but I cannot appeal to my experience of the object in an attempt to provide evidence for it. There is a performative aspect to my utterance: saying that *this* is the object of my referential intention makes it so (even though I can, of course, misdirect the hearer by pointing at the wrong object, say).

The relevant case is secondary perceptual common knowledge. In joint contexts, the evidence for a perceptual claim about an object is constituted by what the subjects perceptually know in common about it. But perceptual common knowledge is not free-standing: an extension of our perceptual common knowledge about a jointly perceived object entails an extension of what you and I each know about it individually. When you tell me that the blob of paint in "Turner" is a buoy, and I come to see that you are right, we have extended the scope of what we know in common about the object of our joint perceptions. And in virtue of that extension the scope of what I know about the object of my perception has been extended as well. In this way, the joint character of the perceptual constellation takes care of the demands imposed by (RSP). Consider again:

P1: "This is a spot of paint" (said by me).

P2: "This is a buoy" (said by you).

C: Something is both a spot of paint and a buoy (known in common by us both).

The argument is noncircular because its premises state what each of us individually knows about the object of our communication and the conclusion states what we perceptually know about it in common. Drawing this conclusion results in each of us perceptually knowing both premises. We have learned something from each other, and we have done so without relying on testimony, simply by exploiting the epistemic power of the joint constellation. The unique feature of such constellations is the public accessibility of the perceptual characteristics of the demonstrated object. Because we already know that we are justifying perceptual claims about a jointly perceived object, we can pass on perceptual evidence from speaker to hearer; the intrapersonal boundary of perceptual justification carried out in soliloquy is lifted. Williamson (2005, 115–116) observes that justification is typically a social practice. You might think that the considerations of this chapter give you a reason to treat public perceptual justification as the unproblematic, standard scenario and to take private perceptual justification to be a special case that has to be developed against the backdrop of the public standard. Developing this view is beyond the reach of the present project, however.

III   Social Space

Introduction

We can know in common how things are in the world that surrounds us because we know where they are: this was, more or less, the upshot of part 2. And we can communicate to each other where things are because we can point them out to each other. This requires the ability to triangulate—to work out the position of the object of our perceptual interest by taking our standpoints as givens, as anchors whence we branch out into the shared world. Here is a dramatic rendering of an attempt at triangulation recounted by Helen Macdonald in *H Is for Hawk* (2014), a memoir in which the taming of a goshawk plays a central role:

> Now I cannot see the hawk because I am searching for the pheasant, so I have to work out what she is doing by putting myself in her mind—and so I become both the hawk in the branches above and the human below. The strangeness of this splitting makes me feel I am walking under myself, and sometimes away from myself. Then for a moment everything becomes dotted lines, and the hawk, the pheasant and I merely elements in a trigonometry exercise, each of us labelled with soft italic letters. And now I am so invested in the hawk and the pheasant's relative positions that my consciousness cuts loose entirely, splits into one or the other, first the hawk looking down, second the pheasant in the brambles looking up, and I move over the ground as if I couldn't possibly affect anything in the world. There is no way I can flush this pheasant. I'm not here. Time stretches and slows. There's a sense of panic at this point, a little buffet of fear that's about annihilation and my place in the world. But then the pheasant is flushed, a pale and burring chunk of muscle and feathers, and the hawk crashes from the hedge towards it. And all the lines that connect heart and head and future possibilities, those lines that also connect me with the hawk and the pheasant and with life and death, suddenly become safe, become tied together in a small muddle of

feathers and gripping talons that stand in mud in the middle of a small field in
the middle of a small county in a small country on the edge of winter. (Macdonald 2014, 183–184)

This is perspective-taking: the ability to work out, by a feat of imagination,
how things are from viewpoints, and for minds, that are not your own. It
is the ability to construe a triangle, the dotted lines with soft italic letters
that connect your own position, the position of your fellow perceiver, and
the object of your interest. Once construed, your imagination can move
between the corners of the triangle, shifting between your own standpoint
and that of the fellow perceiver and fellow being. Sometimes, as in the
passage above, you can shift between all three standpoints and three sorts
of experiences. It takes an elaborate kind of mind to accomplish this feat,
one endowed with a rich imagination, the ability to distinguish between
minds, and kinds of minds, and therefore the possession of the notion of
a mind in the first place. But before any of this is possible, you need to
have a grip on the spatial arrangement of things, and of the occupants of
the corners of your triangle in them. Part 2 was concerned with the knowledge of joint perceivers about the shared environment, the possibility of
communication about and thereby the extension of what we perceptually
know in common. It was about the way in which we learn from each other,
through speech and gesture, about what there is in front of our eyes (and
heads, and bodies). In part 3, I inquire into the spatial framework needed to
learn in this way: a framework that orders things relative to the positions of
a plurality of perceivers and agents.

The issue here is not, in the first place, the conception of space that
underwrites elaborate efforts such as the falconer's attempt to see things
from, quite literally, the bird's-eye perspective of her goshawk. However
breathtaking this ability, the philosophical difficulty begins at a more basic
level. If I am to imaginatively take another perceiver's perspective, I have to
have something to say about how things look from her perspective. But in
order to do that, I already have to have transcended my own. I already have
to be operating with a reflective conception of space that allows me to treat
a variety of positions in it as occupied by perceivers. The question is how
such a reflective conception of space can be available. How can a creature
be able to look beyond itself, as it were, and think of its environment as
arranged around a variety of centers?

This question cannot itself be addressed by an appeal to reflective, intellectual capacities. It requires, so the thought I pursue in this part of the book, a consideration of the role of the body and its doings in the creature's understanding of its surroundings' spatial organization. More specifically, it requires an account of the perceiver's *social* interactions with the environment. It is because we are capable of joint activity that we can transcend our individual spatial perspectives on the environment. We can participate in such activities because we have at our disposal a prereflective social spatial framework that is constituted by a practical know-how. It is because we know how to act with others on objects in our environment that we can come to know, propositionally, where these objects are located relative to our respective positions. The kind of spatial knowledge that is required for linguistic demonstrative communication has its basis in a different, practical kind of knowledge that is exercised in unreflective joint activities. This is the thought I shall be pursuing: we can be linguistic demonstrative communicators only because we are joint agents first.

Part 3 is structured as follows. I begin, in chapter 8, with a general reflection on the notion of a conception of space. In chapter 9, I introduce some psychological work on the nature of perspective-taking, with its crucial distinction between the ability to determine what another is looking at and the developmentally later ability to hypothesize about an object's standpoint-dependent modes of presentation. In chapter 10 I elaborate on the notion of peripersonal space and its relevance for an account of practical, action-relevant knowledge about the environment. Then in chapter 11, I marshal some evidence in support of the existence of a parallel social spatial framework. In chapter 12, I sketch a speculative account of the relation between this kind of practical spatial know-how and the possession of an explicit conception of space.

8 Demonstrative Communication and Conceptions of Space

To be in a position to demonstratively refer to an object, you have to know where the object of your referential intention is. To be in a position to understand a speaker's referential intention, you have to know where the object of his intention is. As soon as you know this, going by CP/1, the demonstrative communication has succeeded. In order to perform and understand demonstrative acts, you need a conception of space: this has been a guiding thought of the discussion in part 2.

Here is one way to spell out what it means to have a conception of space. Having a conception of space means being able to distinguish between an object and its location. It means being able to think of an object as occupying a different location from the one it does in fact occupy and being able to think of a location as being occupied by a different object from the one that in fact occupies it. This seems straightforward enough: I can think of the book that is to my left as being positioned to my right, and I can think of the location that is occupied by the book as being occupied by a writing pad. But it isn't as if the possessor of a conception of space were able to think of locations in complete independence from the objects that occupy them and of objects independently of the locations they occupy. The intricate relation between objects and their locations comes to the fore when you ask what it takes to reidentify places and things. Peter Strawson writes in *Individuals* ([1959] 1996, 36–37):

> The reidentification of places is not something quite different from, and independent of, the reidentification of things. There is, rather, a complex and intricate interplay between the two. For on the one hand places are defined only by the relation to things; and, on the other, one of the requirements for the identity of a material thing is that its existence, as well as being continuous in time, should be continuous in space. That is to say, for many kinds of thing, it counts against

saying that a thing, x, at one place at one time is the same thing, y, at another place at another time, if we think there is not some continuous set of places between these two places such that x was at each successive member of this set of places at successive times between these two times and y was at the same member of the set of places at the same time.

If this is right, what entitles us to think of an object that is at two different locations at different times as the same thing is that we are justified in thinking that the object *moved* from the first to the second location—that it didn't disappear from the first location and then reappear in the second. Then the question arises as to what it takes to be justified in thinking this. One possibility, of course, is that the move of the object from the first to the second location is observed. You focus on the object (a slug, say, as it slowly wanders from leaf to leaf in your vegetable garden) and, not leaving it out of sight, think at t_1, "Now this slug is *here*," where *here* designates the leaf it occupies at that time; then you think, at t_2, "Now this slug is *there*," where *there* designates the leaf it occupies at that later time. The method is not absolutely foolproof (perhaps your attention was briefly diverted, or the slug was replaced by a molecule-by-molecule identical replica at an interval too short for you to notice), but still: if you can form thoughts of this kind, you are able to differentiate between objects and their locations. You are operating with a conception of space. Such a conception may begin with the possession of an egocentric spatial framework, as characterized by Evans:

> Egocentric spatial terms are the terms in which the content of our spatial experiences would be formulated, and those in which our immediate behavioural plans would be expressed. This duality is no coincidence: an egocentric space can exist only for an animal in which a complex network of connections exists between perceptual input and behavioural output. A perceptual input . . . cannot have a spatial significance for an organism except in so far as it has a place in such a complex network of input-output connections. (Evans 1982, 154)

If you are able to act on your environment and perceptually experience the objects in it, you are working with a spatial framework in which things are ordered around you. To be able to reach the cup that is to your left, and that you experience as being on your left, you have to know that moving your arm to the left allows you to reach the cup.

But operating in egocentric space is not sufficient for the possession of a conception of space. To operate in egocentric space merely means operating in an environment whose objects can be described relative to your position as an agent. It does not necessarily mean that the agent herself is able to describe or think about these objects as positioned to her left or right, above or below, behind or in front of her. On Evans's view, this requires that the agent be able to describe the spatial position of an object relative to her own position *for a variety of possible such positions*. To be able to think about space at all, you have to be able to think of yourself as occupying a position in objective space. You have to be able to determine your own location on a map of the region in which you are situated. Thus:

> We say that the subject thinks of himself as located in space (in an objective world that exists independently of him, and through which he moves); only if this is so can the subject's egocentric space be a *space* at all. But what does this thinking of himself as located mean except that the subject can in general regard his situation "from the objective point of view"? And this means that in general he has the ability to locate his egocentric space in the framework of a cognitive map. (Evans 1982, 163)

Evans illustrates his view with an example in which the subject who is able to identify his location on a cognitive map is able to imagine what he would be able to observe from this viewpoint.

> Someone who has a cognitive map of Oxford, for example, must be able to contemplate the imposition of the map in the course of his travels (perhaps in a very dense fog). "If I am here, midway between Balliol and the Bodleian, then that must be Trinity, and so the High must be down there." In such a situation, one may have to choose between several ways of effecting a coincidence between egocentric space and one's conception of space. Each way of effecting a coincidence would generate hypotheses about what one should be able to observe if oriented in this or that direction, and what one would be observe if one moved in this or that direction. (Evans 1982, 162)[1]

To have a conception of space, then, is to *transcend* the egocentric order of the region in which you act. This is what it takes to think about objects and places in that region: you have to see your position as a location in that region and yourself as an object occupying that location.

On such a view, a subject's ability to ascribe a variety of locations to a moving object that is tracked over time, and the ability to ascribe a variety of looks to a static object that is observed while moving around it, are codependent. They can both be explained by the subject's ability to think of himself as part of the objective order, as a perceiver and agent who might be occupying a variety of positions in the region in which he finds himself.

You can ascribe a range of perspective-dependent looks to an observed object because you can think of it as occupying a fixed place in the objective order that can be specified relative to your changing perspectives on it; and you can ascribe a range of locations to a tracked object because you can think of it as occupying changing places in the objective order that can be specified relative to your constant position in it. The ability to ascribe locations and the ability to ascribe perspective-dependent looks are both supported by the idea of yourself as occupying one of many possible locations in the objective order.

Suppose this Evansian view is on the right track.[2] Along its lines, we have reason to take it that the possession of a conception of space, and thus the ability to think of objects and their locations as interdependent in the sense outlined, is tied to self-awareness of some kind: you can have a conception of space only if you can think of *yourself* as occupying a position in the relevant region. The question then is whether such a conception of space is what underwrites demonstrative communication. If you can think of yourself as occupying various locations in space, you are able to think of locations you don't currently occupy as centers of perception and action. That is, in effect, what Evans is doing on his walk through foggy Oxford: he generates hypotheses about how things look from a location that he thinks is his. However, it might not be: he could be mistaken about his whereabouts. And it can seem that the occupation of a given location by another perceiver does not change anything about the subject's conception of space. Of course, the subject needs to have solved the problem of other minds; he must be able to assign to the space occupier the status of a perceiver. But solving this problem, you might think, has nothing to do with the subject's conception of space. As far as space goes, all it takes is that you can think of a variety of locations in the given region as centers of perception and action, and what it means for a location to be such a center can be modeled on your own case: on the location that you, perceiver and agent, in fact occupy.

You can put pressure on this view from a variety of angles. One such approach takes seriously Davidson's notion of triangulation. Here is the concluding passage from his "Three Varieties of Knowledge":

> Our propositional knowledge has its basis not in the impersonal but in the inter-
> personal. Thus, when we look at the natural world we share with others, we do
> not lose contact with ourselves, but rather acknowledge membership in a society

of minds. If I did not know what others think, I would have no thoughts of my own and so would not know what I think. If I did not know what I think, I would lack the ability to gauge the thoughts of others. Gauging the thoughts of others requires that I live in the same world with them, sharing many reactions to its major features, including its values. So there is no danger that in viewing the world objectively we will lose touch with ourselves. The three sorts of knowledge form a tripod: if any leg were lost, no part would stand. (Davidson 2009, 220)

The "three sorts of knowledge" are knowledge of one's own mind, knowledge of other minds, and knowledge of the world of objects. Davidson is not explicitly concerned with joint constellations. But the scenarios he considers typically are of a triadic perceptual kind, in the context of the question of the possibility of translation from one participant's idiom into the other. The idea is that knowledge of any kind requires that the subject have a means of comparison, a secondary access to the event that is perceptually known. You can have knowledge of the environment, in Davidson's view, only if you can think of it as the reality that renders your statements about it true or false. But the notions of truth and reality can only be grasped by a creature that understands the distinction between what there is and the variety of perspectives that can be taken on what there is. And the way to understand them is to be exposed to the contrast between your own perspective and that of another creature.

You could think that a version of this reflection on the mutual interdependency of knowledge about oneself, others, and the environment has a direct application in the question about the conception of space of demonstrative communicators. Triangulation begins, for Davidson, when you try to make sense of another's utterance by interpreting it in the light of a jointly observed stimulus. You might point at the rabbit scurrying past in order to find out whether the native speaker's co-occurring utterance really refers to that event. For this to be possible, self, other, and the observed environment have to be equally constitutive of the triangle: the account cannot get off the ground if you think that your grasp of the other's perspective is the consequence of an imaginative exercise in which you simulate viewpoints other than your own. Along those lines, the knowledge of yourself as part of the objective order is dependent on your knowledge of other persons, and a range of observed objects and events, as being part of this order also. You could then not dissociate the question of perspective-taking, and the conception of space that underwrites it, from the question of how self-knowledge is possible. The conception of space that makes perspective-taking possible has to be one in which it is not merely possible to think of a variety of locations as centers of perception and action; it is a conception of a region that does in fact contain a variety of perceivers.

A somewhat related (though, as will emerge in section 12.2, ultimately quite distinct) idea can be pursued by drawing on Strawson's insistence that addressing the conceptual problem of other minds requires introducing the notion of a person as a basic metaphysical category. In the third chapter of *Individuals* ([1959] 1996), he argues that the possibility of self-ascription of a state of consciousness depends on having the concept of a "person." To give a very rough gloss on Strawson's line of thought: our ordinary human and, in particular, perceptual experience, he says, is such that it enables us to ascribe conscious states to ourselves. But we can do that only if we realize that we are part of the objective order; that we are particular kinds of objects. We are persons, the kinds of objects that certain predicates (Strawson's P-predicates) may be ascribed to. The meaning of these predicates remains constant throughout their first- and third-person uses: when I say of myself that I am in pain, I am talking about the same type of conscious state as I am when I am saying of another person that he is in pain. Understanding the meaning of such predicates thus depends on grasping their general applicability. It follows, for Strawson, that the possibility of self-ascription of conscious states depends on the possibility of also ascribing the same type of state to others. And from this it follows that the concept of a person must be primitive—that it is logically prior to that of an individual consciousness.[3] Only if you have the concept of a person can you understand the generality of P-predicates and only then are you in a position to ascribe experiences to yourself and other persons.[4]

You could build on Strawson's thought to develop the argument that the possession of a conception of space is tied not just to the knowledge of yourself as part of the objective order but as one person among others. On the Evansian view, self-knowledge of a particular kind is necessary for a conception of space: you have to understand that you are an occupant of a position in objective space, and you have to understand that that position affords you a particular perspective on your environment. But if Strawson is right, this understanding can be available to you only if you enjoy the insight that persons can occupy a variety of spatial locations offering distinct perspectives on the environment. You do not, on such a view, begin with the consideration that you enjoy a particular knowledge of yourself as the occupant of a location in objective space; you begin, rather, with the idea that a variety of locations, of which you occupy one, can constitute centers of perception and action and afford distinct perspectives on the environment.

Here, then, are two ways of thinking about the possibility of spatial self-knowledge that situate such knowledge in a social context. They are natural starting points for developing a conception of space that assigns a foundational role to the idea that the possessors of such a conception are demonstrative communicators—that spatial thinking requires the individual to think not merely of herself but of a variety of perceivers as occupying a place in the spatial order. But you might worry that this kind of approach hopelessly overintellectualizes matters. Suppose it does take a particular kind of self-knowledge to enjoy a conception of space, and suppose that an argument can be construed in support of the idea that this self-knowledge requires the subject to situate herself spatially among others. It does not follow that the possibility of demonstrative communication depends on the communicators' deployment of such an elaborate conceptual repertoire. The Evansian account, perhaps suitably enriched by a social element, may spell out sufficient conditions for linguistic demonstrative communication: the person who knows that she and others occupy a position in objective space certainly is able to understand that other perceivers and agents are capable of demonstratively identifying an object in that space. But perhaps possession of this kind of knowledge does not constitute a necessary condition for demonstrative communication. Perhaps these necessary conditions are considerably weaker.

Much depends here on what the target is. If we think of communication in the Gricean terms introduced in part 2, it really can seem irresistible to suppose that subjects capable of demonstrative communication have to be operating with a conception of space that allows them to explicitly attribute perspectives to others that are distinct from their own. But, you might plausibly think, communication about jointly perceived objects does not begin with verbal exchanges that include the utterance of demonstrative expressions.[5] It begins with the ability to follow others' gaze to join one's focus with theirs—with the kind of bodily activity that is part of ordinary visual attention (squinting, moving closer or farther away, adjusting one's bodily position) but acquires a communicative function in joint contexts. As soon as we are interested in the demands on nonverbal communicators' spatial frameworks, it seems unlikely that a full-fledged Evansian conception of space is a prerequisite of demonstrative communication. And there are excellent reasons to be interested in this topic. For one thing, I have been maintaining that demonstrative communication, even in the Gricean paradigm, relies heavily on demonstrations and thus bodily gestures. Regardless of whether you think that these gestures have semantic content, there can be no doubt that they serve a communicative function: they direct the hearer's attention to the object of the speaker's referential intention. And it would be a mistake to suppose that because the Gricean hearer's understanding of the speaker's referential intention rests on her ability to triangulate the object's location relative to the speaker's position, all demonstrative communication requires the deployment of an explicit spatial frame of reference. Humans begin to communicate, through looks and gestures, from a very young age;[6] they share aspects of their environment with others toward the end of the first year of life (see for instance, Hobson and Hobson 2005; Tomasello 2008) and thus well before they are able to engage in Gricean-type demonstrative communication. The spatial frameworks that facilitate these heavily body-reliant forms of communicative sharing are not simply superseded by an allocentric conception of space once it is acquired. Bodily, action-centered spatial frameworks play a vital role in explaining the demands on the conception of space that enables linguistic demonstrative communication.

In order to do justice to these considerations, I begin by distinguishing between various kinds of perspective-taking, and I ask what spatial frameworks are involved in demonstrative communications that are body centered and less demanding than those requiring something like the Evansian conception of space sketched above. The hope is to develop a richer, empirically informed account of the role of spatial frameworks in demonstrative communication than would otherwise be possible and that this approach will result in a deeper understanding of the kind of conception of space that full-fledged Gricean communicators operate with.

9 Perspective-Taking

Demonstrative communication presupposes the ability to take perspectives. If you have no grasp of the notion of a viewpoint; if you are not in a position to know that the same things you are perceiving are perceivable from another's perspective also, it is impossible for you to demonstratively point out some object or situation in the environment to others. It is hence tempting to think of the capacity for perspective-taking in terms of the ability to generate hypotheses about how things look from viewpoints other than one's own.

But it would be a mistake to think of this capacity exclusively in such conceptually demanding terms. Developmental psychology distinguishes between two kinds of perspective-taking that children master at different times in their lives. Broadly, level 1 perspective-taking is the capacity to judge *what* another perceiver can see. Children pass level 1 tasks at about two and a half years of age. Level 2 perspective-taking is the capacity to judge *how* an object looks from another's point of view. Children pass level 2 tasks significantly later, around four and a half years of age. But the ability to communicate demonstratively does not begin with the capacity to solve level 2 tasks. Children can work out what object another speaker intends to communicate about without being able to judge how that object looks from the speaker's perspective. They know where the object of the speaker's intended communication is, and this is what enables them to produce, and understand, demonstrative utterances. The developmental evidence suggests that we should not place too much emphasis on the capacity for full-fledged perspective-taking, and the conception of space that enables it, in our attempt to understand the spatial demands facing demonstrative communicators. Rather, we should begin with the question of what spatial framework is enjoyed by children capable of passing only level 1 tests, since the possession of such a framework appears sufficient for demonstrative communication. In this chapter I introduce the distinction between the two levels of perspective-taking in some more detail.

Flavell characterizes the distinction as follows:

> At later-developing Level 2 . . . children clearly understand the idea of people having different perspectives or views of the same display. Level 2 children can represent the fact that although both they and another person see the very same thing—"same" qua thing—from different station points, the other person none-theless sees it a bit differently, or has a somewhat different visual experience of it, than they do. Level 2 knowledge thus is essentially the kind all of us had assumed we were studying beginning with Piaget and Inhelder (1956). At earlier-developing Level 1, children understand that the other person need not presently see something (again, qua thing) just because they do. Conversely, they also recognize that the other person may currently see something they do not.
>
> However, they do not yet conceptualize and consciously represent the fact of perspective-derived differences between their and the other person's visual experience of something both people both currently see. Level 1 children know that others also see things and that they and others need not see the same things at any given moment. They may also be able to infer exactly what things others do and do not see, given adequate cues. Thus, they are clearly not profoundly and pervasively egocentric in the Piagetian sense; they definitely do have some Existence-type knowledge about visual perception. Level 2 children possess this same knowledge and ability, of course, but are additionally aware that the same things may look different to others viewing them from a different position. (Flavell 1985, 119–120)

Moll and Meltzoff (2011) introduce the turtle task (Masangkay et al. 1974) as a classic level 2 task that tests subjects' capacity for visual perspective-taking. A child and an adult sit at opposite ends of a table with a picture of a turtle between them. Children who are four and a half years old or older are able to acknowledge that the adult sees the turtle in a different orientation, whereas younger children tend to describe the turtle from their own perspective. For this acknowledgement to be possible, the child has to be able to take the perspective of the adult and generate a hypothesis about the object's orientation from a viewpoint that is distinct from her own. This is a more demanding task than that mastered by two-year-olds who, when witnessing an adult searching for something, prefer to hand her an object that is blocked from the adult's view over a mutually visible one. It is more demanding also than a task in which an adult holds up a card between herself and a child, each side of which shows a different animal. The children had previously been shown both sides of the card. Most children of two and a half years old or older could say what they and the adult saw, respectively. Moll and Meltzoff (2011, 401) describe level 1 perspective-taking as the ability to determine "what objects another sees from a certain spatial position or where an object has to be placed in order to hide it from a person's view"; they describe level 2 as "the understanding that people may not only see different things but see things *differently*. In this level, a child can determine, in philosophical terms, the specific "mode of presentation" (Frege 1892) in which an object is given."

You might think that the difference in the demands on subjects' perspective-taking capacities is reflected in the demands on their spatial frame of reference. Creem-Regehr et al. (2013, 5) suggest that the capacity for level 2 perspective-taking requires the subject to operate with what they call the "transformation of the egocentric reference frame onto the other's viewpoint." The ability to generate imaginative hypotheses about an object's looks, or about the spatial relation of objects relative to a variety of perspectives, requires them to imagine perspectives other than their own, where these possible perspectives, and objects' corresponding looks, are not already defined. Level 2 perspective-taking thus requires subjects to operate with a conception of space in which many locations can serve as centers of perception.

The important question for present purposes is what frame of reference is required for level 1 perspective-taking. Creem-Regehr et al. (2013, 5) suggest that level 1 perspective-taking tasks require the deployment of an allocentric framework in which "inter-object relations" are used to determine what is visible from another's perspective. That is, tasks in which a perceiver is asked to judge whether a given object is visible from another's perspective are mastered by exploiting the visual spatial relation between the object and the other perceiver. They cite evidence from Kelly, Beall, and Loomis (2004), who asked observers to judge which aspects of a target object that was partly occluded by a building others could see. The finding was that subjects were generally good at this task but overestimated what the other could see as the distance between viewer and subject increased. Creem-Regehr et al.'s explanation of this finding is that subjects make use of an allocentric frame of reference in which subjects match various distances and angles to infer the line of sight of another.

How plausible is this conclusion? It will be useful to distinguish between two kinds of allocentric frames of reference. The Evansian account I sketched earlier is one such kind: it amounts to the full-fledged ability to map egocentric perspectives onto locations in objective space, and thus to a reflective conception of space. This is the framework that Creem-Regehr et al. ascribe to subjects in level 2 perspective-taking tasks. The second kind of allocentric frame of reference is less demanding. It is what Grush (2001, 79) describes as "egocentric space with a nonego reference point": it is the framework employed by someone who thinks of himself as the center of space, so that other objects in the same region can be described relative to his own position (left-right, above-below, and so on); and who then uses one object in space as a reference point for the description of the position of other objects. You might speculate that this is the spatial framework in use in level 1 perspective-taking tasks: when I have to make a judgment about what is visible from your perspective, I use your location as a nonego reference point in egocentric space. You can think of this process as a form of triangulation, albeit not of the social Davidsonian kind. Burge (2010, 204), in his discussion of Evans's account of the prerequisites of spatial thinking, notes:

> If, from position e(1) I see and think about an object x at a certain distance 45 degrees to my right and another object y at a certain distance 45 degrees to my left, I should be able to determine the approximate distance between the two objects. And I should be able to determine the approximate relation between the distance from me to object x and the distance from me to object y. This determination depends on computational transformations in the perceptual system. If the transformations are to be regular, all the principles governing the three distance relations must attribute the same metric properties (or be ordinarily comparable), and must employ the same geometrical principles.

The perceiver in this example relies on triangulation to work out the spatial positions of perceived objects relative to himself and to the other object. He is using the position of the perceived objects as non-ego reference points in Grush's sense. Could the perceiver be exploiting the same spatial framework to work out, as in Kelly et al.'s experiment, what aspects of an object remain visible behind a barrier that partially obstruct someone's view of the thing?

Creem-Regehr et al.'s suggestion is, in effect, to think of the location of the other perceiver in level 1 perspective-taking as a nonego reference point, which allows the subject to construe the line of sight of that perceiver so as to be in a position to judge what is or is not visible from her perspective. But the crucial difference between Kelly et al.'s experiment and the operation Burge describes is that the subject in Kelly et al. treats the location as a center of perspective. The subject is not concerned with the question of spatial distances between a variety of perceived objects; she is concerned with what is visible from a location distinct from her own. She does not have to perform an imaginative rotation so as to form a view about how the object looks from someone else's perspective; but she still has to treat the other's location as a viewpoint. And the resources of a strictly allocentric spatial framework are not sufficient to explain how this is possible: the notion cannot explain the social character of the frame of reference with which the subject is operating. A creature capable of perspective-taking, even of a level 1 kind, has to be operating with a spatial framework in which a variety of locations are treated as the positions of perceivers and agents. A purely allocentric spatial framework in which a creature is able to compute the spatial relations of objects relative to a variety of reference points is not a social framework in this sense.

The difficulty, then, is to make sense of the idea of a social spatial framework that is available to creatures not (yet) capable of level 2 perspective-taking. It can seem compelling to think that if you are to judge what another can see, you must also be in a position to judge how she sees it. After all, visual objects are always presented in particular standpoint-dependent ways. To suggest that it is possible for a creature to judge what is visible to another but not how it looks to her is, as Moll and Meltzoff (2011, 400) put it, counterintuitive. Grip on sociality in perceptual thinking appears to be tightly linked with grasping that the objects of other perceivers' visual experiences are presented to them in a perspective-dependent way. Visual objects, you might think, cannot be presented shorn of their perspective-dependent properties, and perceivers' standpoints toward these objects cannot be made sense of unless one understands the standpoint-dependency of these properties. Kessler and Rutherford (2010) approach this problem by asking what role the perceiver's body plays in the two forms of visuospatial perspective-taking. They suggest that "in front of" and "behind" judgments rely on level 1 perspective-taking that does not require the subject to simulate a bodily rotation, while understanding "left" and "right" requires such a rotation, and hypothesize that the two kinds of perspective-taking rely on quite different forms of embodiment. Level 2 perspective-taking requires a simulation of a body rotation into another perspective, while level 1 perspective-taking might rely on motor resonance.[1]

These reflections do not provide a definite answer to the question of how to think of the spatial framework of creatures capable of level 1 perspective-taking. But they give us a first clue as to how to approach the issue: to make sense of the notion of social space, of the kind that facilitates level 1 perspective-taking, it is necessary to go beyond the classic distinction between egocentric and allocentric spatial frameworks. We need to consider the way in which the subject's body, with its capacity for action, is spatially presented in its environment. The next two chapters develop this suggestion.

10 Space and Action

10.1 The Spatiality of the Body

As we have seen, Evans thinks of the ability to locate oneself in the objective order, and thus to map one's egocentric framework onto what he calls a cognitive map, in practical terms. In the passage from *The Varieties of Reference* quoted earlier, he highlights the conceptual connection between a creature's capacity for action and its spatial framework (Evans 1982, 154). The view is that the egocentric spatial organization of the objects of a creature's experience depends on the creature's ability to act on these objects. To have practical knowledge of an object's location is to know in which direction to move in order to act on it. An egocentric frame of reference is a frame of reference for action, where "action" connotes a bodily know-how. Spatial reasoning, along those lines, is possible only for agents. And since perspective-taking is a form of spatial reasoning, it follows on this view that creatures capable of perspective-taking must be agents.

Action-relevant practical knowledge involves the awareness of your internal spatial constitution. If you are to act on the cup to your left by stretching out your left arm and closing your fingers around its handle, you must know the position of your arm and how to move it to reach the cup. Gallagher highlights the role of the body in providing an egocentric frame of reference:

> One of the important functions of the body in the context of perception and action is to provide the basis for an egocentric spatial frame of reference. Indeed, this egocentric framework is required for the very possibility of action, and for the general structure of perceptual experience. The fact that perception and action are perspectivally spatial (for example, the book appears to my right or to my left, or in the center of my perceptual field), is a fact that depends precisely on the spatiality of the perceiving and acting body. (Gallagher 2005, 59)

It is not clear, though, what it means to treat one's body as the center of an egocentric frame of reference. At first sight, it seems uncontroversial that we regard our bodily location as the origin of agency and perception—as the place we could think of as "here" (more on this in section 12.3). But since bodies are spatially extended, the question arises whether "here" denotes the entire area taken up by the body in external space or whether it denotes a bodily center that itself may or may not be spatially extended. You might think that the notion of such a spatial center is in use when we describe the location of our limbs relative to each other by means of a range of bodily axes ("above" and "below," "left" and "right," and "in front of" and "behind"). Wouldn't these axes have to be centered around some common core (the body's trunk perhaps)?

Campbell (1994, 14) highlights a problem with this suggestion: the axes defining the movement of the hand in writing, for instance, are not the same ones as those defining the movement of the whole body in walking. He also points out that some axes used to direct bodily movement, such as the axis that defines above and below, are not given in bodily terms at all (but rather, in this instance, in terms of the magnetic field). There is no unified bodily center relative to which we understand the spatial orientation of our bodily axes and whose location could be designated by thinking of it as "here." There is no single place that would define the center of the body, and thus of action space. The agent's awareness of the bodily axes must in some sense be taken as primitive; it simply is the sense one has of one's body and its internal spatial order that allows one to interact with the environment.[1]

To sum up where we stand: in order to make progress with the idea that perspective-taking is possible without the ability to generate, imaginatively, hypotheses about how an object looks from viewpoints other than one's own, we need to consider bodily spatial awareness. It appears that whatever the social spatial framework underwriting demonstrative communication turns out to consist in, it is not the conceptually demanding kind that abstracts from the body's capacity for action. But it is not at all easy to spell out what it means to treat one's bodily location as the center of perception and action. The bodily axes by means of which one can describe one's internal bodily arrangement are not unified around a common center, a core you could designate as "here." It appears, rather, that our sense of our internal bodily constitution is fluid and that it can only be described relative to the environment in which we find ourselves and the actions we are performing.

10.2   Proprioception and the Relational Character of Action Space

Gallagher (2005, 140) suggests that "perceptual space is already pragmatically organized by the construction, the very shape, of the body," and that this organization facilitates the ecological interaction between body and environment. If you are able to lift a cup to your mouth (say), you have to know in which direction to move your arm and hand, how to close your fingers around its handle, and how to move it upward. This requires more than knowing the internal relation of your limbs and knowing the spatial features of the cup and its position in external space. You have to know the position of your body relative to the environment in which you act.

Awareness of one's body thus is a prerequisite of an egocentric spatial framework that allows the individual to act on this environment. Gallagher appeals to the necessary "implicit reference" to one's bodily spatial framework in egocentric space:

> If one accepts the premise that sense perception of the world is spatially organized by an implicit reference to our bodily framework, the awareness that is the basis for that implicit reference cannot depend on perceptual awareness without the threat of infinite regress. To avoid the infinite regress one requires a pre-reflective bodily awareness that is built into the structures of perception and action, but that is not itself egocentric . . . the proprioceptive spatiality of the body is not framed by anything other than the body itself. (Gallagher 2005, 137)

On this view, which has its roots in Merleau-Ponty ([1945] 2002), proprioceptive bodily awareness should not be thought of as a form of perception; it is a primitive given.[2] But the line of thought I have been developing casts doubt on the contention that proprioceptive bodily awareness can by itself provide the agent with a spatial center around which the objects of action are grouped. Rather, you have to think of bodily awareness as, necessarily, the awareness of the body in its environment, and thus as drawing on both proprioceptive and perceptual information. While there can be no doubt that bodily awareness plays a vital role in one's practical know-how, the bodily axes cannot constitute the basis of an egocentric spatial framework. You can know how to move your body in order to reach for and move objects in the environment only if this environment is already present to you.[3] There are several reasons for thinking this. First, given what was said in the previous section about the diversity of the axes that shape bodily awareness, it is not clear exactly which location should form the ego center of the spatial organization of one's environment. The bodily axes that enable you to reach for objects with your hands are not the same as those that allow you to walk toward them, and they are not, if the earlier considerations are on the right track, centered on a common core. Hence, there is the question of just where the center around which the environment is organized should be located.

Second, while it is true that an agent's grasp of her internal spatial constitution and movement is primarily proprioceptive, visual perception in particular also contributes to and can on some occasion overrule proprioceptive information in the self-ascription of actions (Bermúdez 2000, 152–153; I discuss this topic in more detail in section 12.4. And, as Bermúdez (141) points out, there are good reasons for thinking that there is a common coding structure between visual input and motor output. If so, it is a mistake to think of our internal spatial organization as constitutive of the spatial order of the external environment.

Third, the idea that agents base their understanding of the environment's spatial order on their grasp of their internal spatial arrangement provokes the question of how the agent could be in a position to distinguish between objects that are within her reach and those too far away to be acted on. You might speculate that the agent can find out whether an object is within reach by mapping the proprioceptive location that marks the outer limit of her action space (perhaps the location of the tips of her fingers when she stretches out her hand) onto her surroundings. As you are sitting at your desk, you can work out which perceptual objects are within your reach (the keyboard, the mouse), which ones can be within reach if you move your body (the desk lamp if you lean forward, the plant at the other end of the room if you walk over), and which ones cannot be reached in principle (the sun that is shining through the window). You can find this out because you know the length of your arm (three feet, say) and because you can come to perceptually know, at least roughly, which objects are three feet or less from your position, which ones are within walking distance, and which ones are not. But this method can be put to use only if you are already operating with a spatial framework that allows you to think of the objects in your surroundings as grouped around you and of your body as an object in external space.

You already have to have solved the problem of how to integrate proprioception and perception into a common spatial framework. You could not
explain your ability to distinguish between what is and what is not within
reach if you began with the idea that the egocentric spatial order of the perceived environment is grounded in proprioceptive spatial awareness.

Generally the picture that is emerging suggests a relational account of
bodily and perceptual awareness, on which the acting subject is always
drawing on both sources of information to situate himself in the environment. The discussions of peripersonal space and the body schema in the
next sections fill in that idea.

10.3   Peripersonal Space

We should not, then, think that creatures like us rely solely on two kinds
of spatial representation: the personal space that is primarily propriocep-
tively constituted and the extrapersonal space of vision and some of the
other senses. On such a view, it remains mysterious how we could be able
to integrate the two domains, which seems indispensable if we are to act
in the environment at all. Hence you might hypothesize that there is a
third, equally basic spatial domain that is characterized by its sensitivity
to both perceptual and proprioceptive cues.[4] You could think of such a
domain, phenomenally, as the region in which objects are presented as
ready-to-hand—the domain, that is, in which they are presented so as to
offer opportunities for action. Matthen (2005, 300) suggests that there is a
kind of motion-guiding vision whose objects have a "feeling of presence":
it "furnishes us with the capacity to come into contact with and physically
manipulate physical objects." This kind of vision can be available only for
objects that are within reach. If Matthen is right, there is a phenomenological difference between the experience of objects in a perceiver's action
space and those outside it. Suppose (to take an example from Holmes and
Spence 2004) you are walking down a path in the forest on a windy day
and a tree branch swings toward you. Your natural reaction will be to duck
out of its way or perhaps protect your face with your hands. It is because
of the sensitivity of your perceptual system to the events in your immediate environment that you are able to avoid being hit by the branch. The
relative distance of the perceived event matters for how you react: had the
branch snapped in the far distance, it would not have elicited the bodily

response that allowed you to avoid getting hit. You are sensitive to events in your close surroundings in an automatic, nonreflective mode that is not activated by events farther away. What counts as close here is determined by a variety of factors; it depends, for instance, on your action capabilities. A perceiver's estimate of an object's distance depends on whether she holds a tool with the purpose of reaching for the thing (Witt, Profitt, and Epstein 2004); on how difficult she thinks it is to grasp the object (Linkenauger et al. 2009); whether you are by yourself or with other people (whether an event is within your action space is modulated by the presence of others in your vicinity; Costantini and Sinigaglia 2011); and whether the event is relevant for the execution of your action intention or because it necessitates a protective reaction (De Vignemont and Iannetti 2015).

In a seminal article, Rizzolatti et al. (1997) argued that peripersonal space is represented in the brain in the form of a specific spatial map that is critical for the control of motor movement. Much of the empirical support for the existence of a separate spatial framework for action comes from studies of tactile extinction.[5] Di Pellegrino, Làdavas, and Farné (1997) studied a patient suffering from left tactile extinction following right hemisphere brain damage. Such patients fail to detect a sensory stimulus on the opposite "contralesional" bodily side of their lesion when a competing stimulus in the same sense (such as sight or touch) is presented on the same "ipsilesional" side. Di Pellegrino et al. found that in their patient, an ipsilesional visual stimulus could cross-modally induce the extinction of a tactile stimulus. If the patient was touched on the left hand that was screened from his view and the experimenter wiggled his finger, in a touch-like movement, just above his right hand, the patient could not reliably detect the touch. However, if the visual stimulus was presented at the level of the patient's eye and thus far from his hands, he was able to reliably detect being touched on his left hand. This finding provides evidence that visual and tactile stimuli are represented in an integrated, bimodal format; and it also supports the view that this integration is possible only close to the subject's body. Summing up the past decades' research into peripersonal space, De Vignemont and Iannetti (2015, 327) write, "It is now well accepted that the central nervous system represents differently and separately sensory stimuli happening on the body, in the space immediately surrounding the body, and in the space beyond reach, in which the individual navigates."

10.4   "Coping" in Peripersonal Space

How should we think of the agent's involvement in peripersonal space? One way to approach the question is this. Think of the agent as a detached observer who is related to the objects available for action in the same way in which you are related to the plastic goldfish that can be angled, with difficulty, at a fishing booth at a fair. Then you think of the agent as being at one remove from her environment. Although the agent exploits visuo-sensory representations in order to know which objects are available for angling, she is not embedded in that environment; she is, rather, presented with choices that she may or may not execute. Something like this picture is implicit in Wu's (2011) notion of a "behavioral space," which he introduces in the context of outlining his idea that attention is selection for action. He asks us to imagine a simple scenario in which two objects are in your view: a baseball and a basketball. You could kick either ball with your right or your left leg, so there are four possible actions available to you. These four possibilities constitute the agent's behavioral space, which Wu thinks of in terms of the possible "input-output linkages" that are available to the agent at a given moment. For there to be action, he says, "appropriate selections must be made whereby an input informs a specific output. Thus, a path in behavioural space is selected" (Wu 2011, 99).

On this model, the objects or situations in peripersonal space offer a variety of opportunities for action that can be paired with a variety of bodily responses to satisfy whatever the agent's motivational state is. Wu's account of behavioral space is of a functionalist kind, in which perceptual inputs (from the perceived objects) are paired with behavioral outputs (the agent's responses). So there are, on this view, two independently defined variables whose selection yields different functions. Each of these variables is defined without reference to any of the other. In particular, the perceptual variables are defined independently of the behavioral variables. This is what it takes for what Wu calls the "many-many problem" to arise: the problem of how to select inputs and outputs so as to satisfy the agent's motivational state. To solve this problem, the agent has to look at the environmental opportunities for action in isolation from the bodily response: there is a choice between two balls and a choice between two feet with which to kick either. Much will depend, of course, on how you think of this selection:

whether you think of it in the explicit conscious terms of a choice or the implicit terms of a selection underwritten by the agent's embodied motor system. But in either case, the spatial framework in which these selections or choices are presented could only treat the agent as being at one remove from his surroundings. Behavioral space is static, akin to a snapshot taken of the spatial arrangement of objects affording opportunities for action, at the moment before the action is carried out: it is like the array of goldfish laid out for you to angle at the fishing booth.

It would be a mistake to think of peripersonal space as a kind of behavioral space (to be clear, Wu does not recommend this view). This becomes apparent when you consider the crucial role of touch in studies of tactile extinction, as introduced in the previous section: the observed cross-modal effect involves vision and touch. And it is not surprising that touch should play this vital role in the empirical study of action space: in ordinary human agents, touch is simply indispensable in motor action.[6] As Martin (1992, 206) points out, the awareness of the spatial arrangement of your fingers' grasp of an object makes you aware of the shape of the thing; the arrangement of your body mirrors that of the object. Touch is an experience of the body in relation to objects in the environment that conveys vital practical information about these objects.[7] And touch is a dynamic sense: it is by moving your fingers around an object that you acquire knowledge of its shape. It is hence unsurprising that action space, in which touch plays such an important role, is itself dynamic.[8] This dynamic character of peripersonal space puts it at odds with Wu's notion of behavioral space, since on such an account you could not explain the integration of proprioceptive and visual information in the way necessary for bodily activity. In an account of peripersonal space, you cannot prise apart sensory input and behavioral output in the way that gives rise to the many-many problem. Action space is really space-in-action; it is not a representation that abstracts from the agent's actual involvement from his doings in the particular action context.[9]

You can substantiate the notion of peripersonal space further by means of a proposal by Costantini and Sinigaglia (2011), who argue in favor of an affordance-relative notion of space. Gibson introduced the notion of an affordance as follows: "The affordances of the environment are what it offers the animal, what it provides or furnishes, either for good or ill" (Gibson 1979, 127). Affordances, according to this view, are properties of the environment, but, as Chemero puts it, "taken relative to an animal"

(Chemero 2003, 182). Chemero develops a different proposal: on his account, affordances have to be thought of as relations between the abilities of organisms and features of the environment. He discusses the affordance relation between a set of stairs and a subject's climbing ability. The relation has two relata—the relevant feature of the environment and the stair-climbing ability of the individual—and it is determined by both. For instance, the affordance relation between a subject with longer legs and stairs with greater riser height may be the same as the relation between a subject with shorter legs and stairs with smaller riser height.

Costantini and Sinigaglia (2011) build on Chemero's view. They suggest that the distance between an object and the agent matters for the agent's perception of the opportunities for action provided by the object. They show that "micro-affordances" (opportunities for action immediately dependent on what is within the agent's reach) are space-dependent by means of an experiment in which they use the "spatial alignment effect." The effect consists in a decrease in reaction time when a subject executes a motor act congruent with that afforded by an object (Costantini and Sinigaglia 2011, 438). Subjects carry out motor movements more quickly if the object on which they act is conducive to that movement. Thus, subjects were instructed to replicate a grasping hand movement when a go signal appeared. They were presented with a three-dimensional scene in which a mug, placed on a table, had its handle oriented toward the left or the right, thus being congruent or incongruent with the grasping action. Costantini and Sinigaglia found that the alignment effect occurred only if the cup was placed within reach of the subject—when the mug was, as they say in a Heideggerian vein, "ready-to-hand." Their conclusion is as follows:

> Overall our findings suggest that, at least for micro-affordances, the relation of affordance depends on a further relation between its relata, that is, a spatial relation which is not constitutive of the affordance but makes it possible. In order for something to be graspable with respect to an individual endowed with the appropriate motor abilities, it has to fall within his or her own peripersonal space—better, it has to be ready to her own hand. (Costantini and Sinigaglia 2011, 440)

This quotation highlights an important point: when thinking about the role of action in perception, a common move is to focus on the question of *how* sensorimotor action shapes the subject's perception of it.[10] But this requires that the object of perception be available for action in the first place.[11] An explanation is needed for how it can be that some objects are presented as available for action and others are not without presupposing that the perceiver already has a grip on the practical spatial relation between herself and the object. The appeal to the notion of peripersonal space can help here. The practical spatial relation obtains in regions in which the agent is sensitive to both proprioceptive and perceptual cues; it is the region in which objects are presented as offering affordances for action.

But not everything that is within an agent's reach is within her action space. In the example of the walk through the woods, there are countless ways in which I could interact with my environment. I could grab the branch that is moving toward me and swing off it, Tarzan style. I could collapse onto the ground and pretend I'm dead. I could bloody-mindedly ignore the branch and just take the knock. Yet that's not what I do: I duck out of its way so as to avoid getting hit. You might think that Costantini and Sinigaglia's experiment, in which the reaction time to a visual stimulus varies depending on whether the object is ready-to-hand, supports the idea that peripersonal space should be thought of as presenting opportunities for action that the agent can select or not. But it would be a mistake to think that. It is not, after all, as if the agent had, in one scenario, been presented with a variety of possible action opportunities. Rather, she is presented with two distinct scenarios (one in which the handle of the cup is convenient to reach and another in which it is not), in which she performs differently. The evidence for the affordance relation is the spatial alignment effect that consists in a decrease in reaction time if the object is ready-to-hand. The evidence consists, in other words, not in the selection of options but in what you might call, with Dreyfus ([1993] 2014), "coping"—the actual bodily engagement with one's surroundings, which varies in the two conditions. As Dreyfus (81) points out, it is not necessary to appeal to the notion of the agent's intentions, or (as in Wu's model) his motivational states, to make sense of such an engagement. The experience of acting is, as he puts it, "the experience of a steady flow of skillful activity in response to one's sense of the environment."[12] Rietveld, in his discussion of the role of affordance in perception, offers this quote from Merleau-Ponty:

> The subject, when put in front of his scissors, needle and familiar tasks, does not need to look for his hands or his fingers, because they are . . . potentialities already mobilized by the perception of scissors or needle, the central end of those "intentional threads" which link him to the objects given. . . . [It] is the piece of

leather "to be cut up"; it is the lining "to be sewn" (Merleau-Ponty [1945] 2002, 121–122), quoted after Rietveld (2008, 992).

Rietveld sees this case as

> a good example of the way the motor potentialities of the body are provoked or recruited by affordances. The body that is attuned to its environment does not deliberate but allows itself to be invited, so to speak, by the perceived possibilities for action in the given situation. The body's skills are immediately potentiated by some of the meaningful or alluring objects around it, responding to the piece of leather as that which is "to be cut up"; to a possibility for action in this situation (affordance). (Rietveld 2008, 992)

This is just the thought I have been pursuing: it is a mistake to understand the notion of an "affordance" or "opportunity for action" as implying the need for a selection between alternatives. The mistake is to think of the body and its responses to environmental stimuli as distinct from the environment so as to require a choice that links the inner with the outer domains. The body is already presented in its relation to the environment; it is already interacting with it.

The failure to acknowledge this consideration makes it impossible to explain the notion of peripersonal space. Action space is context dependent in that it presents the agent's body and environment directly in relation to each other, and it is dynamic in that this relation is continuously changing as a consequence of both bodily and environmental events. The relation changes if the order of things in the agent's environment is altered (if, say, the orientation of the cup's handle is moved from one side to the other), and it changes when the agent produces a bodily response to the way things are in his vicinity. There is no selection to be made here: the rock bottom is the relation between body and environment that is presented to the agent in peripersonal space.

To sum up this chapter: Motivated by the question of the role of the body in level 1 perspective-taking, I considered some views on spatial bodily awareness and highlighted its peculiar nature. Although the body's spatial organization can be thought of as involving a variety of axes, these axes do not originate in some common core. This consideration supported the view, in section 10.2, that action space had to be thought of as a relation between the body and its environment: the agent could not know which objects are within reach by means of a calculation that takes the bodily axes as a starting point. This observation was borne out by the notion of periper-sonal space, introduced in section 10.3, which is defined as the area around the body in which the agent can exploit both proprioceptive and percep-tual cues. Finally, I asked how we should think of the relation between agent and environment that obtains in peripersonal space and suggested that it should be thought of as a kind of coping: an actual bodily involve-ment with one's surroundings.

11   Social Action Space

In this chapter I begin to substantiate the notion of a social spatial frame-work. So far I have been interested in spatial frameworks quite generally. The upshot of the discussion has been that we need to take seriously the idea of an action space in which both proprioceptive and perceptual cues can be exploited and that underwrites organisms' ability to perform motor actions in their environments. This chapter builds on this idea in order to develop an account of social space in the practical terms I have been intro-ducing. Along those lines, social creatures like us act in environments that not only present them with affordances for action; they present them with opportunities to act jointly.

11.1   Introduction

When thinking about joint action, you have at least two distinct options. You can begin by asking what kinds of intentions creatures need to enter-tain if they are to act together, which then largely means that they are able to jointly pursue a shared goal.[1] *How* they are able to realize their collec-tive intentions is not at the heart of this (predominantly philosophical) research program; indeed, it is not a prerequisite of a collective intention that any coordinated motor movement take place at all.[2] Alternatively, you can begin with a focus not on the agents' mental states but their actual bodily doings. You will then be interested in the coordination of the agents' motor activities that enable them to act jointly. This may involve research into their ability to predict others' bodily movements (for instance, Sebanz and Knoblich 2009), and it involves asking what the format is for the representation of one's own and the other's body (for instance, De Vignemont and Fourneret 2004).

Both of these research programs are well established. They have produced an impressive and rapidly growing body of literature that attests to philosophers' and psychologists' increasing interest in the social domain. By contrast, the empirical research into social spatial frameworks is in its infancy. Much of the work I will be drawing on has been carried out only in the past few years. But the accumulated evidence is substantive enough, I think, to allow at least an exploration of the ways in which we might think about the notion of a social spatial framework, even if we are not yet in a position to draw definite conclusions about its nature.

11.2   Empirical Studies of Social Action Space

Suppose that the line of thought I pursued in the previous chapter is on the right track: we should endorse the idea of a multisensory action space in which the agent is sensitive to both perceptual and proprioceptive cues and in which things are presented relationally so as to facilitate motor action. Then the question arises how to accommodate the observation that some of the things we do are done jointly with other agents. Humans are intensely sensitive to the presence and doings of others. We mimic each other's posture and mannerisms (Liu et al. 2016), imitate facial expressions from birth (Meltzoff and Moore 1983) and in adulthood (Chartrand and Bargh 1999), take up each other's speech behavior (Zajonc et al. 1987), breathe and synchronize our heart rates with our partners (Levelt and Kelter 1982), and even synchronize our skin conductance (Helm, Sbarra, and Ferrer 2012). These attunements are automatic or motoric in nature; they do not require a deliberate, reflective, conscious mental act, such as the formation of an intention. The bodily presence of others influences us quite profoundly and in ways we are not always aware of. Does this kind of motoric influence have an impact on the spatial framework underwriting joint action?

This question is only beginning to be investigated, but the findings are intriguing. In the previous section, I introduced Costantini and Sinigaglia's (2011) discussion of peripersonal space. As we saw, they draw on the spatial alignment effect to argue that affordance relations between perceivers and their environments depend on a further relation that presents action-relevant situations in peripersonal space. They then build on this view to shed light on the notion of what they call "affordance in a social context." They investigate whether the spatial relation on which the affordance relation between environmental features and an animal's abilities depends can be modulated by the action space of an individual other than the agent herself. In a version of their first experiment, an avatar (that is, a virtual reality simulation of a person) is seated at the table on which the mug is placed. As before, the spatial alignment effect occurs when the mug is within the peripersonal space of the agent. But, remarkably, the effect occurs also when the mug is within the action space of the avatar even though it is not reachable by the subject. The effect does not occur, however, if the avatar is replaced by a cylinder with the same volume as the avatar. Costantini and Sinigaglia (2011, 445) draw the following conclusion:

> All of this suggests that the space constraint of the micro-affordances should not be construed only as relative to one's own peripersonal space because the affordance relation can be mediated by the peripersonal space of another individual. According to our data, the situational features may evoke a motor behaviour to the observer even when they are outside his or her own reaching space, provided that they fall within the peripersonal space of a potential coactor. Our proposal is that the extension of the space modulation of the affordance relation from an individual to another one is likely to be due to a space mirror mechanism that allows the individual to match others' surrounding space with his or her own peripersonal space, thus mapping others' action potentialities onto his or her own motor abilities.

More evidence in support of the existence of a spatial framework for social action, albeit of an auditory rather than visual nature, comes from Maister et al. (2015). They investigate whether shared sensory experiences can elicit changes in the way subjects' peripersonal space is represented and whether these changes amount to an expansion of a subject's own action space or a remapping of the other's action space onto her own. In the experiment (which I am rendering in somewhat abbreviated form), the subjects are exposed to an audio-tactile integration task in which they have to respond to an electrical stimulus at predefined intervals. Meanwhile, they hear pink noise (a kind of noise with the same frequency as the color pink) that seems to move between themselves and a confederate. In the first round of the experiment, Maister et al. find that subjects react more quickly to the stimulus when the noise is perceived as being situated near their own bodies. After the first round, the subjects undergo an asynchronous interpersonal stimulation during which they experience being touched on the face and subsequently see a confederate being touched at the same location on her face. This experience does not affect their reaction time to the tactile stimulus. The subjects then undergo a shared experience in the form of the so-called "enfacement illusion," in which they are simultaneously being touched on their faces and seeing the other person being touched in the same place. Maister et al. find that their subjects now react comparably faster to the auditory-tactile stimulus when it occurs at a location close to the other's body, while reaction times at intermediate positions between the participant's and the confederate's body remain unchanged. However, the response times to stimuli experienced as close to the other's body are still longer than responses to stimuli occurring close to the subject's own body. Maister et al. conclude that the shared experience of the enfacement illusion results in a spatial framework during social interactions that is best described as a remapping of the representation of the other's peripersonal space as one's own; the difference in reaction times between events experienced as occurring close to one's own and the other's body shows that this remapping remains incomplete.

A third study investigates the social modulation of the boundaries of peripersonal space. Similarly to Maister et al., Teneggi et al. (2013) use a tactile detection task to measure the scope of subjects' peripersonal space. Subjects are asked to respond as quickly as possible to a series of tactile stimuli on their face while task-irrelevant sounds move between the subject and either a mannequin or a person. Similarly to Maister et al., Teneggi et al. take reaction time as an indicator of the boundary of the subject's peripersonal space: a disproportionate drop in reaction time between two stimuli is taken as evidence that the sound has entered the subject's action space. They find that the boundaries of subjects' peripersonal space shrink when they are facing a person rather than a mannequin. In further rounds of the experiment, subjects play either a cooperative (equal payoffs) or a competitive (unequal payoffs) economic game with the other person prior to the task. Reaction times follow the same pattern as in the first round after the competitive game. After the cooperative game, by contrast, subjects' reaction times remain unaffected by the sound's perceived distance. Teneggi et al. take this finding to indicate that the boundary between the subject's own and the other's peripersonal space has vanished, suggesting a unified action space for both.

Maister's et al.'s (2015) experiments and their conclusions bear some similarity to those of Costantini and Sinigaglia (2011). It is not news that humans are sensitive and responsive to others' motoric bodily expressions and movements, such as smiles and nods. What is news is that they also appear to display sensitivity to objects and events in the peripersonal space of perceptually present other agents, particularly those with whom they engage in some form. In both studies, the observed effect appears in areas that are grouped either around the subject's own or the other's body, with increased reaction times in between. Affordances in the space around others with whom we are engaged appear to be presented in the same way in which affordances are presented in peripersonal space—that is, in a format that integrates perceptual and proprioceptive cues. In Maister et al.'s study, the effect occurs after the subjects' experience of the enfacement illusion. By contrast, the spatial alignment effect is present after the mere observation of the cup being oriented toward the avatar; no interaction or common experience was necessary. A somewhat different picture is presented by Teneggi et al.'s (2013) study, in which an individual's peripersonal space is modulated by the presence of others and, in a cooperative activity, appears to be extended toward, or perhaps fused with that, of the other participant.[3]

For Costantini and Sinigaglia (2011) as well as Maister et al. (2015), reference to the neural underpinnings of spatial resonance mechanisms constitutes an important part of their account. They explain their findings by appeal to a particular class of neurons, the famous (or, depending on your view, infamous) mirror neurons, that are responsive both to stimuli occurring on (or close to) the agent's own body and to stimuli on (or close to) another person's body.[4] Constantini and Sinigaglia (2011, 442–443) draw on a study by Caggiano et al. (2009), in which F5 mirror neurons were recorded both when a monkey executed a goal-directed motor act and when it observed an experimenter executing the same motor act in its own peripersonal and extrapersonal space. Caggiano et al. found that over half of the tested F5 neurons responded selectively to the monkey's peripersonal or extrapersonal space, while the remaining mirror neurons responded to the visual presentation of actions irrespective of their spatial location. Further support for a social mirror mechanism that modulates action space comes from a study by Ishida et al. (2009), which provides evidence for the existence of bimodal neurons that are activated not only by tactile or visual stimuli in the peripersonal space of the monkey but also by visual stimuli presented in the peripersonal space of another individual facing it. Costantini and Sinigaglia refer to these two studies to support their claim that the occurrence of the spatial alignment effect in peripersonal but not extrapersonal space, including its social version, can be explained by appeal to mirror neuronal activity. Similarly, Maister et al. (2015, 456) appeal to a somatosensory mirror system that gets activated both when we are touched and when we see others getting touched.

What can we learn from these studies? I do not think the behavioral evidence is robust enough yet to support definite conclusions about the nature of social action space. In particular, it does not allow for a detailed discussion of the conditions under which subjects' action spaces are extended, so as to include those of other cooperating agents, and when they are presented as distinct regions that are grouped around separate individuals. At the same time, it appears robust enough to support the view that there really is a social kind of action space—that subjects who cooperate with others make use of a spatial format in which they are sensitive to proprioceptive and perceptual cues in regions relatively remote from the area surrounding their own bodies so that these regions can present them with opportunities for action.

With regard to the neurophysiological aspect of some of the studies presented here, it is important to bear in mind that there has been a backlash against some of the more extravagant claims put forward by defenders of the view that the discovery of mirror neurons constitutes a breakthrough in the empirical study of social cognition and, in particular, action recognition.[5] It is beyond the reach of my project to take a view on this debate. It suffices to note that the debate is tangential to the discussion here. I am interested in the way in which joint perceivers can exploit spatial frameworks in order to jointly act on and demonstratively communicate about perceptual objects. In the previous chapter, I suggested that this inquiry needs to take seriously the notion of action space. In this section, I looked at some recent work that supports, however tentatively, the contention that there is a social kind of action space. If you think that neurophysiology provides additional evidence in support of such a framework, you have a stronger reason to take the work considered here seriously. But even if you think that arguments that appeal to the properties of mirror neurons show us absolutely nothing of relevance for social spatial frameworks, the behavioral evidence remains in place.

11.3   Merged and Aligned Action Spaces

Suppose you take the evidence considered in the previous section to support the view that there really is such a thing as social action space. It is nevertheless not at all easy to make sense of the notion. How can there be a spatial framework in which the subject is receptive to proprioceptive and perceptual cues from areas centered around locations other than the one occupied by her own body? After all, I cannot proprioceive your bodily movements, and I cannot see (or otherwise perceptually experience) objects from your perspective. In some way, the subject must be making use of her body to get a grip on the other's point of view. Costantini and Sinigaglia use the notion of "mapping" to accommodate this point; Maister et al. talk about the "remapping" of the subject's peripersonal space onto that of the other agent. Thus, Costantini and Sinigaglia (2011, 445) write:

> Our proposal is that the extension of the space modulation of the affordance relation from an individual to another one is likely to be due to a space mirror mechanism that allows the individual to match others' surrounding space with his or her own peripersonal space, thus mapping others' action potentialities onto his or her own motor abilities.

Similarly, Maister et al. (2015, 459) suggest:

> In our study, sharing a sensory experience with another person did not lead to an expansion of the PPS representation, as it only induced changes in the way information was integrated within the other's PPS, and not in the interim space between self and other. This pattern of results is therefore more accurately described as a "remapping" of the representation of the other's PPS; after stimulation, participants' responses to events occurring in the other's PPS were enhanced.

The question is how to understand these proposals: what spatial framework is required for the mapping or remapping another's action opportunities onto one's own? Pezzulo et al. (2013) distinguish between two distinct spatial frames of reference that agents involved in joint undertakings can deploy; in their view, social space is not unitary. They introduce a variety of parameters that include the angular disparity between agents in relation to the object of their action and whether the activity requires complex operations that cannot be carried out by resonance mechanisms of the agents' motor systems. If joint agents more or less share a common angle on an object or scene (if the angle is below 60 to 90 degrees) and if the tasks demanded of them are simple, they can "merge" their action spaces. This, Pezzulo and colleagues suggest, preserves an egocentric frame of reference, as no perspective-taking is necessary, and can be accomplished through resonance mechanisms of the motor system. If the angular disparity between agents' perspectives is greater than 60 to 90 degrees but the demands on agent's activities are simple, a merger of action spaces is still possible, though the agents will then not share a common frame of reference. If, however, great angular disparities are combined with demanding tasks (Pezzulo et al. mention tasks requiring the ability to distinguish between left and right from the other agent's perspective), then a simulated rotation is required and the action spaces are "aligned," rather than merged, to achieve a common frame of reference. Along the lines of this taxonomy, there is nothing specifically social to the spatial framework that underwrites joint motor action: merged action space is egocentric because no conscious calculation of perspective (by an exercise in imaginative rotation, say) is required to make it possible; all that is needed is the activation of the resonance mechanisms that make an attunement of the agents' motor actions possible. It is when a subject aligns her own action space with that of her co-agent, through an act of reflective perspective-taking, that the agent becomes aware of the distinctness of her own and the other's perspective.

But the studies discussed in the previous section suggest that the distinction between merged and aligned spatial frameworks does not capture the entirety of ways in which agents exploit spatial frames of reference to perform joint actions. The distinction covers cases in which a mere attunement of motor activity is sufficient to coordinate individuals' doings. Such social activities really do not require a spatial framework in which others feature as agents. On the other end of the spectrum, the distinction covers cases in which an explicit act of perspective-taking is required. Examples include the various kinds of demonstrative communication discussed in part 2. What the distinction does not cover is the kind of case in which a fellow subject's location is treated as a center of perception and action, as in the studies discussed in the previous section. Yet this is the interesting kind of case for my purposes. I argued that accounting for the notion of communication-enabling sense requires you to explain how subjects can know in common the location of an object in social space. But neither the aligning nor the merging of perspectives accomplishes this task: merged action spaces are egocentric; aligned ones are allocentric.

11.4   The Joint Body Schema

I cannot proprioceive your bodily movements: this plain observation is the cause of significant difficulties for a plausible account of social space. As noted in the previous section, some kind of mapping appears necessary for the subject to transcend her own bodily location and achieve a frame of reference that allows her to treat a joint subject's position as a center of agency. I now approach this thorny issue by inquiring into the body schema of joint agents.

Gallagher (2005, 24–25) distinguishes between body schema and body image. By *body schema*, he means, roughly, a system of "motor capacities, abilities, and habits that both enable and constrain movement and the maintenance of posture." The body schema is contrasted with the *body image*, which "consists of a system of perceptions, attitudes, and beliefs pertaining to one's own body." The two systems are complexly interrelated. The body schema, says Gallagher, can "enter intentional activity," though it is more basic than that. Gallagher likens the difference between body image and body schema to "the difference between a *perception* (or conscious monitoring) of movement and the actual accomplishment of movement" (24).

It is only because the body schema processes both information about the subject's own body and information about the environment that it can enable the body's movement in its surroundings. The body schema relies on "intermodal communication" (Gallagher 2005, 24) between vision and proprioception even in simple cases of bodily movement. This is a striking parallel to the key feature of peripersonal space, which also facilitates motor action because it is able to integrate both perceptual-environmental and bodily information. At the same time, the representations of personal space (within the subject's body), peripersonal space, and external space are thought to be distinct despite their close integration. As Fulkerson (2013, 160) points out, they "can be dissociated from one another, and there exist pathologies that leave a subject without the ability to represent only one level of representation through forms of spatial neglect."

Soliman et al. (2015) suggest that social tasks requiring the joint manipulation of an object are accomplished by drawing on a joint body schema, in which the subject uses her own body to obtain information beyond what is visible to solve the problem of coordination. In their fascinating study, two participants were given the respective ends of a wire and instructed to saw through a candle by jointly pulling it to and fro. Because the wire was flexible, each participant had to be acutely sensitive to the other's movements so as to keep it taut. The study found that the joint activity resulted in a modification of the subject's body schema and that this modification persisted after the task was completed. To give an abbreviated description of one of the experiments: a pair of LEDs was flashed next to the experimenter's thumb and index fingers on her left hand, which she used to perform the sawing activity. The subject performed the sawing activity with her right hand; her thumbs and index fingers on her (task-irrelevant) left hand were fitted with vibrating devices. The subject's feet had access to two pedals. The task was to press the pedal under her toes when she experienced a vibration at her index finger and to press the pedal under her heels when she experienced a vibration at her thumb. Soliman et al. found that after a five-minute joint sawing activity, the subject was slower in locating a buzz on her left hand when her partner's left hand was flashed at an incongruent location (that is, when the flash was at the partner's thumb and the buzz on the participant's index finger, or vice versa). By contrast, if the subject carried out the sawing activity by herself (with a weight placed at the wire's other end), the effect of congruity with the observed stimuli on the experimenter's hand was much reduced and unreliable. Soliman et al. (2015, 877) conclude:

> When required to coordinate for smooth joint-sawing, the participant's seemingly idle left hand engages continuously in a process of modeling the partner's task relevant hand. . . . Even after joint-sawing is over, the participant's implicit spatial awareness of her left hand continues to be interlocked with the perceived state of the JBS [joint body schema]-relevant partner's left hand so that a flash at the partner's hand, for example, is mapped onto the participant's hand, referencing a given location in the participant's JBS of this hand. If, in addition, a different spatial location is simultaneously referenced by a vibration on the participant's same hand, localizing this vibration becomes less efficient, incurring accuracy and/or delay processing costs.

You might object that Soliman et al.'s findings can be incorporated into a view that takes joint agents to be operating with "merged," and thus egocentric, spatial frameworks. Then you don't think that the subject who is using her body to model her partner's task is operating with a joint body schema; she is, rather, using her own body's pragmatic relation to the manipulated object in order to generate predictions about what the other will do and to thus facilitate smooth movement of the wire. On this view, what is within reach is defined relative to the subject's own location, not relative to the locations of both cooperators. The other's location does then not serve as a center of action; it is, rather, treated as a nonego reference point in egocentric space along the lines of Grush (2001).

Soliman et al. (2015) consider an objection of this sort. The objection is that the term *joint body schema* is unjustified because the grasp of the partner's movements is achieved by a resonance mechanism that originates within the agent's own body. It is not, after all, that the participant somehow transcends her own body and its location; she simply uses her own body schema to generate an adequate motor response to the other's movements. Soliman et al. defend their view by pointing out that it is not just, in the joint condition of the experiment, that an incongruence between the LED signals at the partner's and the buzzing signals at the subject's left hands result in a delay of reaction time; congruence between the two signals in the joint condition also speeds up reaction time and thus facilitates the "processing of one's own body state." This "bidirectionality," Soliman et al. suggest, justifies treating the body schemata of the experimental subjects as joint. The view is, in other words, that the congruence/incongruence relation between signals at the partner's hand and the subject's own does not merely interfere with the completion of the task; it can also play a supporting role if the signals are congruent. So it cannot be that the own body schema is treated by the subject as the basic case whose deployment in the subject's motor activity is merely being interfered with by outside disturbances. Rather, the deployment of the joint schema is the basic case, since congruence between signals at the partner's hand and the subject's own aids the completion of the task.

Why not suppose, though, that the subject operates with an *extended* rather than a joint body schema, as is the case in tool use (Soliman et al. 2015, 885)? In this case, the partner's body is, again, not treated as an independent center of action; it is, rather, integrated into the subject's own bodily activity. Then the idea that the subjects operate with a spatial framework in which distinct locations are represented as centers of agency comes under threat; the view is, rather, that the own body's boundaries are extended so as to encompass the other's arm. There would then be only one (extended) location of bodily activity; the body schema would not be joint, and the agent would be operating with an egocentric spatial framework. But Soliman et al.'s findings speak against this interpretation: if the participant carried out the sawing activity by herself, the effect of congruity of the visual and felt stimuli on her reaction time was reduced. So it does seem to matter, with respect to the force of the congruity effect, whether one or two agents are involved in the activity. The second agent does not appear to play the role of a tool that extends the subject's own body schema but rather of a distinct, yet jointly involved, agent.[6]

Soliman et al. think of the agent's use of her own body schema to model the activity of her co-agent as a simulation:

> A uses visual, auditory, and proprioceptive information specifying her partner's left-hand movement to adjust her own right-hand movement toward smooth interpersonal coordination. Importantly, however, we propose that A uses, in addition, her own body as another source of information to solve the coordination problem. That is, the visually perceived kinematics of B's left hand are modeled by the multisensory spatial circuits underlying the body schema of A's inactive left hand. The mirror-neuron system (MNS; Rizzolatti & Craighero, 2004) then kicks in. The motor controllers of A's left-hand simulate the dynamic forces underlying B's left hand movement, guided by the spatial parameter values instantiated in A's own left-hand body schema. This motor simulation, in turn, enforces the dyadic sensory model developing in A's left hand schema (i.e., the JBS). (Soliman et al. 2015, 874)

Simulation theory (ST) proposes that subjects come to understand observed others' mental states by imaginatively "putting themselves into the other's shoes." To understand the other person, you simulate the thoughts and feelings that you would be experiencing if you were in the other's situation (for instance, Gordon 1986, 1995; Goldman 2006; Heal 1986, 1998). This simulation can, but need not, be explicit; Goldman (2006) allows for the possibility of a "low-level," nonconscious simulation that nevertheless results in the awareness of the resulting understanding. The discovery of mirror neurons is often taken to offer empirical support for simulation theory, as mirroring processes might facilitate the nonconscious (subpersonal) simulation that results in the understanding of the other's mental state. Thus, Gallese and Goldman (1998, 498), in the course of their argument that the discovery of mirror neurons supports ST, maintain that "[mirror neuron] activity . . . creates in the observer a state that *matches* that of the target [person]" (quoted after Gallagher 2005, 221; italics added).

The thing to note for present purposes is that regardless of whether you think that simulative processes (and mirror neuron systems; see section 11.2) are involved in the subject's modeling of the participant's left-hand movements, ST cannot explain how the use of visual information from the cooperator's hand results in the generation of a joint body schema in which the location of the cooperator is presented as a center of perception and agency that is distinct from the subject's own. Such a center is characterized, if my line of thought is on the right track, by the availability of both proprioceptive (bodily) and perceptual (exteroceptive) information at it; so much is required to facilitate action at this location. If the joint body schema is to be distinguished from a merely extended one, the cooperator's location must be presented as a distinct standpoint. The joint agent must be operating with a map on which a variety of places are treated as centers of agency and their occupants as bodily agents. To put it bluntly: for mapping to be possible, you have to have a map. The map, as the representation of the region in which joint agents operate, must already be in place for simulation to be possible.

11.5   The Multilocation Hypothesis

How, then, should we explain the joint agent's capacity to treat locations other than her own as centers of agency? Soliman et al.'s study suggests that the agent, by exploiting visual information about the cooperator's bodily doings, uses her own body to model the other's activity. Since this modeling process relies on the subject's own bodily resources, it ought to be relying on proprioceptive as well as perceptual information. Hence a hypothesis that would be compatible with the approach taken here is that the agent is assigning proprioceptive information from her own bodily movements to a location distinct from her own in allocentric space. It can seem natural to suppose that proprioceptive information is necessarily presented to the agent at her own location; after all, her own location is simply the location of her body. But consider the virtual reality experiments by Lenggenhager et al. (2007) in which subjects saw their own backs in a virtual room. If they experienced their backs being stroked while seeing their backs being stroked synchronously in the virtual room, they were likely to identify the figure in the virtual room as themselves, thus mapping their somatosensorily experienced body onto a location it did not occupy. This study provides some prima facie support for thinking that the ascription of "internal" bodily information to locations distinct from the body's position in allocentric space is possible. If so, you can hypothesize that the process of mapping consists in assigning proprioceptive information obtained from one's own body to places other than one's own location so that it can be integrated with perceptual information from objects occupying these places and so that these places can be presented as centers of agency. Call this the *multilocation hypothesis*.

In section 10.2, I argued that the relational character of action space puts pressure on the proposal to see the proprioceived body as the center of the egocentric framework. Rather, we should conceptualize proprioception and perception as necessarily integrated. The multilocation hypothesis is aligned with this view: if egocentric space is organized around a center that is the result of the binding of proprioceptive and perceptual information at a particular location, then the door is open for the idea that such binding need not occur at the agent's position in allocentric space. Fridland (2011, 533) observes that the body schema may be a better candidate than the proprioceived bodily domain for the center of egocentric space. And the body schema, like peripersonal space, is constituted by both perceptual and proprioceptive information that are integrated in movement (see section 11.4). It is not a big step from this observation to the idea that the bodies of others, with whom we are jointly interacting, can be presented through body schemata that require the binding of proprioceptive and perceptual information in movement. It is just that they are centered on locations other than one's own.

How is such centering possible? To a large extent, this is an empirical question, and an answer will not be available before the evidence is in. But I can outline a few possible moves and their implications for an eventual theory. One such move is to build on the notion of a "master map" of locations, as it is familiar from feature integration theory (Treisman 1988; Treisman and Gelade 1980). The theory aims to explain how processing of objects takes place in the nervous system. It suggests that the representation of elementary features precedes the combination of these features into visual objects. Features belonging to separable dimensions are processed in parallel in preattentive maps, which are glued together by focal attention into unitary objects on a master map. This map contains all the locations at which features have been detected, with each location on the master map having access to the various feature maps. Campbell (2002, 28–29) draws on this theory in his account of the role of visual attention in demonstrative reasoning. Importantly for my purposes, he distinguishes between two distinct uses of feature maps. Their first use, to bind features at a particular location to visually single out an object, is accomplished in early vision and is what makes experience of the object possible. The second use is the verification of demonstrative propositions through conscious attention. There is, on this view, a difference between the ability to single an object out visually and the ability to attend to it consciously.

The proposal is to think of proprioceptive information along the same lines as the features of objects that are combined into objects through binding at particular locations. Just as shapes and colors are features that are processed in early vision, so that they can be integrated into objects through a low-level kind of attention, you might think that the proprioceived movements of particular limbs are action-relevant features found at particular locations. There are, according to the hypothesis, what you might call *movement maps* that allow a low-level action system to integrate proprioceived movements found at particular locations with perceptual features found at the same locations, so as to represent these movements in a format that binds proprioceptive and perceptual information at particular places. This binding secures the connection between proprioception and perception; it places the moving body in its environment by connecting it spatially to the objects around it. Once this binding has taken place and the experience of bodily movement in a given environment is thus possible, you can then consciously focus on an object in your vicinity so as to be able to select it for demonstrative thinking and intentional action. And you can focus on your movements so as to guide them consciously. An example of the first kind of case is a scenario in which you focus on a perceptual object and consciously pick it up. An example of the second kind of case is a scenario in which you consciously exercise a bodily movement, as you do when you perfect a yoga pose, say. Along the lines of the present proposal, these two capacities exploit the same mechanism: they both build on the integration of proprioceptive and perceptual information at particular locations.

The hypothesis has some intuitive appeal. First, it can explain our ability to effortlessly shift our focus in intentional action from environmental to bodily aspects: it is because proprioceptive and perceptual information is integrated below the threshold of consciousness that we do not experience

a rift in mode of presentation when we attend to the body in its environment. Second, it can help substantiate the notion of a body schema.
The body schema, remember, is a system of motor capacities that enables
and controls bodily movement in a given environment. As such, it must
draw on both perceptual and proprioceptive information. If these kinds
of information are bound at particular locations prior to the possibility of
conscious attention to one's intentional doings, it follows that these doings
are never just perceptual objects or internal bodily movements: the agent
always attends to a relation between the two. Along those lines, the body
schema covers the area in which perception and proprioception can be
integrated, so as to facilitate action.[7]

The stipulation of a master map for the binding of proprioception and
perception opens the door to the idea that such integration may be possible
at locations other than the agent's, and perceiver's, own position in allocentric space. It helps with the multilocation hypothesis, since the master map
is a map of all locations at which the relevant features are found. Along
those lines, if proprioceptive and perceptual information is integrated at a
particular location, an agentive event is presented to the perceiver at that
location. Now everything hangs on the proposal that proprioceptive information can be assigned to locations other than the perceiver's own. There
are two distinct ways to give substance to the proposal. The first is to think
that interaction plays a vital role for the agent's deployment of a social
spatial framework. The coordinated, attuned movements exercised by joint
perceivers and agents explain how a location other than one's own can
be presented as a center of agency. This approach is supported by a long
tradition of intersubjectivity research in developmental psychology (for
instance, Trevarthen 1980; Hobson [2002] 2004; Reddy 2011), according
to which interactions that involve both bodily coordination and the har-
monization of their subjective, felt experiences play a vital role in human
sociocognitive development. It is aligned with the findings of Maister et al.
(2015), Teneggi et al. (2013), and Soliman et al. (2015) that I have already
discussed, all of whose experiments are set in interactive constellations.

Here is how you might try to account for the multilocation hypothesis
on the intersubjectivist approach. Begin with the observations from chapter 10: action spaces and body schemata are fluid with regard to their core
and their boundaries. They can be extended through tool use, are affected
by emotional attitudes toward the social environment, and have no fixed

core. The core shifts depending on the activity that is being carried out: your bodily center in walking is not where it is when you play the piano, for example. Where your bodily center is depends on what you do; it is where the part of the activity is located that affords opportunities for particular movements. Along those lines, you can argue that the hallmark of joint interactions is that this location can shift to places outside the boundaries of one's own body and onto places occupied by the cooperator. When we are jointly sawing through the candle, as in Soliman's experiment, the center of agency is in constant flux between your body and mine, depending on who is pulling the wire: it shifts from my hand to yours and back. It shifts to wherever the kind of movement is afforded that keeps the undertaking going: in the experiment, it is located wherever the longer end of the wire is. So for each participant, this location shifts between a place occupied by the agent herself and a place occupied by her cooperator. This is what makes the body schema joint rather than merely extended: it enables the binding of proprioception and perception at places not occupied by the individual agent and thus supports a (temporary) shift of the center of agency to such places.

An alternative approach would be to suppose that a very basic human ability to distinguish between agents and things is at work in the social spatial framework. It is then not the interaction between agents that explains how places not occupied by oneself are represented as centers of agency but rather the recognition of particular kinds of movements as actions (for instance, Luo and Baillargeon 2005). This kind of account draws on the finding that infants as young as five months engage in some basic form of psychological reasoning—that it is not the contact with other human agents but rather the exposure to objects with particular kinds of features that enables them to draw a foundational distinction between agents and things. This is, of course, a very different kind of proposal. According to this view, it is not cooperation and shared activity but the activation of a specific system of reasoning that explains the ability to represent agency.

The thrust of the argument developed here is overwhelmingly aligned with the first rather than the second proposal. It is important to note, though, that the evidence I have been marshaling in support of the existence of social space does not unambiguously support the intersubjectivist account: Costantini's and Sinigaglia's (2011) experiment does not involve social interaction: the subject's reaction time decreases if an object is ready-to-hand relative to an avatar with which she does not cooperate. Quite generally, the ideas sketched in this section are highly speculative. They are not meant to constitute definite arguments in favor of a particular account of the psychological mechanisms that underwrite a social spatial framework. Any such theory could only be developed in the light of much more robust evidence than is currently available. Still, we can at least see what direction such an empirically minded inquiry might take. If you can find empirical support for the contention that proprioceptive and perceptual features are processed in parallel, prior to their binding into an event that is presented as an action at a particular location, you will have made a big step toward an empirically grounded theory of social space. Such a theory would allow for a new and, to my mind, promising take on a range of problems arising in the broad context of the problem of other minds. It would have overcome the explanatory gap between the knowledge of your own mind and your bodily activity, and that of others. The theory would take as basic the notion of activity, as characterized by the integration of proprioceptive and perceptual information at particular locations. And you could then, in a second step, ask how some such locations come to be treated as occupied by oneself. In the next chapter, I make a tentative move in that direction.

11.6 Summary

Here is where the inquiry stands. I began with the consideration that we should think of the subjects of spatial frameworks, and ultimately the possessors of a conception of space, as agents. In order to be able to act, you have to know where to move in egocentric space. Knowing where to move requires that the objects of your action be presented to you as being within reach. This is accomplished by peripersonal space, in which bodily and environmental information is integrated. You are at the center of your action space, but this center is not to be thought of as a static, fixed point; body and environment are always presented relative to each other in action. Intriguing recent research suggests that in joint action, the agents are operating with a frame of reference that contains two (or, conceivably, more) centers of action: there is more than one domain in which they are sensitive to proprioceptive as well as perceptual cues. Other recent work suggests that these centers are presented in relation to each other via a joint body schema in which the subject uses proprioception in order to attain spatial awareness of the other's action-relevant limb, and thus comes to treat it as a center of (joint) agency. If the experimental findings discussed here are anything to go by, proprioceptive information is allocated to the other's body in joint activity. It is through this allocation that the other's position becomes a center of agency. What is within reach, and thus available for action, is now presented to the agent, triadically, relative to her own standpoint and that of her cooperator: this establishes the spatial joint affordance relation. The resulting spatial framework is neither merged nor aligned: it is joint in the sense that it presents objects as available for action relative to the two standpoints of the joint agents.

In section 10.4, I argued that the notion of peripersonal space should not be understood in functional terms. It is not adequately characterized as a kind of behavioral space in which possible inputs are paired with possible outputs so as to generate a list of options for action. Because peripersonal space integrates proprioceptive and perceptual information and therefore presents the acting subject in relation to her surroundings, we should think of the agent as being situated *in* these surroundings. By extension, the same considerations apply to social action space: it too integrates bodily and environmental information and thus presents the acting subject in a dynamic relation to her surroundings. But the relation is of a different kind: what objects present opportunities for action is determined relative to two standpoints rather than one. We can now begin to see the nature of the environment in which joint perceivers operate: it is of a social kind that contains the perceivers themselves, as agents in the surroundings that they help constitute. In the next chapter, I suggest that the engaged spatial relation in which joint agents are standing to their surroundings forms the basis on which explicit perspective-taking, and linguistic demonstrative communication, becomes possible.

12 Indexical Spatial Thinking

Suppose there really is a social spatial framework in which opportunities for action are presented relative to the standpoints of both cooperators. It does not follow that joint agents *know*, propositionally, where the object is in social space. On the account developed here, social spatial frameworks are of a pragmatic kind: they make possible particular kinds of action, but the capacity to perform these joint actions does not require that their subjects possess propositional knowledge about the location of their objects. In this chapter, I develop the idea that such knowledge is nevertheless rooted in subjects' possession of a social spatial framework, and thus their capacity for joint agency. It is because subjects are able to treat, pragmatically, locations other than their own as centers of joint agency that they can come to know, propositionally, where an object is placed relative to these locations. The capacity for joint action, on this view, facilitates the ability to explicitly take perspectives.

12.1 Introduction

In his *Past, Space, and Self*, Campbell (1994, 42) introduces the notion of "causal indexicality."[1] Understanding a causally indexical notion means understanding its implications for one's own actions. Such notions include "is a weight I can easily lift" or "is too hot for me to handle." An understanding of such notions may be linked, Campbell says, to a reflective grasp of the object's properties and one's own capacities. But it need not be linked in this way: we can imagine creatures that are capable of thinking of their relations to the environment in purely indexical terms. Campbell (1993) suggests that the notion of causal indexicality can be brought to bear on spatial frameworks: an egocentric framework that is defined by the axes left or right, above or below, and up or down, and that is used for guiding simple action, is a causally indexical frame of reference. He suggests also that a creature can use this framework to work out the pragmatic implications for actions in locations other than its own without transcending egocentric space:

> Suppose we have an animal which is capable of thinking in terms of egocentric frames centred on places other than its own current location, such as the places occupied by other animals, or places which it occupied in the past. Is this animal thinking in causally indexical terms? It depends on how it gives physical significance to the spatial relations it represents. If it did this in a disengaged way, thinking only in terms of the causal relations between the places represented and the creature occupying the place on which the frame is centred, then we would have here a non-indexical mode of thought. If, however, its grasp of these causal relations is ultimately a matter only of the pragmatic implications for its own actions of the way things are with the creature at the other location, or the lessons to be learnt from its own past self, then the mode of thought that we have here is still causally indexical. (Campbell 1993, 86)

The creature in Campbell's example is deploying an egocentric spatial framework in which it can work out, pragmatically, the implications of another creature's activity for its own doings. This is an instance of a spatial framework that is merged in Pezzulo et al.'s (2013) sense: it enables the creature to exploit the action opportunities it is presented with in a region containing other agents because the other's doings are presented relative to its own spatial position and the actions it affords. The idea I have been pursuing is that there is a kind of spatial causal indexicality that is relativized not to an individual creature but to joint agents. And this kind of causally indexical framework can also be available to creatures not (yet) capable of a reflective stance on the acted-on object's properties and their own capacities.

Consider the case of human infants who, in their second year of life, are capable of social triangulation but not yet reflective spatial perspective-taking (Moll and Meltzoff 2011; Moll and Kadipasaoglu 2013).[2] Is the infant treating the location of the adult with whom she is jointly attending to an object in terms of an egocentric frame of reference, and thus in terms of the opportunities for action they make available to her? There are good reasons to doubt this. The infant is operating in a spatial context that allows her to treat the adult's location as a center of perception and action; otherwise you could not accommodate the consideration that the infant, in her demonstrative efforts, is attempting to draw the adult's attention to objects of interest. It appears that demonstrative communication of some kind can get off the ground without the capacity for explicit level 1 perspective-taking. But such communication could not be concerned with the transmission of propositional knowledge; the infant who is not yet able to take explicit perspectives is not in a position to engage in demonstrative reasoning. She is, however, able to make use of the sociospatial order in which she finds herself to engage in joint activities, such as the shared attention to some third object. On the picture I am sketching, we can think of the period (broadly the second year of life) that begins with the capacity for joint attention and ends with the ability to solve explicit level 1 perspective-taking tasks as the development of a reflective grasp of the causally indexical spatial framework that facilitates joint attention.[3] Social space does not come into existence with the capacity for explicit perspective-taking; it comes into existence, rather, with the capacity for communicative demonstrative activity, which requires participants to treat locations other than their own as centers of perception and action.

12.2   The Significance of Joint Action for Spatial Thinking

In the previous chapter, I began to give substance to the idea of a social spatial framework that is deployed in joint motor action. Such a framework, according to the claim, constitutes a genuine alternative to both the egocentric frame of reference with which individual agents operate and the objective conception of space that is required, on the Evansian view, to think about one's place in the perspective-transcendent spatial order. The framework I have been describing so far is strictly pragmatic; it makes available to joint agents the practical knowledge of what is within their reach, without necessarily enabling them to think of their locations as "here." This, though, is an ability that needs addressing in the context of the present project. I said, at the beginning of chapter 9, that the capacity for level 1 perspective-taking was sufficient for communicative demonstrative reference, and therefore an account was needed of the conception of space of hearers capable of knowing what object a speaker demonstratively identifies, without being able to distinguish between the object's standpoint-relative modes of presentation. This chapter expands on the idea of a social spatial framework in order to address that question. The general line of thought I have been pursuing thus far points toward a Strawsonian rather than a Davidsonian answer: the primary distinction that the social agent needs to be able to draw in order to demonstratively refer in communicative contexts is that between (joint) agents and the objects of their agency, not the distinction between self, other, and a third object. It is the Strawsonian distinction between "persons" (or, on the view pursued here, "joint agents") and "things" that is required for the acquisition of the concept of a perspective and that can be enjoyed by creatures (such as children in their third year of life) capable of ascribing perspectives to themselves and others, without being able to reliably distinguish between these perspectives (see section 14.1). Such agents are able, so the view, to individuate an object in terms of its location relative to the standpoints of joint perceivers and agents, and thus meet the requirements imposed by CP/1. They are then capable of linguistic demonstrative communication.

I have introduced two ways to determine the location of an object through an exercise in triangulation. You can either determine its location by using what Grush (2001) calls a "nonego reference point." Then you are operating with an egocentric spatial framework: you can define the location of the reference point relative to your own standpoint and the location of a third object relative to the reference point. This kind of triangulation does not require you to transcend your own perspective. But you can also determine the location of an object by means of an exercise in social triangulation. Then you treat the location of another perceiver as a center of perception; you do not define it relative to your own position but treat it as being on a par with your own. This is what demonstrative communicators do. Their ability to socially triangulate explains, along the lines of the view developed here, how they can know in common which object they are communicating about, even though this object may have standpoint-dependent modes of presentation.

If you are able to use your location as a reference point, you are able to think of it as "here." "Here" is an indexical: its meaning is dependent on the context of a token utterance of the term. The location indexed by a token of "here" is the one occupied by its producer. For creatures like us, this producer is a perceiver and agent, whose location provides her with a particular perspective and particular opportunities for action. The question is what it takes to think of a position that is not occupied by oneself as one that could be designated as "here," were one to occupy it. One approach is to appeal to the capacity for joint agency. To see how attractive such a move is, consider first what it would take for a solitary creature to be able to think of locations other than its own as centers of perception and agency. Begin by imagining (perhaps *per impossibile*[4]) a creature that is stationary, though it enjoys the capacity for both conscious vision and visually guided motor action. Suppose the creature has limbs with which it can reach for objects to its left and its right in the execution of its action plans. Could the creature be in a position to identify in egocentric space the location of the objects it consciously perceives? Could it think, *This thing is to my left*, about a thing that it can reach by using its left limb? Doing so would require the creature to identify the location of these objects relative to its own position in space and thus to think of this position as "here." Like humans (see section 10.1), it may not be in a position to exactly give the internal spatial coordinates of the extended location it occupies; the frames of reference used by the creature in its actions may be diverse and grouped around varying, constantly changing centers. But why not suppose that such a creature could, in principle, be capable of "here" thoughts?

Remember the considerations from chapter 10. There, I said that you could not come to enjoy the practical knowledge of an object's location in egocentric space by simply relying on your awareness of your body's spatial constitution, that is, the relative position of your bodily axes and your bodily boundaries. What is needed, rather, is the awareness of your body's internal spatial arrangement relative to the environment in which you find yourself. And it is hard to see how an immobile creature could enjoy this awareness. What allows a mobile creature to have practical knowledge of an object's location is that whenever it moves through its environment, it is exposed to a modification of the relation between its internal spatial axes and the objects in the environment. This modification accounts for the difference in content between the "here" thought that is available to the creature at an earlier location and the "here" thought available to it at a later one: if the creature moves around an object, so that the object's location shifts from the creature's right to its left, it needs to use its limbs in different ways to act on the thing and can thus come to think of a distinct location as "here." But this way of giving content to a "here" thought is not available to the stationary creature; it could not spell out what it means to be "here" for different locations in terms of the different movements required to act on the thing at these locations.[5]

Suppose we think of the creature as mobile. Then the visual information it receives from its surroundings changes as it moves through its environment. It can think of the location it occupies at a particular time as "here" in terms of the practical knowledge of how to act on its surroundings at that time, and it can think of the location that it occupies at a different time as "here" in the same terms. Now the creature can distinguish between the locations occupied by it at distinct times in terms of the difference of the practical knowledge of what it would take to act on its surroundings at these times. Grasping this temporal dimension appears indispensable for a creature's capacity to think of locations as "here."

But being able to move between different locations is still not sufficient for "here" thoughts. A creature who can form them has to be capable of keeping track of its movements; it has to be capable of distinguishing between the locations it occupies at various times (see Campbell (1994, 38) for a discussion). How can it accomplish this? The natural answer is that the creature remembers its earlier location. But now the problem is that this further requirement presupposes an answer to the question raised in the first place. It presupposes that the creature is capable of thinking of itself as occupying a variety of locations in external space, and thus of locations it does not currently occupy as centers of perception and action. Yet just this capacity is what needs to be explained. It turns out that it is not at all obvious how a nonsocial creature, even if it is mobile and has the capacity to keep track of its movements by memorizing its past locations in terms of the practical knowledge of how to act from them on the objects that surround it, can be in a position to think of itself as being "here."

You can render the problem in terms of Evans's (1982, 103) "generality constraint": in order to entertain a thought of the form "A is b," you have to be in a position to entertain a range of thoughts of the same form but with different subject and predicate terms. You also have to be able to think, say, "C is b" or "A is f."[6] Applied to spatial indexical thinking, the constraint is that in order to think "I am *here*," you must also be in a position to think "I am *there*" (where "there" is an indexically identified location other than the one designated by "here"), or "She is *here*." In other words, you have to be able to think of the indexically identified location designated by "here" as being occupied by agents other than yourself, and you have to be able to think of yourself as occupying indexically identifiable locations other than the one designated by "here." This, on the view sketched in this section, requires you to deploy the kind of memory that allows you to keep track of your movements over time and to think of places you occupied at particular past times as "here (at t_1)" and of places you occupied later as "here (at t_2)." The problem is that this way of indexical thinking about your past locations is available only if you already are operating with a conception of "here" that allows you to meet the generality constraint. It already requires you to distinguish between yourself and the place you occupy; it requires you to operate with a conception of yourself as occupying a position in the objective spatial order and of various locations as centers of perception and agency.

These brief reflections are not meant to provide a decisive argument in support of the view that solitary creatures cannot be capable of spatial reasoning; the point is merely to highlight some difficulties that arise for any attempt to defend the opposite view. These difficulties can be avoided if you allow that the spatial reasoner is social; that she is capable of joint activities in which she is pragmatically treating the other's location as a center of perception and agency. All such a reasoner has to do is to make explicit in thought the spatial constellation that underwrites her capacity for joint action. If you can explain how the reasoner makes explicit the triadic spatial constellation of which she is a constituent, you have provided one explanation (though perhaps not the only possible one) of how she can come to entertain "here" thoughts; and you have thereby explained how she comes to acquire the concept of a perspective. In the following two sections, I consider some evidence that can help with such an explanation. In section 12.3, I inquire into the role of vision in the identification of locations as centers of perception and agency, and thus as referents of "here" thoughts. In section 12.4, I suggest that awareness of location has a crucial role to play in the ascription of motor actions to oneself and others.

12.3 "Here"

To think of yourself as being "here," you must understand yourself as part of the objective order—as occupying a position in objective space. You must have a grasp of yourself as an object in space. But if the considerations of the previous section are on the right track, you must also have an understanding of yourself as an agent. As Evans (1982, 153) puts it, "Where there is no *possibility* of action and perception, 'here'-thoughts cannot get a grip." An account is needed of how these two dimensions are integrated in spatial thinking. One important consideration is the finding that visual information has two distinct roles to play in our psychological economy: it supports our conscious experience of our perceptual environment, and it underwrites our motor actions on its objects. It can appear as if conscious attention to an object facilitated motor action on the thing: it can seem that it is because I consciously focus on the tennis ball on my side of the court that I can volley it to your side. But motor action does not always demand reflective attention, and often it appears to go smoothly precisely because you are not reflectively involved: consider what happens when you, an experienced skier, begin to think about the motor movements by means of which you navigate a steep slope. The idea I pursue in this section is that the capacity for "here" thoughts can be explained in terms of a creature's ability to integrate conscious and action-guiding visual information about its body in one location: it is this location that is designated by a token of "here."

In a version of Nielsen's (1963) experiment, Fourneret and Jeannerod (1998) devised a task in which subjects were instructed to move a stylus with a hand that was hidden from view toward a visual target. Only the trajectory of the stylus was visible on a computer screen. They found that if a directional bias was introduced electronically, subjects unconsciously corrected for this bias by moving their hand in the opposite direction. Jeannerod and Pacherie (2004, 120) highlight that the visuomotor system is able to accurately use visual information to make corrections in order to achieve a consciously presented target, but that these corrections are not themselves accessible to consciousness. The subject is aware of what she intends to do but not in detail of how she does it. It is also possible, they point out, that a patient who has no visual experience of his body is under the illusion of doing something when doing nothing, as in a case reported by William James in which a patient with an anesthetized arm who was blindfolded and then asked to move his arm reported an experience of moving his arm. And, as they also point out, it is possible for a patient to experience a voluntary movement in a phantom limb if the patient's existing limb is mirrored to be on the side of the amputated limb and she is asked to move both limbs simultaneously.

These observations suggest that vision has two roles to play in action: it facilitates the movement of the body in its environment and the conscious attribution of actions to oneself or others. Somewhat counterintuitively, the two roles do not appear to be fully integrated. Georgieff and Jeannerod suggest that action-related information is "double-coded":

> Signals for controlling motor execution would be different from those used for generating conscious judgement on an action. In other words, consciousness of an action does not depend on those informations which come into place during automatic control of movements. (Georgieff and Jeannerod 1998, 470)

Conscious experience (including visual experience of one's own body) and the awareness of agency present their objects in different spatial frameworks. Conscious visual experience presents its objects in a spatial order that enables perceivers to describe their locations relative to each other; it presents them in allocentric space. When you consciously attend to your body in vision (perhaps you are contemplating your face in a mirror), you perceive it as an object whose location can be defined relative to other objects in its vicinity: *I am in front of the bathroom cabinet*, you may think as you look at yourself.

By contrast, when you are exploiting visual information in the performance of motor actions, you are relying on a spatial framework in which visual and proprioceptive cues are integrated. If my earlier remarks are on the right track, we should think of peripersonal space as the area around the body in which this integration is achieved. You can draw on this distinction between the spatial frameworks deployed by agents and conscious perceivers in order to account for the dissociation between action execution and action attribution in Jeannerod's and his colleagues' experiments: when moving the stylus, the subject is relying on the sensorimotor information available in peripersonal space, but when judging the traces produced by her action, she is relying on her conscious experience of the marks in external space. The double role of vision corresponds to a double role of spatial frames of reference. The subject's failure to consciously ascribe to herself her own motor movements illustrates a dissociation not just between the two forms of vision; it also shows that the corresponding frames of reference are not fully integrated.

Intriguing support for the view that movement plays a crucial role in binding personal and peripersonal space comes from a study by Vaishnavi, Calhoun, and Chaterjee (2001) that investigates binding mechanisms in tactile extinction patients. This attentional disorder was briefly introduced in section 10.3: these patients, who have suffered brain damage, are unaware of being touched on a contralesional limb (that is, a limb away from the side of the brain on which the lesion is located) if they are simultaneously being touched on the corresponding ipsilesional limb. Vaishnavi and colleagues found that patients' awareness of being touched on their contralesional limbs improved both when they were asked to look at the limb and when they were actively moving on tactile probes rather than receiving tactile stimuli. They thus hypothesize that cross-modal integration (between vision and touch) and sensorimotor integration (between touch and intentional movement) help bind personal and peripersonal space.

This finding gives us an idea of how to square the view that personal and peripersonal space are distinctly represented with the consideration that bodily awareness and the action-relative presentation of one's close surroundings are integrated and, in ordinary cases, mutually informed (see also section 10.2). The spatial bodily framework is not of a static kind; it is a frame of the body in motion. By the same token, action space is distinct from external space precisely because it presents opportunities for bodily action, and it presents these opportunities relative to the body moving through its environment. We can hence think of body schema and peripersonal space as constituting a relation between personal and peripersonal space in motor action: it is through sensorimotor movement that the agent is integrating personal and peripersonal space.

This proposal, with its appeal to a distinction between action- and conscious-perception-related forms of perceptual information-processing, has a natural ally in Milner's and Goodale's ([1995] 2006) "two-systems hypothesis," according to which the primate brain supports two distinct systems for action and conscious perception. Evidence comes from visual form agnosia, in which the subject is unable to report what object she is viewing while still being able to make precise movements directed at the target; and optic ataxia that does not impair visual attention while impairing visual control of hand movements directed at objects in the periphery of the contralesional visual field.[7] Here, again, you could think that the sufferer who is unable to integrate conscious and action-related visual information is not working with a unified spatial framework: what is seen in conscious vision, in allocentric space, does not correspond to what is done in peripersonal space, even though the visual information in both cases is from the same object.

The question then arises how, in the ordinary case, these distinct frames of reference are integrated, so as to allow the subject to think of the perceived hand as the one with which she is acting. This question is important because the capacity for "here" thoughts depends on this integration: along the lines introduced earlier, "here" thoughts are entertained by subjects who are perceivers and agents. The capacity for such thoughts amounts to the ability to think of the location occupied by the thinker as a center of perception and agency. So they require the integration of allocentric and peripersonal space: if you are to think of a place as "here," you have to identify a location in action space as a location in allocentric space.

As I noted in section 11.5, Campbell (2002, 53-57), in his discussion of how demonstrative reference enables you to act on an object, proposes the "binding thesis" to explain the integration of action- and perception-directed information in the visual system. He takes his initial cue from Treisman's (1988) feature integration theory, according to which all features found at a single location are bound as features of a single thing on a master map of locations. This kind of binding takes place in early vision. But there is a second role for feature maps in conscious attention. Conscious attention allows the perceiver to verify propositions about the perceptual properties of objects, and it allows her to act on them. The question then is how conscious attention can single out the object of demonstrative reference as the one on which you can choose to act. This is the binding problem. How, Campbell asks, "do we make sure that the 'action' and 'perception' systems are dealing with one and the same external object?" (Campbell 2002, 55). He endorses Jeannerod's (1997) proposal that location is the binding principle: conscious attention to an object involves awareness of the object's location, and the target for visuomotor processing can be identified as "the object at that location." The role of conscious attention is to provide enough information about the object to make it a target for the visuomotor system. And this is possible, Campbell thinks, even where the experience of the object is inaccurate; what informs the visuomotor system is not the target's actual but its experienced location.[8]

This view is not uncontroversial: Matthen (2006) argues that Campbell overestimates the role of location and that although the view that binding of features takes place on a master map of locations is correct for early vision, it is not plausible that the maps used in conscious attention are those of early vision (see Campbell 2006 for a response). But suppose the binding thesis is sustainable and location does play the role Campbell ascribes to it in conscious attention and intentional action: Then you have a way of explaining how the integration of locations in peripersonal and allocentric space is achieved, so that you can think of your location as "here."

As we have seen, the visual information that supports motor action is integrated with proprioception in the presentation of the body in its environment in peripersonal space. Peripersonal space is the domain in which cues from both proprioception and vision can be exploited. Peripersonal space is not in the first instance consciously presented. Success in motor action, which is enabled by the integration of proprioceptive and perceptual information, does not depend on conscious attention, on the contrary. But you can bring your activity to conscious attention: you can consciously focus on what you are doing, as you are when learning a new skill, for instance. Along the lines of the binding thesis, attention binds visual information from motor action and from conscious vision in one location. Suppose that what you are attending to is not a visual object in your environment but your own bodily doings: you focus on your activity of playing a piano sonata perhaps, in the effort to master a particularly difficult passage. Your attention then is of both a visual-exteroceptive and proprioceptive-interoceptive kind: you visually attend to the movement of your hands, but as an activity that involves your intense proprioceptive awareness of what you are doing. Your conscious attention is directed at your own body as it is active in its environment. The information from motor action and conscious vision that is integrated in a common location in this kind of attention is of a specific kind: it is information about *you*. And the location that is thus summoned to conscious awareness is your location. It is the location at which information about your body as a physical object and information about your body as an agent are bound together.

This line of thought exploits the binding thesis to sustain a point Campbell is not himself making. He is concerned with the role of conscious attention in demonstrative reference and intentional action, and thus with attention to external objects. But since the body is an object that can be perceived in visual experience, you can use his view to argue that when an agent's conscious attention is directed at her own active body in its environment, she is integrating perceptual and proprioceptive information at the location she is occupying. She is mapping her location in peripersonal space onto a location in allocentric space. And it is this operation that allows her to think of that location as "here." On this view, your location, and the attention that binds your various kinds of bodily awareness in that location, plays an important role in the self-attribution of action. It also plays a vital role in the ascription of motor actions to others. The next section is concerned with this topic.

12.4   The Role of Location in the Self- and Other-Attribution of Motor Actions

There are various ways in which you can come to ascribe an action to yourself. You can, for instance, judge that the typing hands whose image you see in a mirror are yours. This kind of self-ascription requires an act of visual identification. As such, it is fallible: perhaps the mirror arrangement is tricking you into thinking that someone else's hands are yours.

But not all thoughts you can have about your own agency are fallible in this way. Some are "immune to error through misidentification," to use Shoemaker's (1968) phrase (it is subsequently taken up by Evans, 1982, 215–220). If you have an experience of typing on the keyboard, it would not make sense to ask whether it is you who is having the experience. Consider Wittgenstein's classic distinction in the *Blue Book* (1958, 66–67) between the use of the first person as a subject and its use as an object, with which Shoemaker begins his argument:

> There are two different cases in the use of the word "I" (or "my") which I might call "the use as object" and "the use as subject." . . . The cases of the first category involve the recognition of a particular person, and there is in these cases the possibility of an error. . . . On the other hand, there is no question of recognizing a person when I say I have a toothache. To ask "are you sure that it's you who has pains?" would be nonsensical.

Wittgenstein's point generalizes to the self-ascription of action: when I identify a bodily event as mine, perhaps on the basis of visual information, I see myself as an object, part of the perceivable furnishings of the world. But when I ascribe to myself the experience of acting, I don't identify myself visually; I am simply the acting subject. It is tempting to think that this distinction corresponds neatly to two ways in which we can acquire knowledge about our own agency. We can, first, come to know about our bodily doings through proprioception, by an internal sense of our bodily limbs and their movements. And we can, second, come to know about our bodies through perception—most importantly (for present purposes), by seeing ourselves acting in the environment. Initially, it can seem that this distinction is vital for thinking about joint action and the spatial order in which it takes place. While perception can be of your own and others' actions, proprioception is necessarily about yourself; you could not proprioceive another person's doings. If so, we should focus on the perceptual awareness of others in our thinking about social spatial frameworks. But we have already seen one reason to doubt that this view is correct: If social space is a form of action space, both proprioceptive and perceptual cues are exploited in the interactions it facilitates with its objects. Whatever it is that accounts for the social character of the framework, it cannot be that proprioception plays no role in acquiring knowledge about its occupants.

This section sketches an account of how joint agents come to ascribe actions in social space to themselves and their cooperators. This task is the last step of the main project pursued in this chapter. The project is to substantiate the suggestion that the capacity for joint action helps explain how a creature comes to acquire a conception of space. The guiding thought is that a creature has a conception of space when it is able to think of locations other than its own as centers of perception and agency: when it can think of these locations as picked out by their occupants' "here" thoughts. In chapter 11, I developed the idea that joint actions are presented in a spatial format in which the locations of the agents are areas at which each can exploit proprioceptive and perceptual cues. I presented some recent evidence that supports the idea of a social action space. This kind of spatial framework is practical, not theoretical; it enables action rather than spatial thinking. The question thus remains how agents can acquire a reflective understanding of this framework. And this question simply amounts to the demand for an explanation of joint agents' ability to ascribe activity in social space to themselves and their co-operators: once they are capable of that, they are already treating locations other than their own as the referents of their occupant's "here" thoughts. They have acquired a conception of space.

The general idea is as follows. If agency is assigned to the occupants of locations at which proprioceptive and perceptual information is available, and if a variety of locations are presented as centers of action in social space, the question arises as to what area (or areas) is designated by the joint agents' "here" thoughts. There are two unattractive options. One pos-sibility is that a token use of "here" designates the entire area in which the agent is sensitive to proprioceptive and perceptual cues, including the location occupied by the cooperator's body. Thus, in Soliman et al.'s (2015) experiment, "here" would designate the area around the subject's hand that manipulates one end of the wire with which the candle is being sawed; and it would also designate the area around the collaborator's hand, onto which proprioceptive information is transferred. The subject would be thinking of two distinct locations as "here"; that two distinct locations in allocentric space are being designated by her use of the indexical would have no bear-ing on the reference of a token of "here" in social space. This proposal is not promising: the joint agent would then not be in a position to differentiate between her own location as a center of agency and that of the cooperator. But the ability to so differentiate is vital for social triangulation: only if I can think of your and my locations as distinct centers of perception and agency can I determine the position of third objects relative to them. And only then have I transcended my own perspective.

The alternative is that social space itself is not ordered around two dis-tinct locations (those occupied by the joint agents) in allocentric space; there is just one center of perception and agency, which occupies a spatially extended area containing the standpoints of both agents. This approach is incompatible with Maister et al.'s (2015) and Soliman et al.'s (2015) studies (though it appears to be in line with the findings of Teneggi et al. (2013). Also, it is unable to accommodate scenarios in which the joint agents are operating on an object that is placed between them: since the location occupied by the object would be part of the area designated by "here," the idea that the location of an object in social space can be determined by means of an exercise in social triangulation would, again, be lost. Nei-ther of the two options, then, appears at all attractive. What is wanted is an account that can both explain how agents come to think of their own locations as "here" and how they can come to treat the locations occupied by their cooperators as centers of perception and agency, without having to engage in the kinds of inferences necessary to solve the traditional problem of other minds.

Pertinent empirical evidence comes from Jeannerod and his colleagues' studies of the self- and other-ascription of actions. A comprehensive account of this rich research program is beyond the reach of the current project.[9] I restrict myself to introducing two of a wide range of experiments they discuss (for a third one, see section 12.3), with the aim of illustrating those of their views that are of immediate relevance for present purposes.

Van den Bos and Jeannerod (2002) simultaneously showed two hands to a subject on a video screen; one hand was the subject's own. The hands could be presented at a rotation of 90 or 180 degrees relative to their actual positions. On some trials, subjects were instructed to wiggle their fingers. Unsurprisingly, they made attribution errors when the hands were presented in positions other than their actual one. However, when the observed finger movements matched the proprioceived movement, agents correctly attributed the observed action to themselves, even when the display was rotated by 180 degrees. The experiment highlights that action attribution is fallible: it appears to rely on some kind of "matching" of felt and perceived bodily movements. If such a match is achieved, it overrides the perceptually presented location of the acting part of the body.

What determines whether there is a match? Jeannerod (1999, 18) introduces an experiment by Daprati et al. (1997), in which a subject's hand and the experimenter's hand were simultaneously filmed with two cameras. Both were wearing the same kind of glove so that the hands could not be visually distinguished. Subject and experimenter were each instructed to perform a given hand movement. In some trials, these instructions deviated for subject and experimenter: in some trials, the subject was shown the experimenter's hand and in other cases she was shown her own hand. The subject always correctly identified her own hand, and she correctly identified the filmed hand as not being hers when the hand's movements dramatically deviated from her own. But if the experimenter's hand carried out the same kind of movement as she did herself, the subject misjudged the alien hand as her own in about a third of all cases. Jeannerod suggests that this result can be explained in terms of slight differences in timing and kinematics between the movement of the subject's own hand and the movement of the experimenter's hand: self-attribution of an observed movement appears to require a temporal and kinematic match between the movement that is consciously seen and the movement whose execution is felt; the less perfect the match, the greater the possibility of misattribution.

In order to explain how this match (or mismatch) is effected by the action-monitoring system, Jeannerod proposes a comparator that receives action-related signals from internal and external sources:[10]

> During a self-generated action, internal signals, which are a copy of the commands sent to the effectors (and which therefore reflect the desired action) are sent to the comparator. These internal signals create therein an anticipation for the consequences of the action. . . . When the action is effectively executed, sensory signals related to changes in the external world also reach the comparator. If these sensory signals match the anticipation of the comparator, the desired action is registered by the system; if they do not, a mismatch is registered between the desired action and the action that has been produced; finally, if sensory signals arrive in the absence of internal signals, a change in the external world independent of the agent is registered. (Jeannerod 1999, 17–18)

The matching procedure, on this approach, is intramodal rather than intermodal: the comparison takes place between representations in the same informational currency (if you want). This is a virtue of the approach, since it is not at all easy to explain how a matching of events that are presented in different modes (proprioception and vision) might be achieved. You could try to stipulate some kind of "supramodal framework" into which both kinds of inputs can be fed and that "translates" them into abstract geometrical and temporal patterns.[11] But then you face the intractable problem of spelling out what constitutes a correct translation into the supramodal lingua franca. After all, there is no means of comparison, such as an external world, pointing to which could deliver, in a Davidsonian vein, the rough meaning of the basic sentences of the language.

The comparator model does not suffer from this problem: Since it compares the anticipated external state of affairs with the environmental changes produced by the action, the comparison is not dependent on a translation of proprioceptive and perceptual information into a common currency.[12] However, Jeannerod and Pacherie (2004, 125–126) think that the central monitoring theory suffers from a different kind of problem: it cannot cope with the ascription of "covert" actions that are not actually executed but merely imagined; and it cannot, vitally for present purposes, account for the understanding of observed actions. A better way to explain action understanding, they suggest, is in terms of a simulationist approach that takes action execution and observation to be underwritten by the activation of the same neural processes, and both to be represented in the same format. In case of an action that is executed rather than observed, these "shared representations" (Daprati et al. 1997) are accompanied by neural activity in "canonical neurons," and this neural difference is thought to be the cue for the self-attribution of an action.

In section 11.4, I said that ST could not by itself explain how a spatial location distinct from one's own comes to be represented as a center of perception and agency: For this to be possible, the egocentric frame of reference already has to be transcended. But it is not obvious that ST is useful in explaining how, in a cooperative action, the other's movements are integrated into a joint body schema either. The core idea behind the notion of a low-level simulation is that the other's bodily activity is understood by an activation of the same neural resources that are correlated with the agent's own doings. But if the same neural processes are activated in both cases, we lose track of the consideration that the motor actions of the perceiver's fellow agent are not the same ones as her own. As Gallagher (2005, 222) points out, it is not that the simulation of another's action activates the neural process supporting the action representation *twice*; the same, token-identical single neural event is taking place in both the execution and the observation of an action. If the joint agent were to simulate the partner's action using the neural resources that underwrite her own doings, she would end up with a model of the other's activity that replicates her own. But for many joint actions, that model would simply be inaccurate. The fact that joint agents, though they are cooperating, have to be able to differentiate between their own and the other's doings, in terms of both the locations whence they act and the kinds of movements they each perform, is not easily accommodated in a simulationist framework. Nevertheless, a significant aspect of Jeannerod and Pacherie's (2004) view[13] is in line with my approach: They too think that there is, sometimes at least, no fundamental asymmetry between action recognition and attribution in one's own case and that of others. But their argument does not take into consideration the crucially important notion of joint action, and it is here that the case for the priority of agency over the attribution of action can be most forcefully made.

To briefly take stock: I suggested that spatial thinking required the ability to identify one's own location as "here"—as the origin of a perceptual viewpoint and of actions. On the broadly Evansian approach I have been adopting, "here" thoughts could only be available to agents, since a conception of space requires the subject to give meaning to spatial locations in terms of the action-related requirements they impose. Locations occupied by oneself are those at which both perceptual and proprioceptive bodily information can be exploited. You can think, then, of the capacity for spatial indexical thinking as the ability to consciously bind these two kinds of information at one location. In the non–joint case, actions that are ascribed to others are typically occurring in an action space distinct from one's own.[14] Such actions are simply observed; they are not presented to the observer in a format that includes a "felt," proprioceptive dimension. Hence, they are not the interesting case in the attempt to explain what enables subjects to transcend their egocentric spatial framework. The interesting case is, rather, that of actions that are presented in peripersonal space but are not correctly attributed to oneself. This case obtains in joint actions. If you can explain how a joint agent comes to think of the cooperator's location as a center of agency, you have explained also how the agent has transcended her egocentric perspective and thus acquired a conception of space.

In the case of an individual action, the capacity to think of a location as "here" is, if my remarks in section 12.3 are on the right track, effected by the binding of conscious and pragmatic action-guiding visual information at that location. The subject who attends to her own doings and thus comes to think of her location as "here" is an agent, a doer rather than a spectator: only so can she be in a position to evaluate the success of her execution of a motor intention in terms of the effects it generates. Now consider a scenario in which the perceiver is focusing on a cooperator's doings. The situation is in some important respects exactly comparable to her self-directed attention. Here, too, her focus allows her to exploit both visual and proprioceptive information, whose integration at the place occupied by the other's body ensures that the other's movements are directly presented as actions. So the question arises how the agent comes to self-ascribe her own movements and not those of her cooperator. The key consideration here is that the prediction of the motor movement that is possible on the basis of information from one's own body is likely to be accurate for what one does oneself but not for the actions of one's fellow agent. In Soliman et al.'s experiment, the subject's reliance on proprioceptive information from her idle left hand to predict the movement of the experimenter's left hand (which is active in the task) will not, typically, lead to a match of what is seen with what is felt; it was for this reason that the appeal to ST in the attempt to explain the joint body schema appeared unconvincing. If there is no match between predicted and observed movement, the action is not attributed to oneself: the agent is not in a position to think of the location of the bodily movement as "here." But, since it is a location at which proprioception and perception can be exploited, she can still think of it as a center of agency. She can think of it as "*there"; as the location of her cooperator about whose doings she has no motor control. Pacherie (2007) argues that a match between an internal prediction of a perceptual event generated by a motor command and the event that is in fact produced results in a sense of control. So you might think that a joint agent's "here"-thoughts pick out the location of motor movements over which she experiences a sense of control, while her "*there"-thoughts pick out the location of movements over which she does not experience control even though they are still presented as part of the joint activity. When the agent has acquired the capacity to distinguish between these two locations, she has transcended her egocentric perspective. She has acquired the kind of conception of space that renders her capable of explicit level 1 perspective-taking.

IV Joint Attention

Introduction

Remember the remarks about *The Raft of the Medusa* with which I began this book: you can see the shaky vessel as a metaphor for action space and its role in the acquisition of perceptual common knowledge. The latter depends on the former: only joint agents can possess propositional perceptual common knowledge, and the communication that facilitates the acquisition of such knowledge is a joint activity. Possessors of common perceptual knowledge are necessarily joint agents; it is hard to overestimate the importance of this point. It is because the occupants of the raft hold on to each other, prop each other up, and point out the spot that may be a sail on the distant horizon that they can come to know in common that the rescuing ship is near. It is because creatures interact that they can come to treat the areas around the locations of others as peripersonal spaces, and it is because they operate with a social spatial framework that they can extend their common knowledge about perceptual objects by means of demonstrative expressions.

The survivors on the raft are more than intensely physically involved cooperators: their bodily activity enables them to focus on a distal object of perception and communication. There is a difference between social forms of action and social forms of attention, just as there is a difference between an individual's object-directed activity and her conscious focus on the thing. Philosophical treatments of perceptual attention may, but need not, frame the notion as an agentive phenomenon.[1] On the view I am presenting, shared perceptual attention is, always and necessarily, based on some kind of bodily interaction. It need not be as pronounced as the activities of the people on the raft; but it always necessitates treating the fellow perceiver as the occupant of a center of perception and action, and thus her position as one of the corners of the social triangle that makes it possible to determine the location of objects in social space. However, not all bodily joint interaction, of the kind discussed in part 3, amounts to reflective, propositional common knowledge-producing joint attention. In chapter 13, I develop the notion of what I call "joint perception" and situate it within the philosophical debate about joint attention. Here it is important to distinguish between the kind of interaction that takes place in a social spatial framework and agents' attention to objects presented in that framework. The two are developmentally and conceptually distinct: a creature can be capable of the former but not the latter (though, on my view, not vice versa), and only the latter produces in the communicators the kind of propositional common knowledge that I considered in the first part of this essay. But they are also deeply related: attention to a jointly perceived object is possible only in social space, and the linguistic demonstrative communication through which common knowledge about the perceptual object is acquired is necessarily also a bodily communication. I argue that in the light of this distinction, the label "joint attention" turns out to be something of a misnomer: there is a particular form of enacted perception in which objects are presented in a social spatial framework; and there is individuals' conscious attention to these objects that underwrites linguistic demonstrative reference in communicative contexts. I end this chapter by asking how my theory can explain the capacity of joint perceivers to attend to distal objects that are beyond their reach and consider some recent evidence from psycholinguistics to that end. In the fourteenth and final chapter, I put the account developed in this book to use. One success criterion for any theory is its explanatory power, and so I try to show how the current proposal can help with some questions in psychology and the philosophy of perception.

13 Joint Perception

13.1 Background

Joint attention is the ability, possessed by humans and possibly (depending on your views[1]) by some nonhuman primates, to look at objects together with others.[2] It is a perceptual constellation with three constituents—two subjects and the object they are attending to—that allows its subjects to act together on the thing and acquire common knowledge about it. So much is uncontested, but complications arise immediately. What does it mean to look at an object "together" with someone? How do you make sense of the notion of "joint" attention if, after all, perceivers are individuals who each have to be alternating their gaze between the object and the co-attender in order to know what the co-attender is looking at? How can the attention of two perceivers to the same object, in conjunction with their mutual awareness of the other's focus on the thing, make *common* knowledge about the perceived object possible? We struggle with the notion of joint attention, even more so than with the somewhat cognate notion of a collective intention. Intentions have the advantage of being more or less unanimously thought to be mental states with a mind-to-world fit.[3] Once so much is accepted, you can then ask who the bearers of collective intentions are, and how (the preferred move)[4] various individual intentions can combine so as to account for the joint pursuit of a shared goal. But the literature on joint attention does not enjoy this modest advantage. Nobody knows what attention is, in William James's oft-quoted remark, so the work on joint attention cannot begin by endorsing some widely defined account of attention and build the joint case from there.

Although the concerns I am pursuing here are predominantly philosophical, no attempt to come to terms with the rich and complex notion of joint attention can get by without at least acknowledging its origins in developmental psychology. Despite the interest of the classic developmental theorists in infant cognition, the beginnings of academic interest in joint attention can be traced back to two pioneering papers in the mid-1970s (Racine 2011). Scaife and Bruner (1975) presented evidence of early gaze following and proposed a framework for its systematic study; Bates, Camaioni, and Volterra (1975) documented the transition from nonintentional to intentional communication involving gestures and, eventually, verbal reference. Trevarthen (1980) introduced the notions of primary and secondary intersubjectivity to describe a sharing of experiences and feelings that, he suggested, provides the foundation for the cognitive mastering of meaning. Tomasello's and his colleagues' early work on the communicative aspect of joint attention, documented, for example, in Tomasello and Farrar (1986), led to the suggestion that it holds the key to human cognitive uniqueness (Tomasello 1999).[5] Baron-Cohen (1999) developed a theory of mind–based account of autism, whose sufferers exhibit difficulties in achieving social attention. Hobson ([2002] 2004; Hobson and Hobson 2011) studied autism by drawing on intersubjectivity research, and Reddy (2008, 2011) explored the role of emotional engagement in social understanding. Since joint attention research is closely tied to the study of interpersonal relations, the still-face paradigm (Tronick et al. 1978) and Meltzoff and Moore's (1983) groundbreaking work on facial imitation in infancy should be mentioned also.

This snapshot of the trajectory of joint attention research can clearly not begin to do justice to the rich and fruitful discussion about the social aspect of the mind that started in psychology in the mid-1970s and continues to this day; all it can achieve is highlight a few prominent names at the expense of others. But it may do as a brief sketch of the wide-ranging empirical work that predates and makes possible the philosophical interest in joint attention. It provides the grounding for a conceptual inquiry that situates the social aspect of the mind at the heart, rather than the periphery, of its perceptual, agentive, and cognitive capacities.

13.2   Joint Attention and Joint Perception

One reason joint attention research is so philosophically interesting is that it requires the theorist to consider *in tandem* individuals' perception and cognition of third objects and their perception of other subjects. Thinking about joint attention in these integrated terms puts pressure on the idea that there are two quite distinct, and unrelated, ways we have of coming to act on and know about our environment. This idea begins with the consideration that there are, first and foremost, ordinary, physical objects that we can perceptually know and manipulate; and there are, second, persons, creatures about whose mental lives we can acquire knowledge inferentially or perhaps through the deployment of simulative capacities or a theory of mind. Supposing that the acquisition of knowledge about these two kinds of objects requires distinct mental faculties gives rise to the long-standing problem of other minds (see Avramides 2001 for an overview). But in joint attention research, this sharp distinction comes under threat: when you and I are contemplating Turner's seascape together, it isn't that I perceive you and thus come to know something about your mental life, *and also* perceive the painting and thus come to know something about its perceptual characteristics. A promising approach to joint attention will not begin with the attempt to solve the problem of other minds. If the line of argument I have been advancing is on the right track, we should begin by reflecting on the environment in which joint agents and perceivers operate; then the door is open to the idea that the fusion of ordinary cognition and its social counterpart that facilitates joint attention is to be found in the structure of joint perceivers' surroundings.

Begin with a simple, and deliberately loose, characterization of the phenomenon:

JA: Joint attention is a triadic perceptual and agentive constellation that obtains when its subjects know in common which the object is of their perception and action, and when they know this in virtue of the perceptual constellation they help constitute.

This characterization will appeal to readers who think of joint attention in the 'rich' terms of a phenomenon that can only be adequately described by invoking some aspect of the involved creatures' cognitive lives, whatever that aspect may be. It will not appeal to those who want the term to also cover instances of cued looking that are sometimes conceptualised as its 'lean' form.[6] That is fine: the point here is not to enter the debate about what does or does not qualify as an instance of joint attention. JA is meant to capture the capacity of social agents to jointly perceive, act on, and communicate about an object and to thereby extend their stock of knowledge about it that I have been concerned with in this book. The important thing to see is that the notion of 'knowledge', in this characterisation, covers both the propositional variety I have been discussing in part 2 and the practical kind of part 3. JA applies both to linguistic demonstrative communication and nonverbal joint activity. In both cases, the agents determine the location of the object of their attention and action by means of an exercise in social triangulation and thus by deploying a social spatial framework.

JA thus covers two capacities that, though intimately related, are also quite distinct. It covers the kind of triadic social interaction that Trevarthen (1980) calls 'secondary intersubjectivity' and that human infants begin to participate in around the end of their first year of life; and it covers the kind of linguistic communication in which speakers seek to transmit knowledge about perceptually present objects to their hearers by means of the use of demonstrations and demonstrative terms. This is not just a quirk of my classification. Quite generally, the term 'joint attention' is used in both contexts[7], and with good reason: the term denotes the peculiar ability to direct one's attention towards an environmental object or feature together with someone else that is in play in both.

But you might think that indiscriminate usage of the term glosses over crucial differences in the two capacities; and you might think that, despite having been instrumental and enormously useful in framing the discussion of social perception, it is strictly speaking a misnomer. It is hard to see quite what a social form of attention could amount to: no matter whether you understand it in terms of a kind of experiential highlighting as proposed by Campbell (2002), or a structuring of your conscious life along the lines of Watzl (2017), or a selection for action (Wu 2011), attention appears to be an ability deployed by individual minds. This observation is in line with the argument I have been developing: the social nature of our joint interactions with the environment is not to be explained primarily in terms of our mental capacities; it is, rather, to be accounted for by the structure of the environment in which joint perceivers operate. Along those lines, it is not their attention that makes the relation to the objects of their perception and action social; it is, rather, the way in which the environment is ordered in perception. What changes when I visually attend to an object and you join me is, first and foremost, that we are now exposed to it in a spatial format in which, for each of us, both your location and mine form centers of perception. This change comes about, along the lines of the view I have been developing, through communicative interaction: the social ordering of the environment is something that is not simply given to but produced by us. This interaction is better thought of as a form of enacted perception than a form of attention:

JP: Two subjects jointly perceive an object just when, due to their communicative interaction, they locate it relative to their respective positions and thus in social space.

Joint perception is an intensely bodily undertaking: it requires its subjects to nudge, point, and otherwise direct each other's gaze so as to achieve demonstrative communication. This activity does not require language; pre-verbal infants master it with their caregivers. It is, however, a prerequisite of the kind of linguistic demonstrative communication that I considered in part 2 and that leads to propositional common knowledge about the object of reference. I have tried to show that this kind of communication relies on a reflective appropriation of the triadic spatial constellation that underlies joint perception; once the linguistic communicators can distinguish between their respective positions and locate the demonstratively identified object by means of a reflective exercise in social triangulation, they have acquired a minimal kind of perceptual common knowledge about it and are in possession of a conception of space.

How, then, should we think of the kind of attention that is required for the singling out of a perceptual object in social space, for the purposes of demonstrative thinking, reflective perspective-taking, and linguistic communication? The important thing to note is that the social element of demonstrative communication has already been accounted for. A speaker's attention to the object of her communicative and referential intention already plays out in social space. And so you can think of the speaker's attention to the object of his referential intention in the ordinary, individualist terms of a "perceptual highlighting" that Campbell (2002) adopts. Consider what happens when you focus your attention on an object in a social context for the purpose of demonstrative communication. As I noted in section 4.3, the way in which you attend to your environment in such a context will differ significantly from a situation in which you focus on an object by yourself: you will change your direction of gaze between the object and your co-attender, to whom you will try to make salient the target of your focus by appropriate gestures and verbal utterances; you will try to share what it is you are attending to. But it is still you who is doing the attending: there is no mode of attention in which the individual's act of highlighting an object for communication would be superseded by some kind of collective focus. We should not look for the social element of joint attention on the level of highlighting; there is, strictly speaking, no such thing as joint attention. There is joint perception, in which the triadic perceptual constellation is established that facilitates communicative activity directed at third objects; and there is the individual perceiver's attention to objects in social space. That joint perceivers end up perceptually singling out the same object in communication, and come to know in common that they do, is to be explained not in terms of a special form of perceptual attention; it is explained by the spatial framework in which the object is presented.

13.3   Subject- and Object-Based Views

You can broadly distinguish between two ways of conceptualizing joint attention, which I call the "subject-based" and (following Campbell 2011a) "object-based" views. Both have to address the core problem for any theory of joint phenomena: for a triadic constellation to qualify as joint, the subjects must mutually feature in each other's perceptions. The theory has to explain how this is possible. Gallagher (2011, 295), who in turn refers to Naomi Eilan (2005, 2), describes the difficulty inherent in this project:

> Philosophers often support the view that the coordination involved in joint attention is a coordination of mental states. Traditionally, they explain this psychological coordination in terms of propositional attitudes, or being in certain propositional states, like belief or desire—states where we mentally recognize something to be the case. With respect to joint attention, the object of such propositional states is the other person's mental states. Naomi Eilan rehearses this "typical philosophical analysis." . . . This [analysis], Eilan rightly suggests, leads to questions about the infinite iterations of beliefs, which she also rightly rejects.

If these remarks are correct, what is wanted is an account of the joint character of triadic perceptual constellations that avoids the "typical philosophical analysis." There are really only two basic moves you can make in the pursuit of such an account. You can take the triadic constellation to be basic, in the sense of being irreducible to a relation, or relations, between two of its constituents. Then you have to either say how the appeal to this basic relation allows you to avoid the problem Gallagher outlines or incur the charge of mysterianism. Alternatively, you can maintain that the subject-subject side of the triangle is more basic than the other two flanks.[8] Simulationist accounts of joint phenomena endorse this strategy: they attempt to explain the joint constellation in terms of its subjects' ability to understand their fellow perceivers' (perhaps embodied) mental states. I briefly introduce both approaches below, by considering one example of each.

The Subject-Based View of Joint Attention

Stueber (2011, 280) writes:

> Particularly significant for simulation theorists . . . is the fact that the crucial developmental milestone of joint attention involves a capacity for perspective taking. . . . The capacity for joint attention does not involve only the ability to recognize that one is jointly attending with another person toward an object in the external world. Rather, the infant actively monitors whether joint attention between persons is maintained. . . . Accordingly, the infant has to recognize whether the object is in a shared sphere of perceptual attention or whether the other person's perceptual sphere of attention is directed toward another part of the external world.

The capacity for perspective-taking, then, is at the heart of a "shared sphere of perceptual attention."[9] For this to be possible, the subject has to have some understanding of the other's mental life. Stueber thinks of this understanding as being achieved through acts of what he calls "basic empathy," which rely on "quasi-perceptual mechanisms creating 'perceptual similarity spaces' that allow us to practically grasp the other person to be minded like ourselves" (Stueber 2011, 276). This "bodily feeling of familiarity" (elsewhere he talks about "like-me-" familiarity) is egocentric; it takes as its starting point the familiarity with one's own bodily doings, which makes it possible to gain a practical understanding of those of the other person. If basic empathy is at the heart of the capacity for perspective-taking and if joint attention requires perspective-taking of some kind, it follows that the simulation theorist must account for the triadic perceptual constellation reductively, in terms of an explanation of how the joint perceiver comes to understand the other's state of mind by drawing on the acquaintance with her own bodily feelings.

How, though, does the simulation theorist make use of this explanation in the attempt to accommodate the triadic character of joint phenomena? Here is how the story might go: the perceiver is, through an act of basic empathy, able to simulate the other's perspective on the perceptual environment. She also perceives this environment herself. In order to transform the perceptual relation into a joint one, she has to somehow determine whether the other person is attending to the object or scene that she is perceiving herself. She thus has to map the other's simulated perception onto her own. This consideration is familiar from the brief discussions of ST in sections 11.4 and 12.4. There, the idea was that in order to explain how an agent uses his own bodily resources to integrate the cooperator's perceived doings into the joint body schema, you might appeal to low-level simulative processes. I argued that this proposal was problematic. And the same problems that arise for ST in the context of the discussion of the joint body schema also beset the idea that implicit, nonconceptual simulation procedures underlie the capacity for joint attention. First, it is not clear how ST copes with the consideration that the neural processes facilitating the simulation can only be activated once, not twice: just how does the simulating system distinguish between the perceiver's own actual perception and the simulated perspective of the other person, given that both take place simultaneously? Second, and more importantly, in order to map the other's simulated perspective onto your own perception, you already have to have in place a framework that allows you to determine whether the other's attention is directed at the same object as your own. You already have to have, quite literally, a map on which you can locate yourself and your fellow perceiver. ST, given its egocentric bias, does not have the resources to explain what this framework consists in. It can only get off the ground once you already have in place an account of the triadic constellation that the two perceivers help constitute. You already have to have an explanation of how the individual subject can have transcended her own perspective.[10]

This is not to dismiss Stueber's and other simulationist approaches to joint attention as fundamentally misguided. I have said nothing about the role of simulation and empathy in understanding another's mental life, where there are excellent reasons to think that they play a crucial role. It is just that as far as the problem described by Gallagher (2011) is concerned, an appeal to ST alone will not be able to provide a solution; the triadic character of joint perceptual constellation requires an approach that does not begin by taking the subject's own perspective on her environment as foundational.

The Object-Based View of Joint Attention

The supporter of the object-based view proposes to investigate joint attention by focusing directly on the perceptual relation between the subjects and their object of attention. This theorist denies that the best way to get a grip on joint attention is to begin by considering the ability of the involved creatures to acquire an understanding of their respective mental lives. Campbell (2011a, 426) thinks that questions about social cognition arising in the context of joint attention can be fruitfully addressed only once you have in place a view of the perceptual relation between the jointly involved subjects and their object of attention:

> The point I want to emphasize is that the basic ability to identify *what* the other person is attending to, so that one can attend to it oneself, is foundational for the subsequent perspective-taking capacities. . . . There is no such thing as coming to grasp the other person's perspective on the world without having first identified which things it is that the person is attending to.

Campbell goes on to argue in favor of an externalist conception of joint attention, according to which we begin to make sense of joint encounters by describing the phenomenal character of the subjects' experiences in terms of their perceptual relations with their surroundings. What makes the joint case distinct is that this relation has two subjects. On this view, you begin by asking how each subject can know, on the basis of experience, what object the other person is attending to. Only then can you come to a view about the perspective of the other person on the thing. You ask how the experience yields knowledge of the object, and only then are you able to come to an understanding of the other's perspective on that object.

This externalist approach is, of course, very much in line with the general argument I have been pursuing.[11] But it leaves unanswered significant questions: if you maintain that joint experience explains the capacity for acquiring common knowledge about a jointly perceived thing, the pressing question is what can be said about the nature of this experience. The difficulty is that perceptual experiences are standpoint-dependent, yet joint experiences somehow enable their subjects to transcend their perceptual perspectives. Just how do joint experiences achieve this feat? An answer is urgently needed if the object-based view of joint attention is to be fully convincing. I have been arguing that the answer is to be found in the appeal to a social spatial framework with which joint agents and perceivers operate. The notion of joint perception substantiates the idea of an object-based view.

However, the account I have developed gives rise to a new concern, one that arises specifically for my proposal. I have stressed the importance of joint activity in peripersonal space for the capacity to demonstratively communicate about objects in external space. I have also given an account of how joint perceivers come to acquire a reflective understanding of the triadic spatial constellation they help constitute . But I have not yet explained how joint perceivers can come to attend to distal objects that are beyond their reach. It is not clear what role social peripersonal space plays in our capacity to acquire perceptual common knowledge about objects that are not available for joint action. The next section addresses this difficulty.

13.4   Some Evidence from Psycholinguistics

Call *proximal joint perception* the kind of perception in which the objects of perception are within the perceivers' reach, so that joint action on and demonstrative communication about them becomes possible. Many joint constellations, particularly those discussed in the philosophical literature, are not of this proximal kind. Agents can jointly direct their attention to objects that are not within their reach and thereby come to acquire propositional common knowledge about them. This is what I call *distal joint perception*.

Previously I asked what changes for an individual perceiver who is joined by someone else, so that the ordinary perceptual constellation is replaced by a joint one. As far as proximal joint perception goes, I have developed an answer to this question. If you are folding a blanket by yourself and I take up one end of it in order to help you, you and I are now operating with a social spatial framework in which the areas surrounding our bodies are presented to each of us as peripersonal spaces. In these areas, both of us are receptive to perceptual as well as proprioceptive cues. But, as for instance in "Turner," joint attention does not always require manipulation of the perceived object. It is therefore not obvious that we can answer the above question for scenarios such as "Turner" by appeal to the kind of social spatial framework that is deployed in joint action. How do we account for such cases?

Some recent work in psycholinguistics is helpful here. Peeters, Hagoort, and Özyürek (2015) and Peeters and Özyürek (2016) investigate the spatial meaning of demonstrative terms. They distinguish between two distinct views. The first traditional view is that the meaning of demonstrative terms such as *this* or *that* is determined within an egocentric spatial framework. *This* is used for referents in relative proximity to the speaker, and *that* is used for referents that are remote from the speaker. Peeters and colleagues call this the "egocentric proximity account."[12] The second view is the dyad-oriented account, according to which a speaker uses a proximal demonstrative to refer to objects inside a conversational dyad (that is, within the space between participants in a face-to-face conversation), regardless of whether the object is close to the speaker. By contrast, referents outside the dyad elicit a distal demonstrative. On this view, "establishing reference is a social, interactive process that always takes place in a socio-cultural framework" (Peeters et al. 2015, 66).

To simplify their experimental setup somewhat: in a pre-test, subjects not involved with the main study were shown pictures in which a person (the imagined speaker) sat either at the center of the picture at a table (and thus opposite the participant) or to the left or right of the center of the picture (and thus not directly opposite the participant). The pictures contained two similar objects, one close to the speaker and one farther away. The speaker was looking and pointing at either the proximate or the remote object. The participants were then asked which demonstrative they would use if they were the speaker in the picture. When the speaker pointed to a close object, the participants used a proximate demonstrative; when the speaker pointed to a remote object, the participants used a distal demonstrative. These results were in line with the egocentric proximity account. Peeters and colleagues explain this outcome by suggesting that the pretest tapped into participants' linguistic intuitions, which favor the idea that the reference of demonstratives is determined relative to the speaker's location.

The main experiment began with an introductory round in which the participants were shown pictures that contained two objects on a table, with the speaker placed at the center of the picture and looking at the participant. The participants were subsequently shown the same pictures as the participants in the pretest. They then heard sentences that contained a proximal or a distal demonstrative and a noun that either did or did not pick out a target object. The task for the participants was to carefully look at the pictures and listen to the sentences. They were instructed to push a button whenever the speaker referred to either of the objects in the pictures.

The egocentric proximity account predicts that the speaker's use of a proximal demonstrative to refer to a remote object, and the use of a distal demonstrative to refer to a close object, leads to higher processing costs relative to their inverse uses. But EEG recordings from the subjects' scalp in the main experiment did not support that prediction. When objects were aligned with the face-to-face axes between speaker and participant, higher processing costs were found for the use of the distal demonstrative relative to the use of the proximal demonstrative, regardless of the location of the target object. When objects were not so aligned, there was no such difference in processing cost. Peeters et al. explain this outcome by arguing that the introductory round created a joint constellation in which the speakers looked at the participants when not pointing and looking at the target objects.

In a second round, the pictures in which the speaker was placed to the right or left of the center were modified, so that the speaker was now at the picture's center (and hence aligned with the participant). A further modification was that in the pictures in which the objects were aligned with speaker and participant, the distal object was placed farther away from the speaker so that it was clearly out of reach. The experimental procedure remained the same. Now there was no preference for the proximal demonstrative when the speaker referred to the object close to her. Peeters and his colleagues (2015, 80) interpret this result as showing that subjects prefer a proximal demonstrative for objects in shared space, but only if all possible referents are within that space: if there is another possible referent outside the dyad, this referent introduces a lateral axis and thereby a possible boundary between speaker and addressee, thus eliminating the experience of shared space.

Peeters et al. (2015) take their findings to falsify the egocentric proximity account, although the results of the pretest show that this account is in line with native speakers' linguistic intuitions on demonstratives. Their data support the dyad-oriented account for stimuli with a sagittal orientation of objects (in which the objects are in line with the speaker-addressee axis). But that account cannot explain why participants did not prefer a proximal demonstrative for the object close to the speaker in the lateral orientation of objects. Peeters et al. (2015, 80) introduce a new view, the "shared-space account," to accommodate this finding. This account "underlines that in human interaction physical space is transformed into meaningful space." On this view, what is considered to be shared between participants in a conversation is not merely determined by spatial position. Rather, the account proposes that "interlocutors in a conversation build up shared space throughout the course of a conversation, taking into account previous interaction and mutually shared knowledge." The general view is that demonstrative reference is a "collaborative and cooperative process" (Peeters et al. 2015, 82).

13.5   Proximal and Distal Joint Perception

The findings of Peeters et al. (2015) are intriguing.[13] They offer an explanation of the possibility of distal joint perception that is very much in line with the thought I have been developing. Distal joint perception, on their view, is the result of a constellation that in their experiments is produced by the participants' focus on the faces of the speakers shown in the photographs considered at the beginning of the main experiment. Eye contact appears to matter crucially. It is not a big leap to suppose that the real point here is the establishment of a communicative relation with the other person. This communicative relation has its origin in action space: proximal demonstratives are most obviously used to refer to objects that are within reach; reachability is a strong indicator of proximity.[14] Eye contact, and communicative interaction more generally, activates a spatial framework that is defined relative to the standpoints of both communicators. And, once activated, it can be extended in linguistic communication even if the communicators do not occupy proximal locations or if the object of their perception and action is out of reach: proximal demonstratives are used to refer to objects in the space between the participants.

Peeters et al. (2015) investigate demonstrative reference for objects along the axis between speaker and addressee. Of course, many joint constellations are not of this kind. Demonstrative communication that heavily relies on pointing gestures is often about objects whose location forms the third constituent of a triangle and in which perceivers thus have to alternate gaze in order to achieve the joint constellation. But there is no prima facie reason to think that the view cannot be made to work for triangular constellations: The hypothesis would be that subjects' pointing gestures extend the communicative space in the direction in which they are both looking (though it is unlikely that proximal demonstratives will be used to refer to objects in such locations). The contention of Peeters et al. (2015) that there is a specific kind of spatial framework in which demonstrative communication is accomplished with ease and which is created by means of an extension of an initial episode of eye contact provides an explanation of the connection between proximal and distal joint perception. The distal case is made possible by the extension of a communicative spatial framework that is initially activated by the kind of interaction that facilitates joint activity; it is just that in the distal case, the object of the activity is not within reach.

Another aspect of the conclusions of Peeters et al. (2015) is relevant in our context: they think that the results of the pretest show an "egocentric bias" that guides the subjects in their experiment's preparatory round. Another way to explain these results is to suppose that speakers have two distinct ways to give meaning to demonstratives, depending on whether they are used in communicative contexts: if they are used in soliloquy, they pick out objects in egocentric space; if they are used communicatively, they pick out objects in social space. Such an interpretation would be in line with the view developed here, since it was an important consideration in part 2 that demonstrative reference fixing is to be explained in terms of the speaker's referential rather than communicative intentions. And it would support the idea that the change that is brought about by a co-perceiver's entering the scene is to be thought of as a change in the spatial framework in use to determine the location of the perceived object.

To summarize briefly: When thinking about what is usually called "joint attention," we should begin with the idea that the triadic perceptual relation between the perceivers and the object of their attention is basic. It cannot be explained in terms of the subjects' capacity for perspective-taking (of the level 2 kind), since they can be in a position to appreciate distinctions in perspective on an object only if they know in common that they are attending to the same thing. The way to accommodate this demand is to maintain that joint perceptions occur in social space, in which the perceivers treat both of their locations as centers of perception and action. They can then determine the location of the object of their respective attention by means of an exercise in social triangulation. Social space is, in the first place, action space, constituted by the subjects' joint activity on an object. Such activity is necessarily communicative, and some such activity is exclusively communicative. This is the case when subjects make use of eye contact, pointing gestures, and so on to direct another's conscious attention to particular objects that may (but need not) be out of reach. In these cases, they expand social space into that part of the world that is not available for manipulation. Along those lines, we should distinguish between proximal and distal forms of joint perception: all joint constellations have a proximal aspect, but some of them expand into the distant environment. What unifies them is the social spatial framework that the subjects use to determine the location of the object that they are attending to together, for the purpose of jointly acting on or acquiring propositional common knowledge about it.

14 Some Applications

One crucial test for any theory is its explanatory power. In this final chapter, I show how the approach I have been developing can help with some problems arising for psychologists and philosophers who think about the nature of perspective-taking and social cognition.

14.1 Joint Perception and Level 1 Perspective-Taking

In chapter 4, I introduced the developmental distinction between level 1 and level 2 perspective-taking and pointed out a difficulty: it is not at all obvious how to think of the spatial framework of creatures capable of knowing, perceptually, what another can see but not how the other sees the thing. Full-fledged perspective-taking requires the deployment of what Schellenberg (2007) calls an "engaged allocentric perspective"; it requires the creature to think about a variety of locations as affording perspectives on a perceived scene and to be able to hypothesize about what the scene looks like from such a perspective—perhaps through an exercise of imagined bodily rotation (Klatzky et al. 1998). But such a frame of reference cannot be what underwrites level 1 perspective-taking capacities.

Consider the developmental trajectory. Humans engage in face-to-face interactions from a very young age. They imitate (intentionally or not; see for instance Meltzoff and Moore 1983) perceived facial expressions almost from birth; they may then pursue reengagement in face-to-face interactions (Nagy 2008) and respond with distress in still-face conditions by the time they are two months old (Cohn and Tronick 1989). They actively seek to prolong and take a stance toward interactions with others a few months later (Kopp 1982; Trevarthen and Hubley 1978). At about one year of age, they begin to triangulate, using pointing gestures and gaze to share aspects of the perceptual environment with their caregivers (Trevarthen and Hubley 1978; Bates, Camaioni, and Volterra 1975; Liszkowski et al. 2006). About a year and a half later, they pass level 1 perspective-taking tasks, and, finally, at around four years of age, they can solve level 2 perspective-taking tasks (Flavell 1992, 1985). Perhaps not coincidentally, this is also when they begin to be able to solve classic false-belief tasks (Wimmer and Perner 1983).[1]

Of particular interest for present purposes is the period, roughly between the first and the second year, during which children increasingly attend to objects together with others. They begin to follow the gaze of a caregiver to discern what she is looking at and to deploy pointing gestures to direct the adult's attention to third objects. This is the period in which children engage in what Moll and Kadipasaoglu (2013) call "social perspective-taking." It will still take more than a full year before they are able to master explicit level 1 perspective-taking tasks. The trajectory can seem puzzling: doesn't the capacity for social triangulation already presuppose the ability to take the other's perspective, at least in rudimentary form?

An experiment by Moll, Carpenter, and Tomasello (2011), which I only partially describe here, highlights this question. Caregivers were asked to introduce two-year-old children to some toys. In the first part of the experiment, the caregiver then left the room. In her absence, a new toy was given to the child. The adult subsequently returned to the room and asked to be shown the object she hadn't seen before. The child was able to reliably identify this object. In the second part of the experiment, the caregiver did not leave the room. She remained copresent while a new toy was given to the child. However, the adult's view of the object was obscured by a visual barrier. The adult later asked for the object she hadn't seen before. In this condition, children were unable to reliably identify the right object; they selected the correct object at chance. Moll and Meltzoff (2011, 400) observe:

> Somewhat counterintuitively, children learn what others have or have not become acquainted with *before* they come to determine what they can see from their specific viewpoints. . . . This developmental order, with a broad distinction of others' familiarity versus ignorance of things being in place before the ability to determine what others can see in the here and now, is remarkable as it turns the idea that perception is somehow fundamental or primary on its head.

Moll and Kadipasaoglu (2013) conclude, on the basis of this and a number of other studies, that young children overestimate what another can see if they are mutually engaged with the other person and that physical copresence is the main indicator of a shared experience. They explain this tendency to overestimate what is shared in terms of the failure to differentiate between the subjects' distinct perspectives:

> We argue that young children have a proclivity to treat social interaction as a sufficient condition for shared perceptual availability: "When you and I are co-present and engaged, you should be able to perceive what I perceive." An impression of a shared space is induced, and only later overcome once children learn more about and attend more to the specific defeating conditions of perception, such as a blocked line of sight. (Moll and Kadipasaoglu 2013, 5)

The question is how we should think of this shared space. It cannot (yet) amount to an engaged allocentric conception of space, and it must amount to more than an egocentric spatial framework in which perspectives are merged in Pezzulo's (2013) sense. The two-year-olds in Moll and Meltzoff's experiment were able to make sense in their thinking of the notion of perspective; they understood the question about what the caregiver had not seen. In order to do this, they had to have acquired the concept of a viewpoint. But they could not yet reliably distinguish between their own viewpoint and that of the other person; they tended to ascribe their own viewpoint on the object that they had jointly manipulated to the adult. What needs explaining is how the children could have acquired the concept of a viewpoint without being reliably able to distinguish between various perspectives.

The notion of a social spatial framework can help here. On the present view, the ability to take perspectives has its roots in the practical deployment of such a framework in joint action. When children begin to communicatively point out and attend to objects with others around the end of their first year, they demonstrate a practical grasp of a spatial order in which a variety of locations are occupied by perceivers and agents. But as I highlighted at the end of the previous chapter, this practical spatial knowledge does not have to amount to a propositional knowledge of perspective; demonstrative joint activity does not presuppose a conception of space. You can see the second year of life as the time when children begin to acquire this knowledge. They do this, on the present view, by beginning to develop a reflective understanding of what is within their reach, and of the location whence they act as "'here."

In section 12.4, I suggested that agents can think of locations as "here" if two conditions are met. First, the location has to be presented in action space. That is, it is a location at which both bodily and perceptual information is available, which can be exploited in order to support bodily movements aimed at bringing about changes in the environment. In joint action, this condition is met in both the area surrounding one's own location and the area surrounding a cooperator's location. The second condition is met if the agent experiences a sense of control over an executed motor movement. The location of a cooperator's movement can, so the suggestion goes, be thought of as "*there": as a center of action, but not one over which the agent has control. Once the agent is capable of distinguishing in thought between "here" and "*there," she is operating with a conception of space in Evans's sense: she has acquired the ability to map egocentric space onto a variety of locations in allocentric space. She is now able to reflectively determine the location of objects relative to the positions of joint perceivers and agents. And what this amounts to is that she is able to solve level 1 perspective-taking tasks. Along those lines, the sociocognitive development of children during the second year of life can be described as the acquisition of a reflective understanding of the spatial framework that becomes available to them when they first begin to jointly interact with others on third objects. The view can explain the at first mysterious capacity of children in their third year to judge where an object is relative to another's perspective, without being able to make judgments about the object's perspective-dependent properties. On the present view, the capacity to solve explicit level 1 perspective tasks requires a conception of space in which the location of objects can be determined, in social triangulation, relative to perceivers other than oneself. Because these objects are picked out in terms of the bounded locations they occupy, their perspective-dependent looks are irrelevant in their identification. It is the common knowledge of an object's location that makes demonstrative communication about it possible. And this primary common knowledge forms the basis on which secondary, perceptual common knowledge can subsequently be acquired.

Children begin to solve level 1 perspective-taking tasks at around two and a half years old. Importantly, the children in Moll's experiment are two years old and thus just slightly too young to successfully complete such tasks. You can explain Moll and her colleagues' findings by hypothesizing that the children's process of acquiring a reflective understanding of the social spatial framework in which they operate is not yet complete. They have some awareness of the spatial order in which they operate: they have a grasp of the concept of perspective and are thus capable of ascribing actions and perceptions to particular locations. But they tend to think of these locations as "'here'": as centers of perceptions and actions over whose objects control can be exercised. What they have not yet undertaken is the final step that would make the reflective understanding of the social spatial framework complete: they have not yet mastered the distinction between "here" and "*there." This interpretation is in line with the broadly Strawsonian ([1959] 1996) character of the view I have been developing. The primary distinction, which on his classic account, is between "persons" and "things," becomes the distinction between the occupants of the locations that are presented as centers of perception and agency and those that are occupied by the objects of perception and action. It takes mastery of this primary distinction to then be able to think of a particular person as oneself, and it takes mastery of the parallel spatial distinction to then be able to think of particular centers of perception and agency as "here" and others as "*there." My account supports Moll and her colleagues' view: social interaction really is vital for children's acquisition of the concept of perspective. But it isn't that interaction somehow trumps perception. Rather, social interactions that build on both perceptual and proprioceptive cues activate a frame of reference in which the own standpoint can be transcended and the concept of perspective is thus made available.

14.2 Are Joint Perceivers Mindreaders?

Along the lines of the present proposal, there are two distinct levels to the analysis of perceptual common knowledge. There is, first, the joint interaction in which a practical, embodied relation between agents and environment is established. And there are, second, the agents' mental states of knowing that are individuated by that relation. It is obvious that subjects of propositional common knowledge must have in place a reflective understanding of their own and their cooperators' mental states: when two individuals know in common P(*L), each individual knows that each individual knows P(*L). The subjects of this knowledge must have in place a theory of mind that includes concepts of propositional attitudes such as "knowing that p."[2]

It is less clear what one should say about the mindreading capacities (if any) that are required to participate in joint interactions in social space. You can broadly distinguish between three possible views. You can either think that joint action, including the developmentally early capacity for joint attention, requires that its subjects be able to represent the other's content-possessing mental states (for instance, Fodor 1995; Leslie, Friedman, and German 2004): otherwise you simply lose track of the distinction between *intentional* social action and mere reflexive behavior. Alternatively, you can think that only some minimal capacity for representing others' mental states is needed, where what is represented are not folk psychological concepts such as beliefs and desires (for instance, Bogdan 2009; Tomasello, Call, and Hare 2003). Or you can think that no representational capacities are required to engage in joint activities; all it takes is what Hutto (2011) calls "elementary mind minding," according to which the joint agents display attitudes of intentional directedness without representing mental state concepts at all.

It will be obvious that the present view is incompatible with the contention that possession of a full theory of mind is required for action in social space. The explanation of the possibility of propositional perceptual common knowledge depends vitally on the individuation of the knowers' mental states by a triadic perceptual constellation. You have to take that constellation as basic: if you were to analyze it reductively, in terms of the perceivers' capacity to mentally represent each other's beliefs, you would have deprived yourself of the ability to deflate the threat of regress inherent in the analysis of common knowledge. You could then not be an externalist about common knowledge; common knowledge would amount to the subjects' beliefs about each other's beliefs, and you would have reverted to a conjunctive analysis of the JTB kind. In any case, there are independent considerations that speak against this view: Apperly and Butterfill (2009, 957) note that no study has yet shown the ability of infants to track beliefs about complex contents (such as the location *and* perceptual features of observed objects) that would require the stipulation of their possession of a full-blown theory of mind.

At this juncture it is tempting to take the advocated externalist stance to its full conclusion and argue that mindreading capacities, however conceived, have no place at all in the account of the triadic relation that obtains in social space. What makes the interaction social is not that the subjects understand, by the deployment of a (perhaps very thin) theory of mind, that they are cooperating with other agents, but simply that they treat the standpoint of that agent as a center of perception and action. Joint agency, on this view, is not constituted by social cognition but by social environments. It is, in the first instance, simply a matter of knowing *where* an object is in social space—of being able to act on it jointly and, once a reflective grasp of this spatial order has been achieved, of picking it out by the interpretation of demonstrative utterances and appropriate pointing gestures. I think this view is correct. Although a comprehensive discussion of the literature is not possible here, I can sketch the position by contrasting it with a prominent minimalist view of the mindreading capacities of infants in their second year of life. Apperly and Butterfill's (2009) and, similarly, Butterfill and Apperly's (2013) "two-systems" account of mindreading is ideal for that purpose because it shares quite a bit of common ground with the social externalist view: it too begins with the stipulation that the basic contact between perceiver and environment is to be thought of as a nonpsychological relation between a subject and a location, though on the two-systems account that location is not socially construed. I briefly introduce the account and consider whether it is compatible with the present line of thought.

Apperly and Butterfill (2009) highlight an apparent contradiction: infants are capable of passing false belief tasks between thirteen and fifteen months of age (Onishi and Baillargeon 2005; Surian, Caldi, and Sperber (2007), but they demonstrate reflective understanding of the concept of false belief only at around four years (for instance, Wellman, Cross, and Watson 2001; Wimmer and Perner 1983). Adults are capable of effortless social interaction, but their reasoning about others' beliefs is cognitively demanding. Apperly and Butterfill note a polarization in the debate about the explanation of these findings: either the capacity for mindreading, including developmentally early evidence, is explained in terms of the subject's possession of a theory of mind, and thus of mental concepts such as belief and desire; or it is accounted for in strictly behavioral terms. Apperly and Butterfill suggest an intermediate path. They introduce the view that adult reasoners' flexible (and therefore cognitively demanding) theory of mind is complemented by a separate, efficient (but relatively inflexible) system that processes belief-like states that, though representational, do not have propositional content. The key notions that characterize this system are *encountering* and *registering*. Encountering is defined "as a relation between the individual, an object, and a location, such that the relation obtains when the object is in the individual's field" (Apperly and Butterfill 2009, 962), where a field is "a region of space centered on the individual." You can think of "encountering" as a proxy for "perceiving" in a useful range of cases. The important thing to note is that "the conditions under which an encounter occurs must be specified without appeal to anything psychological."

Registering is introduced as follows:

> One stands in the registering relation to an object and location if one encountered it at that location and if one has not since encountered it somewhere else. Registrations resemble beliefs in having correctness conditions that may not be obtained: A registration fails to be correct when the object registered is not where it is registered as being. Their interest lies in their connections to action. One can understand registration as an enabling condition for action, so that registering an object and location enables one to act on it later, providing its location does not change. This understanding of registration would be useful to an organism, for example, because it would motivate the organism to move objects a competitor encountered in the past. Further, registration also can be understood as determining which location an individual will direct their actions to when attempting to act on that object. This more sophisticated understanding (which requires the notion of an unsuccessful action) enables one to predict actions on the basis of incorrect registrations and so approximate belief reasoning to such a great extent as to pass some false belief tasks (e.g. Onishi/Baillargeon (2005). (Apperly and Butterfill 2009, 962–963)

Registrations thus serve as proxies for beliefs that may be true or false. Crucially, Apperly and Butterfill (2009) point out, they are relations to objects and properties rather than propositions, and they set their parameters for action independently of any psychological states. They enable a subject to track beliefs within a limited range of situations, where those limits exclude (inter alia) the distinction between what is represented and how it is represented. That is, the authors suggest, they make possible level 1 but not level 2 perspective-taking.

Apperly and Butterfill (2009) allow that registrations could include properties other than locations. But the dominance of the role of location in the account of what is registered is striking. Since the most important role of registrations is to enable action, this is no accident: in order to be able to act on an object, you have to locate it. Whatever other properties might be registerable, the necessary one is location. It is the registration of location that enables registrations to play an explanatory role in a minimal theory of mindreading; it is because the individual has registered an object's location that she can predict actions based on incorrect registrations. And it is in virtue of this capacity that she can pass some false belief tasks.

Compare Apperly and Butterfill's (2009) proposal with the externalist account I have been developing. Both views predict that the subject who has the relevant capacities (to register objects at their locations, to operate in social space) will be capable of level 1 but not level 2 perspective-taking. Apperly and Butterfill explain this capacity by appeal to the nature of registrations, which track objects at locations, though they do not permit the tracking of complex beliefs. The social externalist explains it by appeal to the nature of the subject's spatial framework, which allows for the identification of objects in terms of their locations relative to two centers of perception and action. Note that level 1 perspective-taking need not be reflective; it can occur automatically (Michael et al. 2018). The social externalist does not introduce beliefs, or belief-like proxies, in order to explain the subject's knowledge of the object's location: the social environment itself takes care of it. The environment, rather than aspects of the agent's mental life, determines whether she knows where the thing is in social space. Social externalism gets by without stipulating mindreading capacities, even of the thin kind Apperly and Butterfill advocate.

The two-system hypothesis navigates a middle ground between the stipulation of a full-fledged theory of mind for preverbal infants (and possibly other creatures that display behavior suggesting belief-reasoning capacities, such as chimpanzees and scrub jays) and the denial that mindreading capacities are needed to explain their capacity to pass some false belief tasks. Apperly and Butterfill (2009, 957) note that these tasks all test infants' understanding of attitudes to objects' locations. They demonstrate their proposed theory's capacity to solve a simple mindreading task by considering Onishi and Baillargeon's (2005) violation-of-expectation paradigm In this experiment, fifteen-month-old infants are exposed to a scenario in which an actor watches a toy being placed in a green box; subsequently the toy moves to a yellow box while the actor's view is blocked, and later the

actor reaches into one of the two boxes. The infant looks longer at the display if the actor reaches into the yellow box. Conversely, if the actor's view
is not blocked, the opposite looking pattern is found.

Onishi and Baillargeon (2005, 257) interpret their findings as supporting
the view that even young children deploy concepts such as goals, perceptions, and beliefs to make sense of others' actions. Apperly and Butterfill,
by contrast, explain them in terms of the children's grasp of the actor's
incorrect registration of the object's location. A third way of interpreting
the evidence is made available by social externalism. Remember that social
spatial frameworks are constituted by an act of social triangulation: they are
constituted by the triadic constellation between two centers of perception
and agency and a third object. That is, they are constituted by an act of
level 1 perspective-taking. As we have seen, the capacity for conscious level
1 perspective-taking is in place at around two and a half years of age, and
it is the result of children having acquired an explicit understanding of the
social framework with which they are operating. But the triadic constellation itself is brought about when the capacity for joint attention sets in
around the end of the first year of life; this is also the time when children
begin to be able to pass implicit false belief tasks.

Suppose we begin with the view that infants socially triangulate in order
to determine where the actor is going to reach. The view predicts that when
the actor knows the target object's location, the infant expects, as a consequence of an exercise in nonreflective level 1 perspective-taking, that the
actor will reach for the box in which the toy is placed. She will look com-
paratively longer at scenarios in which this expectation is disappointed; so
far, so unproblematic. What, though, does the view have to say about cases
in which the actor holds a false belief about the object's location (because
the object has moved in a way that is visible to the infant but invisible
to the actor)? Here, the infant's prediction of the actor's behavior cannot
be based on an act of level 1 perspective-taking that takes the actor's current perceptual relation to the location of the object as its starting point:
location and target object have, after all, come apart. The question is how
the infant solves this problem. One possibility is that she abandons the
social spatial framework; since the target object's location cannot be determined by social triangulation, she ceases to treat the actor's location as a
center of perception and action. She then falls back on egocentric space
and calculates the location of the target relative to her own position. This

interpretation does not explain the evidence, though: the view predicts that the infant expects the actor to look at the object's actual location. There would be no room for a divergence between the actor's focus and the object's location. In any case, the view is not convincing: why should the discrepancy between the actor's looking behavior and the target object's location provoke the infant to cease treating the actor's location as a center of perception and agency?

The alternative is that the infant continues to operate with a social spatial framework. She continues to treat the actor's location as a center of perception and action. Then her knowledge of the object's location in social space is not current; it has not been updated since the object moved. The infant therefore works with the last location the object occupied in social space—the location of the object prior to its movement. She expects the actor to reach for the object in the location that it occupied prior to its move; this expectation is disappointed if the actor reaches for the box currently containing the object, and this explains why she looks longer at that scenario.

This explanation of the evidence makes two assumptions. The first is the existence of a social spatial framework that underwrites subjects' capacity for level 1 perspective-taking. Substantiating this idea has been a main point of this book. The second assumption is that subjects retain some kind of memory of constellations in social space when these constellations are not being updated by moves of objects in external space. I have no independent evidence to support this assumption; as I pointed out in part 3, the research into social action space is in its infancy. But we can usefully consider scenarios in which the location of objects in egocentric or allocentric space is not updated; there, too, the subject retains in memory the location the object occupied at the last time information from it was available and (for stationary objects) uses this location until it is updated by new information. It is part of our everyday metaphysics that, other things being equal, we take stationary objects in visual space to keep occupying the location at which we last saw them. A similar point applies for action space. Suppose you are driving a car with a manual gearbox. When you shift gears and subsequently remove your hand, perhaps to adjust the volume of the radio, your motor system stores the position of the gear stick in working memory: when (having changed the channel) you want to shift gears again, your hand automatically returns to the position the gear stick

last occupied because you haven't since received new perceptual information about its location (you haven't touched it, and you have been looking
at the road all along). If social space is a sui generis frame of reference that
allows us to order perceptual objects in useful ways, to this extent akin to
egocentric and allocentric space, you might hypothesize that some sort of
working memory is in place that enables subjects to keep operating with
this spatial framework in the absence of real-time perceptual information
about the objects in it. Such a hypothesis would explain Onishi and Baillargeon's (2005) findings in social externalist terms. The hypothesis is, of
course, speculative and in need of empirical testing.

The are three advantages to the view sketched here. First, it has the
advantage of parsimony over its theory of mind competitors. If you can
explain infants' looking behavior without postulating mindreading abilities, it turns out that the stipulation of a mindreading system, however
thin, is not necessary to account for their ability to pass some false belief
tasks. Of course, you might think that postulating a social spatial framework also violates the demands of parsimony, and possibly much more
egregiously. But, and this is the second advantage, there are independent
reasons for thinking that there is such a framework. I have given a conceptual argument in its support in part 2 and considered some empirical evidence in part 3. If you explain Onishi's and Baillargeon's (2005) results by
appeal to such a framework, you have the resources to account for the possibility of demonstrative communication, and you can deflate the threat of
regress inherent in the analysis in perceptual common knowledge. There
is, on the present view, a straightforward connection between the sophis-
ticated mindreading capacities deployed by the possessors of propositional
perceptual common knowledge and their practical knowledge of an object's
location in social space.

The third advantage has to do with developmental considerations. Consider what is required of a creature operating with the notions of encountering and registering (and thus nonpsychological proxies for perceiving and
believing) to solve simple false belief tasks. The point Apperly and Butterfill
(2009) are highlighting is that these proxies, in contrast to the mental states
they stand for, have no content. This is what makes them apt vehicles for
the efficient, if inflexible, solving of simple mindreading tasks. It follows
that the kind of perspective-taking available to a creature that tracks another's registrations can take place only in an egocentric spatial framework.

Since the other subject is not represented *as* a perceiver and agent, the other's position can serve only as a nonego reference point in a space whose objects are grouped around the perceiver. If so, the approach cannot explain how the creature can use its awareness of the other's location in the acquisition of a conception of space; the resources that enable infants to transcend the egocentric perspective, so that the eventual adoption of viewpoints other than their own becomes possible, are not provided by the approach. Of course, they may be provided in another way, for instance by a more fully developed theory of mind. But it is not obvious how such an account might go; as Apperly and Butterfill (2009) note, understanding the relation between infants' earlier and later theory of mind systems remains a major challenge. It is also not obvious how it accommodates the striking observation, stressed by various developmental psychologists (for instance, Hobson and Hobson 2011; Reddy 2011; Moll and Kadipasaoglu 2013), that human infants are not passive observers of others' doings but active participants in their social environments who seek to establish communicative relations with their caregivers. This observation plays an important role on the externalist view: the interactive nature of the social spatial framework explains how locations other than one's own can be presented as centers of perception and action. By freeing ourselves from the idea that prelinguistic children deploy mindreading abilities, however minimal, in making sense of others' doings, we can thus come to a view of human cognitive development that appears much closer to an accurate description of how real-life infants act in their environment.

This is not to say that there can be no room for a system that efficiently tracks attitudes to an object's properties. Apperly and Butterfill (2009) allow that some nonspatial perceptual properties, such as color, could be tracked by such a system. The stipulation of a social spatial framework could not explain this capacity; its "signature limits" are purely spatial. Also, they maintain that other mechanisms, such as automatization (Povinelli and Giambrone 1999; Suddendorf and Whiten 2003) and behavioral association (Baldwin and Baird 2001; Byrne 2003; Perner and Ruffman 2005; Povinelli, Bering, and Giambrone 2000), can have a role to play in the efficient tracking of beliefs. My proposal is not meant to deny that such mechanisms have a role to play in belief reasoning. But where reasoning about location is concerned, the stipulation of social space can explain relevant evidence without having to appeal to mindreading capacities at all.

On my view, then, nonreflective level 1 perspective-taking does not require the deployment of a theory of mind, however minimal. It requires the deployment of a social spatial framework. This framework is activated in social interactions that are directed at visual objects. Social externalism is thus sympathetic to interactionist or enactivist views such as Gallagher's (2011) or Hutto's (2011), on which joint interactions are, simply, activities of a particular kind. Hutto (2011, 329) writes:

> Radical Enactivists do not think of the capacities to mind minds as any kind of conceptual understanding—especially if doing so entails postulating a represented knowledge-base that must be subpersonally consulted. Rather, elementary mind minding can be understood in terms of interactive, unprincipled embodied engagements.

Similarly, Gallagher (2011, 300) observes:

> One learns football by practice and by playing, and one comes to understand the precise actions of others on the field in terms of that practice rather than in terms of some general theory. And as I kick the ball down the field, and try to circumnavigate the adversary player, I don't do so by theorizing about his mental states.

The attraction of these approaches is their minimalism: they get by without attributing to the participants in joint undertakings the ability to reflectively understand anything about their own or the other's mental lives. Joint activities are simply particular kinds of doings, of engaging with one's surroundings. One challenge such enactivist approaches face is that it is quite hard for them to say what *distinguishes* joint undertakings from their individual counterparts. And you need an account of this distinction, since otherwise the social aspect of the activity drops out of the picture completely. You then have deprived yourself of the capacity to explain how joint attention can yield common knowledge about the environment. My account can help by proposing that joint activities play out in specific surroundings: they play out in an environment that is already populated by other creatures with whom the subject interacts. It is the environment, not the individuals' minds, that houses and explains the social character of the activity. The stipulation of a social spatial framework preserves the attractive simplicity of enactivist approaches to joint attention while also having the resources to explain the connection between simple social involvements with the environment and the capacity to demonstratively reason and thereby acquire propositional common knowledge about it.[3]

14.3   Social Space and the Perception of Objects' Spatial Properties

Throughout this book, I have treated social perceptual phenomena in strict separation from their individual counterparts. You may well have gotten the impression that the kinds of perceptual and agentive encounters you enjoy in surroundings that you share with others have nothing to do at all with the kind you have by yourself. There is, you might take me to suggest, an individual's space of action and perception, and there is also the social spatial framework that becomes activated when a second agent begins to interact and demonstratively communicate with the individual about an object that is visible to (and, in the most straightforward cases, within reach of) both. Demonstrative thought does not always occur in social contexts; and even if you are inclined (as I am) to think that we should treat demonstrative acts as, first and foremost, communicative undertakings that we need to understand if we are to give a plausible account of their individual counterparts, there is no denying that the kind of perceptual experience that underwrites the capacity for demonstrative reasoning is not always of a social kind. After all, I can, when contemplating Turner's seascape, form the thought that *this* blob of paint is a buoy even if I am the only visitor in the gallery. Should we conclude, then, that the view developed in this book tells us nothing about the nature of ordinary, nonsocial perception and the knowledge with which it provides us? Does the view that social perceptual experience is the result of a particular spatial organization of our environment have no implications at all for our demonstrative reasoning in the absence of others?

I think that the two modes of experience are much more closely related than this skeptical view allows and that for creatures like us, the character of the objects of ordinary perceptual experience is quite heavily dependent on our operation in a social environment. I can bring out this point by considering an argument put forward by Schellenberg (2007), who is concerned with a core problem for any theory of visual perception: the question of how it can be that perceivers see objects' intrinsic spatial properties (those they have independently of their perceivers' location) even though perceivers see them from a particular perspective. Schellenberg thinks that this question can be answered by appeal to the view that perception is dependent on action, and that perception of an object's intrinsic spatial properties depends on the possession of a practical conception of space: "Perceiving intrinsic spatial properties requires perceiving objects as perceivable from locations other than the one that one happens to occupy" (Schellenberg 2007, 611). She introduces the "spatial know-how thesis," according to which "a subject must have a practical conception of space that involves understanding that there are different possible perspectives on any three-dimensional space-occupier" (614). This view is offered as a middle way between two extremes. One extreme view is that perceiving the spatial properties of objects depends on having learned, through a practical encounter, the sensorimotor affordances of the type of shape that the object exemplifies. The other extreme view is that it suffices to be moved relative to objects to perceive their spatial properties. The moderate view is that the *disposition* to act on a perceived object determines the coordinates of perception and that perceiving an object's intrinsic spatial properties depends on the practical knowledge of what it would take to act on an object from locations other than one's own. This practical know-how requires the subject to operate with an "'alter-ego" conception of space that Schellenberg (614) describes as an "allocentric conception that is engaged." This conception of space meets two distinct requirements: it enables the subject to know how to act on a perceived object from her own perspective; and it enables the subject to adapt her disposition to act on the object relative to changes in its location. For this to be possible, the subject must be operating with an egocentric frame of reference but must also be able to transcend this frame of reference so as to be able to remap her disposition to act relative to different possible standpoints. Schellenberg stresses that this requirement is weaker than the demand that the subject know what the object looks like from locations other than her own; it requires knowing only how to act on it from these locations, were the subject to occupy them.

Schellenberg's (2007) aim is quite distinct from mine: she wants to explain a striking fact about visual perception; I want to understand perception in social contexts. But there are some instructive similarities between the requirements that have to be met (on her view) for the perception of an object's intrinsic spatial properties and those in place (on mine) for demonstrative communication about jointly perceived objects. The most striking parallel between Schellenberg's account and mine is the observation that transcendence of the egocentric perspective is necessary for ordinary spatial perception (her view) or joint perception (mine). Equally remarkably, both proposals advance the broad idea that transcending the egocentric perspective requires action, or at least the capacity for it. Schellenberg notes that only agents are perceivers and that this is no accident; I claimed in part 3 that a plausible explanation of the capacity for level 1 perspective-taking has to draw on the subjects' capacity to jointly interact with their environment.

However, there are some important differences also. I have stressed that a social spatial framework can be available only in the presence of other agents and perceivers. You could not only not be jointly attending to an object by yourself; you could, on the disjunctivist account developed in section 5.4, not enjoy the experience of joint interaction with your environment by yourself. It is the actual presence of others that activates the spatial framework in which joint activity and perceptual common knowledge are possible. By contrast, the "alter-ego" spatial framework is fundamentally individualistic: it is the individual perceiver who is in a position to know what it would take to act on a perceptual object from standpoints other than her own. There is also the further contrast between Schellenberg's focus on the spatial properties of visual objects and my claim that it is common knowledge of location that underwrites demonstrative communication. Both have to do with the ability to take perspectives, but that is where the similarities seem to end. I argue that it takes a spatial framework in which a variety of locations are treated as centers of perception and agency to come to know where the object is in social space; Schellenberg (2007) argues that it takes a spatial framework in which the perceiver knows what it would take to act on an object from a variety of locations to come to see its spatial properties.

One question that arises for Schellenberg's (2007) account is *how* a perceiver can come to operate with what she calls an "engaged allocentric framework"—a conception of space in which the perceiver would know how to act on a visual object from positions that are not her own. Put bluntly, an alter-ego-centric spatial framework can be available only to a creature who knows that other positions in space can be occupied by agents and perceivers; it isn't something that the agent can find out simply by virtue of being an agent (section 12.2). There are really only two broad avenues the theorist can explore in the attempt to explain how perspective-transcendent spatial knowledge, be it of an object's location or its properties, can be available to the kind of perceiver who receives sensory information from objects at her own standpoint. One possibility is that the perceiver has in fact received sensory information from the object from standpoints other than the one she currently occupies. She can have done this on a previous encounter with the object; this is the view Schellenberg ascribes to Noe (2004), on which perception of an object's intrinsic spatial properties requires at least two distinct encounters with the thing. She dismisses this view on the plausible grounds that we can perceive the spatial properties of objects with shapes we have never encountered before. Or the perceiver can have had one extended encounter with the thing, in the course of which she changes her relative position to the perceived object while keeping track of it. But this proposal does not fare any better, since we can perceive the spatial properties of objects without having to move around them.

The alternative is that the perceiver enjoys perspective-transcendent knowledge of her environment because she has encountered it with others. You know where an object is relative to the standpoints of the occupants of positions in social space because you treat these standpoints as centers of perception and agency. That, and how, you can do this even though you do not have perceptual information from these standpoints is a topic I pursued in part 3. The thesis now is that agents' encounters with their environment in social space explain their ability to perceive the intrinsic spatial features of objects. The claim is of a developmental nature: perceivers know that positions other than their own can be occupied by perceivers and agents because they have been parts of constellations in which such positions were in fact occupied by others. Perceivers can operate with an alter-ego-centric conception of space because they have been operating in a social spatial framework. On this view, it is the presentation of the object in social space that permits perceivers to transcend their own perspective. They cannot, of course, see the object from the other's point of view. But they are able, in joint activity, to treat both their own and their cooperators' positions as centres of perception and agency, and are thus capable of implicit level 1 perspective-taking.

Interactions in social space thus play a critical role in spatial perception: it is because of the activation of a social spatial framework that we can come to enjoy perceptual experiences of objects as having mind-independent spatial properties.[4] The fact that we are joint agents answers the question left open by Schellenberg's (2007) proposal: it explains how we can come to know what it would take to act on an object from viewpoints different from our own, were we to occupy them. We can possess an engaged allocentric conception of space because we are agents in spatial constellations in which locations other than one's own are in fact occupied by one's cooperators.

You might worry that this proposal is subject to the same objection as the one raised by Schellenberg (2007) against Noe (2004). Does the proposal not require that subjects must have had a joint encounter with an object if they are to perceive its intrinsic spatial properties? This requirement would make the proposal unattractive: it is obvious that we can perceive the spatial properties of objects we have not jointly encountered before. But I don't think this objection is very worrying. For the proposal to succeed, it suffices that perceivers have come to acquire an engaged allocentric conception of space. The force of Schellenberg's proposal consists in this: once you have in place a spatial framework in which locations distinct from your own can be treated as centers of action and perception, you are in a position to see objects as having perspective-transcendent spatial properties. You do not need to have encountered the particular object before.

If this is right, the role of joint interaction with the environment goes well beyond the acquisition of perceptual common knowledge: it facilitates the kind of perception of the objects in our environment—as having mind-independent spatial properties—that is responsible for our everyday realism. We begin our cognitive lives on the raft, a tightly defined space that is secured, however dubiously, by the presence of others; and we branch out from there into the ocean. Our realism is achieved through and held in place by our joint anchoring in our surroundings with others. We can be naive realists because we are social realists in the first place.

Notes

Introduction

1. The most substantive attempt to date to integrate an account of joint attention into a larger philosophical framework can be found in Campbell (2002).

2. The phenomenological tradition has historically been much more sensitive to the idea that in important respects, the mind is a social phenomenon. See Zahavi (2014) for a recent overview.

3. See Schweikard and Schmid (2013) for an overview.

4. The classic debate here is between defenders of the *theory theory* (for instance, Stich and Nichols 1992; Fodor 1995; Gopnik and Meltzoff 1997), and the *simulation theory* of mindreading (for instance, Gordon 1986, 1995; Heal 1998; Goldman 2006). Various hybrid views are available (for instance, Heal 2003; Perner and Kuehberger 2005). For alternative accounts, see for instance Dennett (1987) and Hutto (2008).

5. Possible exceptions are *plural-subject* accounts, such as Gilbert (1990) and Schmid (2018).

6. See for instance Trevarthen (1980), Hobson ([2002] 2004), and Reddy (2011).

7. The notion of a perceptual constellation features heavily in this book. Here is what I mean by it: a perceptual constellation is the spatial relation that obtains between a perceiver and a perceptual object. If you are perceiving an F, the perceptual constellation between you and the F is constituted by the respective locations of you and the F. If we are jointly perceiving an F, the constellation between you, me, and the F is constituted by the respective locations of you, me, and the F. So you can think of perceptual constellations as kinds of spatial relations that inform the way the object is presented to its perceivers: the spatial relation between perceiver and object has an impact on the character of the perceiver's experience of the thing. Importantly for the argument presented here, this spatial relation changes fundamentally if the constellation is triadic: if there are two individuals who jointly perceive an object, the spatial relation must be thought of as obtaining between the three constituents of the triangle. This has significant consequences for the way the object is presented to the perceivers, as I shall argue.

8. As will become clear, I mean something quite different by that term than does Burge (1979), from whom I borrow it.

9. Williamson (2000) introduces and develops this view.

10. I use the notion of a *physical characteristic* very broadly here to include, in the famous Twin Earth cases (for instance McGinn 1977), a substance's chemical composition.

11. For instance, a reviewer pointed out that my case could be strengthened by working out how various evolutionary arguments in support of enactivist views of perception apply to the social externalist account developed here. I agree; there is a promising line of inquiry there. But in order to pursue it in earnest, I would have to add another chapter to what is already a long book. So I think this opportunity is best reserved for a future occasion.

Chapter 1

1. See Vanderschraaf and Sillari (2014) for an overview.

2. For a history of a decade of discussion about the analysis of knowledge, see Shope (1983).

3. You may object that proposition 12 is open to a Gettier-type treatment: since the justification A has for her belief that S knows that there is a candle on the table is not based on (or consists in) a veridical perceptual experience (A sees S, but her view of the candle is obscured by the hologram), A cannot be said to know that S knows that there is a candle on the table. But I think this objection should be resisted.

Consider again:

(5) A truly and with justification believes that S truly and with justification believes that there is a candle on the table.

Then it follows, along the lines of JTB, that

(5a) A knows that S truly and with justification believes that there is a candle on the table.

Gettier-type considerations have no grip here: A's belief is not accidentally true. Her experience adequately supports her (true) belief that S sees, and thus believes, that a candle is on the table. Her experience is of S looking at what appears to be a candle, which warrants the inference that S truly believes that a candle is on the table. That S's belief is true in virtue of a different object from the one A takes him to be experiencing has no bearing on the adequacy of A's perceptual justification. The perceptual experience justifies A's perceptual belief about S. It cannot *independently* justify A's belief that the object of S's experience is the same thing she is experiencing. And because S's perceptual belief is adequately supported by his experience, it follows that

(12) A knows that S knows that there is a candle on the table.

4. Another reaction would be to attempt to avoid proposition 15 by adopting a conception of perceptual justification on which only veridical experience justifies perceptual belief. But such a disjunctivist move is not easily compatible with the general internalism about the mind implicit in the analysis of knowledge in terms of JTB. See section 5.4 for more on this.

5. Williamson (2000, 93–113) discusses this claim by drawing on a scenario of which the following is only the briefest illustrative sketch. Suppose you wake up in the morning feeling cold, and that feeling cold is what he calls a *luminous condition*: when you feel cold, you know that you do. Suppose you warm up very slowly and that by lunchtime you are feeling hot. From millisecond to millisecond, you are feeling less cold. You consider very thoroughly how you feel from millisecond to millisecond, but you nevertheless fail to track the change in your sense of body temperature. Then you know you feel cold at noon despite feeling hot. This is contradictory, since knowledge is factive: if you know that p, then p. It follows that feeling cold is not luminous. Since Williamson thinks that luminous conditions are curiosities, he takes them to have no bearing on everyday life. For a discussion of his argument, see Steup (2009).

6. I borrow the term from Williamson (2000, 24), who, however, assigns a quite different meaning to it.

7. A good illustration of the difficulty, though it is offered in a slightly different context, can be found in Siegel (2002), 17–19.

Chapter 2

1. See Baron-Cohen (1999) for such a proposal.

Part II

1. I call such communications "demonstrative communications." I say more about how to think about this kind of communication in chapters 3 and 4.

2. By a "demonstrative act," I mean an utterance of a sentence containing a demonstrative expression that is accompanied by a pointing gesture or other deictic bodily movement.

Chapter 3

1. In any case, this is the kind of perceptual common knowledge I am interested in here. A case can be made that not all such knowledge is linguistically mediated (see Sperber and Wilson 1995). And it will become apparent in part 3 that explaining the possibility of the kind of propositional perceptual common knowledge that is acquired in demonstrative communication makes it necessary to think about bodily interactions that help constitute social space.

2. See, for example, Sperber and Wilson (1995), Campbell (2005), and Carpenter and Liebal (2011).

3. Of course, we can think of cases in which no deictic component is required to achieve public salience. For the purposes of the discussion, I am ignoring that kind of case.

4. Campbell (2018) argues that the Gricean intentional model does not provide a suitable basis for thinking about the foundations of communication. As will become clear in part 3, I fully agree: the most basic form of referential communication is to be found in interactions that do not require the expression or recognition of intentions. But as far as the linguistic transmission of propositional knowledge through demonstrative utterances is concerned, Grice's model remains superbly useful. Introducing it here does not amount to the claim that we should analyze all referential communication in its terms.

5. An additional condition is that the speaker has to realize that the hearer has recognized his intention. I assume throughout that this condition is met.

6. You may think that (as in Siegel's 2002, 15, example) a blindfolded speaker who says "That ball is dirty," pointing at random and only accidentally pointing at a ball, can intend to refer to the ball (if any) he is pointing at.

7. In any case, this is so on the view (which I shall introduce shortly) that demonstrative reference is fixed by the speaker's perceptual attention to the object he intends to refer to.

8. Disagreement may be possible here. Both Bob Frederick and a reviewer argued that perceivers can jointly attend to non-visual events, such as a piece of music in which the joint character of the experience is procured acoustically rather than visually. But it is not easy to to see how such an acoustic constellation could perceptually anchor a speaker's referential intention, in a way that facilitates the hearer's recognition of the intention, without making use of visual cues. The point certainly deserves discussion.

9. Siegel (2002) discusses the apparent problem, highlighted by McGinn (1981), that the appeal to perception as the reference-fixing mechanism of uses of demonstratives cannot account for cases in which a speaker demonstratively refers to an object not visible to him. She addresses this problem by arguing that there is no special reason to expect a theory of demonstrative reference to be unified.

10. See Campbell (2002, 2006, 2011b) and Siegel (2002, 2010; Siegel and Silins 2014) for accounts of their respective views.

Chapter 4

1. For a discussion of Heck's notion of cognitive significance and its role in the transmission of information, see Byrne and Thau (1996).

2. You might object that attention shifting does not require eye movement (or any other bodily activity), as Helmholtz showed over a century ago (Warren and Warren 1968) and that Campbell's distinction between reference fixing and communicative

uses of demonstrations is aligned with the distinction between overt (body-involving) and covert attention. I do not think this distinction poses a particular problem for my argument; you can modify my claim to say that *overt* forms of attention have a communicative function in joint contexts without affecting the point, since covert forms of attention cannot generate joint constellations.

Chapter 5

1. Kaplan ([1977] 1989) introduces the term *dthat* to represent the demonstrative "that" together with a type of demonstration.
2. Kaplan (1979) notes some of these difficulties; Evans (1982, 171–172) notes others that, however, do not concern me here.
3. I assume, for the purposes of the following discussion, that discrete objects occupy bounded locations. This assumption is not unproblematic. See Dickie (2015, 27–34).
4. CP/1 cannot account for cases in which two distinct objects occupy one location with identical boundaries. Siegel (2002, n. 11) mentions as an example a lump of clay that is also a statue (the lump of clay is not identical to the statue). But such cases, if they exist at all, are communicatively unproblematic: the hearer can always single out the objects in terms of the location they share, and this is sufficient for communication and the extension of the common knowledge shared by speaker and hearer about the object.
5. If you don't share the intuition, you can simply ignore this section; the discussion does not affect the overall point I am pursuing.
6. For overviews, see Scholl (2002) and Rai (2009).
7. Epistemological disjunctivism need not entail the view that knowledge-generating perceptual experiences are fundamentally different from their counterparts (Byrne and Logue 2008). The kind of disjunctivism I am interested in here is both epistemological and metaphysical, as will become clear.
8. However, see Martin (2002, 2004) for the view that subjective indistinguishability does not amount to sameness of phenomenal character.
9. For a disjunctivist treatment of perceptual illusion, see Brewer (2008).

Chapter 6

1. You may object that I can point out features of objects rather than the things themselves if they are large enough to occupy demonstratively distinguishable regions. But in those cases, the demonstrated features become objects in their own right: they meet the conditions imposed by CP/1.
2. You can think of the distinction along the lines of Dretske's (1993) cognate distinction between awareness of and awareness that, the former of which can be available in the absence of the latter.

Chapter 7

1. Fodor appears to have removed this passage from the ultimate version of his chapter.
2. Parallel distinctions apply if you think of the cognitive mental states produced by joint perceptions in their subjects as beliefs.

Chapter 8

1. For a critical discussion of Evans's use of the notion of a cognitive map, see Bermúdez (2000, 203–207).
2. "Evansian" because I do not want to make any claims as to whether this is exactly what he thought; it suffices for my purposes to acknowledge that the rough view sketched here is inspired by his remarks.
3. A reviewer pointed out an interesting connection between the idea that the concept "person" is primitive and a body of research suggesting that infants from very early on operate with a foundational distinction between agents and objects (Spelke et al. 1992; Luo and Baillargeon 2005). I briefly consider this proposal in section 11.5.
4. See Seemann (2008) for a more detailed account of this view.
5. See Campbell (2018) for a recent defense of this view.
6. See Reddy (2011) for an overview.

Chapter 9

1. Kessler and Rutherford support this hypothesis with their finding that subjects' response time to the question of whether an object is visible to or occluded by an avatar (or in front or behind the occlusion from the avatar's perspective) does not depend on angular disparities between the subject's body and the presented scene, or on changes in their body posture. By contrast, their response time to the question of whether the object is to the left or the right of the avatar (or to the occlusion from the avatar's perspective) varies depending on angular disparities and body posture. This shows, they argue, that level 2 perspective-taking requires an imaginative rotation of the body. But no such rotation is required for level 1 perspective-taking, which, they say, "seems to involve a process that determines object locations in relation to the line of sight of another person" (Kessler and Rutherford 2010, 9).

Chapter 10

1. Bermúdez (2000) suggests, in a similar vein, that there is no good reason to think of any one particular part of one's body as the origin of a proprioceptive frame of reference. The original formulation of this idea is due to Merleau-Ponty (2002, 121).

2. Gallagher (2003) offers three reasons in support of the contention that proprioception is not a form of perception, which are extensively discussed by Fridland (2011). First, it is a stricture on perception that it should meet the "identification constraint" (Shoemaker 1994); perception requires that the perceiver be able to distinguish objects from each other by means of perceptual information and track them through their career. Ordinary, nonreflective proprioceptive bodily awareness does not meet this constraint, Gallagher argues, because it should not be thought of as an identifying awareness of one's body as an object. Second, proprioception does not meet the "multiple-objects constraint," introduced by Bermúdez (2000, 136), who suggests that the objects of proprioception include those of the perceptual modalities. Gallagher argues against this view. The consideration that proprioception contributes to perception does not, he says, thereby show that its objects are like those in other sense modalities. The third reason is the one Gallagher articulates in the above quotation: proprioception does not meet the "egocentric framework constraint." Since all perception is perspectival, it must be organized relative to a standpoint. Proprioception is a good candidate for the awareness of this standpoint. But if proprioception itself were perceptual, an infinite regress would arise. Fridland offers criticisms of the first and third of these arguments. Engaging with this debate is beyond the reach of my project.

3. See Bermúdez (2000) for a discussion of this point.

4. See Holmes and Spence (2004) for a review of the literature on the integrated representation of visual, somatosensory, and auditory peripersonal space.

5. For a review of the neuropsychological evidence for the existence of peripersonal space in humans, see Làdavas (2002).

6. A spectacular case of a person who has retained mobility despite the complete loss of sensation from touch and proprioception is the case of Ian Waterman, who has large-fiber neuropathy and taught himself to rely on visual instead of somatosensory feedback (Gallagher 2005, 43–45; Hickok 2014, 146–150).

7. It is worth noting, however, that sight of a rubber hand can deceive the system coding peripersonal space if the rubber hand is in a position that is plausible relative to the subject's body (Làdavas 2002, 136).

8. Làdavas (2002, 138) highlights one characteristic of this dynamic nature of action space: an agent's peripersonal space can be extended by the use of tools. This is demonstrated by a study in which right-hemisphere damaged patients with tactile extinction were presented with visual stimuli far from their ipsilesional hand. The study found that cross-modal extinction was more severe after patients used a rake to retrieve distant objects than if they did not use the rake.

9. For a somewhat related take on the notion of behavioral space, see Watzl (2017, 108–109).

10. That there is a tight connection between perception and action is acknowledged by enactivist approaches to perception (for instance, Noe 2004).

11. Schellenberg (2007) raises a related problem for Noe's (2004) enactivist view of perception.

12. There is a debate as to whether coping should be thought of as a minded activity at all, a view Dreyfus rejects (see Gallagher (2017, 197–204) for an overview). It is beyond the reach of my project to consider that debate in the context of joint activities.

Chapter 11

1. The notion of collective intentionality, which is concerned with this question, has been discussed and developed intensively over the past three decades or so. For an overview, see Schweikard and Schmid (2013).

2. Thus, Searle (1990) maintains that all intentionality, including its collective version, has to reside "in individuals' heads," and hence cannot necessarily be connected to motor coordination.

3. Taffou and Viaud-Delmon (2014) find that the presence of a feared object also extends the subject's peripersonal space, possibly with the aim of enlarging the area of protection around the body. Krueger and Taylor Aiken (2016) investigate cases in which the sense of social space has been compromised by Moebius syndrome and schizophrenia.

4. Mirror neurons have been variously invoked to explain action understanding. Such neurons have been found in the ventral premotor cortex and the inferior parietal lobule of macaque monkeys. They discharge both during the execution and the observation of goal-directed movements. This discovery has been put to use to explain how monkeys (and, by extension, humans) can draw on the neural activity underwriting their own actions in order to understand the motor actions of others (for a review, see Rizzolatti and Sinigaglia, 2008, 2010).

5. See, for instance, Borg (2007, 2013) and Hickok (2014). For a critical evaluation of Hickok's claims, see Glenberg (2015) and Rizzolatti and Sinigaglia (2015).

6. Further support for the view that joint agents treat their cooperators as agents rather than tools comes from a range of studies that examine the role of shared task representations in joint action. Sebanz, Knoblich, and Prinz (2003, 2005) tested whether the well-known interference in an individual subject's action execution through task-irrelevant stimuli (for example, by adding a finger that points left or right when the task is to press a left key in response to a red ring or a right key in response to a right key) held also in the joint case. They found that this was indeed the case: participants in a joint task responded more quickly to their ring color if the finger pointed toward them rather than the other participant. Sebanz and Knoblich (2009, 357) conclude that knowing a co-actor's task affects one's own performance, even if there is no need to take the other's action into account at all.

7. Readers who remember the discussion of action space in section 10.3. will observe that this suggestion makes it seem as if the term *body schema* were just another name for that notion. And, on the proposal developed here, that view is almost correct: the body schema and action space really do blend into one another; they are not neatly delineated by some boundary. The differentiation occurs at a later stage:

you can have a sense of control over your bodily movements as you manipulate the objects in action space, but you cannot have a corresponding sense over these objects (see the next chapter for a discussion of the role of this sense of control in demonstrative thinking).

Chapter 12

1. See Bermúdez (2000, 200) for a critical discussion.
2. The developmental significance of the social spatial framework will be discussed in section 14.1.
3. Tomasello (2014, 45) points out that young children begin to show an appreciation of perspectives when they begin to jointly attend to objects with others, soon after their first birthday, though solving explicit level 1 tasks comes later (see section 14.1). This appreciation of perspectives is the result of the children's deployment of a sociospatial frame of reference.
4. It is not obvious that vision could be enjoyed by a stationary creature. Schellenberg (2007) argues that it is no coincidence that only agents are perceivers. And you might think that agents are, necessarily, mobile.
5. Perhaps you think that the situation is different if the creature keeps track of an object that moves from its right to its left; then the creature would have to deploy a different motor movement to act on it and could think of its position in terms of changes of the moving target's location. But this presupposes that the creature can remember, and thus compare, the target's earlier location with its later one. And this means presupposing what was meant to be explained. See the next paragraphs.
6. See Bermúdez (2000) for a discussion.
7. See Briscoe (2009) for a comprehensive account of the evidence.
8. See also section 5.3.
9. One focus of their research that is of particular relevance for our project is the distinction between the representation of a bodily movement as an action and the attribution of that action to oneself. Perception and action make use of a common format in which actions are represented. This format codes actions in terms of the perceptual events they produce, and hence perception and action have a common representational domain. Whether actions are attributed to oneself, others, or not at all is determined by a separate "who" system. Closely related to the common coding theory are the notions of shared representations (Daprati et al. 1997) and naked intentions, as introduced by Jeannerod and his colleagues (Jeannerod 1999; Jeannerod and Pacherie 2004; Georgieff and Jeannerod 1998). For a critical discussion of the idea that there are separate systems for action recognition and attribution see De Vignemont (2014). Much of this body of research focuses on the neural correlates action and, in particular, mirror neurons. As I noted in section 11.2, I want to avoid the discussion of the explanatory power of mirror neuron theory. I thus present the relevant findings without reference to their neurological aspect. The aim is to make a case that stands on behavioral grounds alone; if you think mirror neurons help

explain action ascription, this provides additional support for some of the claims put forward here.

10. The idea of a central monitoring system that produces "efference copies" of motor commands, which can then be compared with "reafference inflow signals" generated by the motor movement, so that the state of the motor center can be updated in case of a mismatch, goes back to Sperry (1950) and von Holst and Mittel-staedt (1950). See also Jeannerod and Pacherie (2004, 125).

11. This kind of move is made by Meltzoff and Moore (1997) when they introduce a "supramodal representational system" in their attempt to explain facial imitation in infancy.

12. See Prinz (2007) for a defense of the view that the experience of agency is exclusively perceptual and Briscoe (2011) for a discussion of this claim.

13. It should be noted that I have not attempted to give anything like a comprehensive account of their rich and wide-reaching paper.

14. Pezzulo et al. (2013) discuss cases in which agents' action spaces overlap.

Part IV

1. For an informative collection, see Mole, Smithies, and Wu (2011).

Chapter 13

1. See Leavens (2011) for a discussion.

2. See Moore and Dunham (1995), Eilan et al. (2005), Seemann (2011), and Metcalfe and Terrace (2013) for collections on the topic.

3. In any case, the literature on collective intentionality appears broadly united in this view; see for instance Schweikard and Schmid (2013).

4. For example, the classic Bratman (1992).

5. More recently, Tomasello (2008) has suggested that pointing in humans requires a "shared common ground" that facilitates the pursuit of cooperative goals. If the present line of inquiry is on the right track, this common ground is, in essence, a kind of spatial ordering of the environment of joint perceivers.

6. See Racine (2011) for a discussion of the distinction.

7. Generally, philosophers tend to think about joint attention in cognitivist terms (for instance, Campbell 2005; Peacocke 2005), while developmental psychologists in particular think about it in terms of the ability to intersubjectively "share" aspects of the environment with others (for instance, Hobson and Hobson 2011; Reddy 2011; Moll and Meltzoff 2011).

8. I don't know of any account that attempts to explain joint attention in terms of ordinary attention, thus privileging the subject-object flank of the triangle.

9. Another prominent simulationist account of joint attention is defended in Tomasello (1999). For Tomasello, joint attention requires the recognition of others

as intentional agents, but this does not require the ability to ascribe to them propositional attitudes. This recognition is achieved by means of a nonconceptual simulation procedure.

10. Intentionalist approaches to perception quite generally struggle to account for joint phenomena, since intentional relations are of a two-place, subject-object kind. But see Schmitz (2014), who introduces the notion of a "pragmatic, affectively charged intentional relation" in order to argue that intentionalism is able to accommodate triadic constellations.

11. The other natural ally of my view is the enactivist approach to joint attention recommended by Gallagher (2011) and Hutto (2011). See section 14.2.

12. For a defense of the egocentric proximity account, see Coventry et al. (2008). They argue that spatial demonstratives are used on the basis of an egocentric spatial framework that allows for the distinction between peripersonal space near the speaker and extrapersonal space far from the speaker.

13. As before, cautionary remarks are in order. Readers should not take the experimental findings discussed here as conclusive evidence in support of the view I am developing. The evidence is recent, and it comes from only two studies with the same lead author. Still, the evidence is pertinent for thinking about the nature of distal joint perception and thus well worth discussing here.

14. Thus, Coventry et al. (2008) find that in a game of Memory, speakers of English and Spanish use a proximal demonstrative (*this* and *este*) to refer to objects within peripersonal space and a nonproximal demonstrative (*that* and *aquel*) for objects in extrapersonal space. This suggests, they argue, that spatial demonstratives are used on the basis of an egocentric spatial framework that allows for the distinction between peripersonal space near the speaker and extrapersonal space far from the speaker.

Chapter 14

1. For the view that such tasks are solved only in the sixth year, see Fabricius et al. (2010).

2. Such a theory will be quite different from traditional belief-desire psychologies. It takes mindreaders to work with a conception of knowledge that is individuated relative to the environment. Developing this idea will have to wait for another occasion, however.

3. It should be noted that the social externalist is not committed to the view that representations play no role at all in joint agents' doings. For instance, I have made quite heavy use of the notion of matching (section 5.4), which requires a representational format. Because of the theory's inherent disjunctivism (section 3.4), the social externalist is committed to the view that experience is relational rather than representational. But this leaves open the postulation of representations on the level of subpersonal operations.

4. The view does not amount to a necessity claim; it does not amount to the claim that *only* social interaction can explain the perception of objects as having such properties. But it does amount to the claim that for social creatures like us, joint agency plays a vital role in spatial perception, in both our perceptual grasp of the location of objects of communication and our perceptual grasp of their spatial properties.

References

Apperly, I., and S. Butterfill. 2009. "Do Humans Have Two Systems to Track Beliefs and Belief-Like States?" *Psychological Review* 116:953–970.

Avramides, A. 2001. *Other Minds*. London: Routledge.

Bach, K. 1992. "Intentions and Demonstrations." *Analysis* 52:140–146.

Baldwin, D., and J. A. Baird. 2001. "Discerning Intentions in Dynamic Human Action." *Trends in Cognitive Science* 5:171–178.

Baron-Cohen, S. 1999. *Mindblindness*. Cambridge, MA: MIT Press.

Bates, E., L. Camaioni, and V. Volterra. 1975. "Performatives Prior to Speech." *Merrill-Palmer Quarterly* 21:205–226.

Bermúdez, J. L. 2000. *The Paradox of Self-Consciousness*. Cambridge, MA: MIT Press.

Bogdan, R. J. 2009. *Predicative Minds: The Social Ontogeny of Predicative Thinking*. Cambridge, MA: MIT Press.

Borg, E. 2007. "If Mirror Neurons Are the Answer, What Was the Question?" *Journal of Consciousness Studies* 14 (8): 5–19.

Borg, E. 2013. "More Questions for Mirror Neurons." *Conscious Cognition* 22 (3): 1122–1131.

Bratman, M. 1992. "Shared Cooperative Activity." *Philosophical Review* 101:327–341.

Brewer, B. 1999. *Perception and Reason*. Oxford: Oxford University Press.

Brewer, B. 2008. "How to Account for Illusion." In *Disjunctivism: Perception, Action, Knowledge*, edited by F. Macpherson and A. Haddock, 168–180. Oxford: Oxford University Press.

Briscoe, R. 2009. "Egocentric Spatial Representation in Action and Perception." *Philosophy and Phenomenological Research* 79 (2): 423–460.

Briscoe, R. 2011. "The Elusive Experience of Agency." *Topics in Cognitive Science* 3:262–267.

Brueckner, A. 2009. "E = K and Perceptual Knowledge." In *Williamson on Knowledge*, edited by P. Greenough and D. Pritchard, 5–11. Oxford: Oxford University Press.

Burge, T. 1979. "Individualism and the Mental." *Midwest Studies in Philosophy* 4 (1): 73–121.

Burge, T. 2010. *Origins of Objectivity*. Oxford: Oxford University Press.

Butterfill, S., and I. Apperly. 2013. "How to Construct a Minimal Theory of Mind." *Mind and Language* 28 (5): 606–637.

Byrne, A., and H. Logue. 2008. "Either/Or." In *Disjunctivism: Perception, Action, Knowledge*, edited by A. Macpherson and F. Haddock, 57–94. Oxford: Oxford University Press.

Byrne, A., and M. Thau. 1996. "In Defence of the Hybrid View." *Mind* 105 (417): 139–149.

Byrne, R. W. 2003. "Imitation as Behavior Parsing." *Philosophical Transactions of the Royal Society B* 358:529–536.

Caggiano, V., L. Fogassi, G. Rizzolatti, P. Thier, and A. Casile. 2009. "Mirror Neurons Differentially Encode the Peripersonal and Extrapersonal Space of Monkeys." *Science* 324:403–406.

Campbell, J. 1993. "The Role of Physical Objects in Spatial Thinking." In *Problems in the Philosophy and Psychology of Spatial Representation*, edited by N. Eilan, R. McCarthy, and M. W. Brewer, 65–95. Oxford: Blackwell.

Campbell, J. 1994. *Past, Space, and Self*. Cambridge, MA: MIT Press.

Campbell, J. 2002. *Reference and Consciousness*. Oxford: Oxford University Press.

Campbell, J. 2005. "Joint Attention and Common Knowledge." In *Joint Attention: Communication and Other Minds*, edited by N. Eilan, C. Hoerl, T. McCormack, and J. Roessler, 287–297. Oxford: Oxford University Press.

Campbell, J. 2006. "What Is the Role of Location in the Sense of a Visual Demonstrative? Reply to Matthen." *Philosophical Studies* 127:239–254.

Campbell, J. 2011a. "An Object-Dependent Perspective on Joint Attention." In *Joint Attention: New Developments in Psychology, Philosophy of Mind, and Social Neuroscience*, edited by A. Seemann, 415–430. Cambridge, MA: MIT Press.

Campbell, J. 2011b. "Visual Attention and the Epistemic Role of Consciousness." In *Attention: Philosophical and Psychological Essays*, edited by C. Smithies, D. Mole, and W. Wu, 323–342. Oxford: Oxford University Press.

Campbell, J. 2018. "Joint Attention." In *The Routledge Handbook of Collective Intentionality*, edited by M. Jankovic and K. Ludwig, 115–129. New York: Routledge.

Carpenter, M., and K. Liebal. 2011. "Joint Attention, Communication, and Knowing Together in Infancy." In *Joint Attention: New Developments in Psychology, Philosophy of Mind, and Social Neuroscience*, edited by Axel Seemann, 159–181. Cambridge, MA: MIT Press.

Carr, J. L. 1980/2000. *A Month in the Country*. London: Penguin Books.

Chartrand, T. L., and J. A. Bargh. 1999. "The Chameleon Effect: The Perception-Behavior Link and Social Interaction." *Journal of Personality and Social Psychology* 76 (6): 893–910.

Chemero, A. 2003. "An Outline of a Theory of Affordances." *Ecological Psychology* 15 (2): 181–195.

Cohn, J. F., and E. Z. Tronick. 1989. "Specificity of Infants' Response to Mothers' Affective Behavior." *Journal of the American Academy of Child and Adolescent Psychiatry* 28:242–248.

Costantini, M., and P. Haggard. 2007. "The Rubber Hand Illusion: Sensitivity and Reference Frame for Body Ownership." *Consciousness and Cognition* 16 (2): 229–240.

Costantini, M., and C. Sinigaglia. 2011. "Grasping Affordance: A Window onto Social Cognition." In *Joint Attention: New Developments in Psychology, Philosophy of Mind, and Social Neuroscience*, edited by A. Seemann. Cambridge, MA: MIT Press.

Coventry, K., B. Valdes, A. Castillo, and P. Guijarro-Fuentes. 2008. "Language within Your Reach: Near-Far Perceptual Space and Spatial Demonstratives." *Cognition* 108:889–895.

Creem-Regehr, S., K. Gagnon, M. Geuss, and J. Stefanucci. 2013. "Relating Spatial Perspective Taking to the Perception of Other's Affordances: Providing a Foundation for Predicting the Future Behavior of Others." *Frontiers in Human Neuroscience* 7:1–14. doi:10.3389/fnhum.2013.00596.

Daprati, E., N. Franck, N. Georgieff, J. Proust, E. Pacherie, J. Dalery, and M. Jeannerod. 1997. "Looking for the Agent: An Investigation into Consciousness of Action and Self-Consciousness in Schizophrenic Patients." *Cognition* 65:71–86.

Davidson, D. 2009. *Subjective, Intersubjective, Objective*. Oxford: Clarendon Press.

De Vignemont, F. 2014. "Shared Body Representations and the 'Whose' System." *Neuropsychologia* 55:128–136.

De Vignemont, F., and P. Fourneret. 2004. "The Sense of Agency: A Philosophical and Empirical Review of the 'Who' System." *Consciousness and Cognition* 13:1–19.

De Vignemont, F., and G. D. Iannetti. 2015. "How Many Peripersonal Spaces?" *Neuropsychologia* 70:327–334.

Dennett, D. 1987. *The Intentional Stance*. Cambridge, MA: MIT Press.

Di Pellegrino, G., and E. Làdavas. 2015. "Peripersonal Space in the Brain." *Neuropsychologia* 66:126–133.

Di Pellegrino, G., E. Làdavas, and A. Farné. 1997. "Seeing Where Your Hands Are." *Nature* 388 (6644): 730.

Dickie, I. 2015. *Fixing Reference*. Oxford: Oxford University Press.

Dickie, I., and G. Rattan. 2010. "Sense, Communication, and Rational Engagement." *Dialectica* 64 (2): 131–151.

Dretske, F. 1993. "Conscious Experience." *Mind* 102:263–283.

Dreyfus, H. (1993) 2014. *Skillful Coping: Essays on the Phenomenology of Everyday Perception and Action*, 76–91. Oxford: Oxford University Press.

Eilan, N. 2005. "Joint Attention, Communication, and Mind." In *Joint Attention: Communication and Other Minds*, edited by N. Eilan, T. Hoerl, Theresa McCormack, and Johannes Roessler, 1–33. Oxford: Oxford Unversity Press.

Eilan, N., C. Hoerl, T. McCormack, and J. Roessler, eds. 2005. *Joint Attention: Communication and Other Minds*. Oxford: Oxford University Press.

Evans, G. 1982. *The Varieties of Reference*. Oxford: Oxford University Press.

Fabricius, W.V., T. Boyer, A. Weimer, and K. Carroll. 2010. "True or False: Do Five-Year Olds Understand Belief?" *Developmental Psychology* 46:1402–1416.

Flavell, J. H. 1985. *Cognitive Development*. Upper Saddle River, NJ: Prentice Hall.

Flavell, J. H. 1992. "Perspectives on Perspective-Taking." In *The Jean Piaget Symposium Series. Piaget's Theory: Prospects and Possibilities*, edited by H. Beilin and P. B. Pufall, 107–139. Hillsdale, NJ: Erlbaum.

Fodor, J. 1995. "A Theory of the Child's Theory of Mind." In *Mental Simulation*, edited by M. Davies and T. Stone, 109–122. Oxford: Blackwell.

Fodor, J. 2007. "Revenge of the Given." In *Contemporary Debates in the Philosophy of Mind*, edited by B. P. McLaughlin and J. Cohen. New York: Blackwell.

Fourneret, P., and M. Jeannerod. 1998. "Limited Conscious Monitoring of Motor Performance in Normal Subjects." *Neuropsychologia* 36:1133–1140.

Frege, G. (1892) 1984. "On Sense and Meaning." In *Collected Papers*, edited by B. McGuinness. Oxford: Blackwell.

Fricker, E. 2009. "Is Knowing a State of Mind? The Case Against." In *Williamson on Knowledge*, edited by P. Greenough and D. Pritchard, 31–59. Oxford: Oxford University Press.

Fridland, E. 2011. "The Case for Proprioception." *Phenomenology of the Cognitive Sciences* 10:521–540.

Fulkerson, M. 2013. *The First Sense: A Philosophical Study of Human Touch*. Cambridge, MA: MIT Press.

Gallagher, S. 2003. "Bodily Self-Awareness and Object Perception." *Theoria et Historia Scientiarum: International Journal for Interdisciplinary Studies* 7 (1): 53–68.

Gallagher, S. 2005. *How the Body Shapes the Mind*. Oxford: Oxford University Press.

Gallagher, S. 2008. "Direct Perception in the Intersubjective Context." *Consciousness and Cognition* 17:535–543.

Gallagher, S. 2011. "Interactive Coordination in Joint Attention." In *Joint Attention: New Developments in Psychology, Philosophy of Mind, and Social Neuroscience*, edited by Axel Seemann, 293–306. Cambridge, MA: MIT Press.

Gallagher, S. 2017. *Enactivist Interventions: Rethinking the Mind*. Oxford: Oxford University Press.

Gallese, V., and A. Goldman. 1998. "Mirror Neurons and the Simulation Theory of Mind-Reading." *Trends in Cognitive Sciences* 2 (12): 493–501.

Georgieff, N., and M. Jeannerod. 1998. "Beyond Consciousness of External Reality: A 'Who' System for Consciousness of Action and Self-Consciousness." *Consciousness and Cognition* 7:465–477.

Gettier, E. 1963. "Is Justified True Belief Knowledge?" *Analysis* 23:121–123.

Gibson, J. 1979. *The Ecological Approach to Visual Perception*. Boston: Houghton Mifflin.

Gilbert, Margaret. 1990. "Walking Together: A Paradigmatic Social Phenomenon." *Midwest Studies in Philosophy* 15 (1): 1–14.

Glenberg, A. M. 2015. "Big Myth or Major Miss? Review of Hickok's 'The Myth of Mirror Neurons.'" *American Journal of Psychology* 128 (4): 533–539.

Goldman, A. 2006. *Simulating Minds: The Philosophy, Psychology, and Neuroscience of Mindreading*. Oxford: Oxford University Press.

Goldman, A. 2009. "Williamson on Knowledge and Evidence." In *Williamson on Knowledge*, edited by P. Greenough, and D. Pritchard, 73–91. Oxford: Oxford University Press.

Gopnik, A., and A. N. Meltzoff. 1997. *Words, Thoughts, and Theories.* Cambridge, MA: MIT Press.

Gordon, R. M. 1986. "Folk Psychology as Simulation." *Mind and Language* 1:158–171.

Gordon, R. M. 1995. "Simulation without Introspection or Inference from Me to You." In *Mental Simulation: Evaluations and Applications,* edited by M. Davies and T. Stone. Oxford: Blackwell.

Grice, H. P. 1957. "Meaning." *Philosophical Review* 66:377–388.

Grush, R. 2001. "Self, World and Space: The Meaning and Mechanisms of Ego- and Allocentric Spatial Representation." *Brain and Mind* 1:59–92.

Habermas, Jürgen. 1999. *Moral Consciousness and Communicative Action.* Cambridge, MA: MIT Press.

Heal, J. 1986. "Replication and Functionalism." In *Language, Mind, and Logic,* edited by J. Butterfield, 45–59. Cambridge: Cambridge University Press.

Heal, J. 1998. "Co-Cognition and Off-Line Simulation: Two Ways of Understanding the Simulation Approach." *Mind and Language* 13:477–498.

Heal, J. 2003. *Mind, Reason, and Imagination.* Cambridge: Cambridge University Press.

Heck, R. G. 1995. "The Sense of Communication." *Mind* 104 (413): 79–106.

Heck, R. G. 2002. "Do Demonstratives Have Senses?" *Philosophers' Imprint* 2 (2): 1–33.

Helm, J. L., D. Sbarra, and E. Ferrer. 2012. "Assessing Cross-Partner Associations in Physiological Responses via Coupled Oscillator Models." *Emotion* 12 (4): 748.

Hickok, G. 2014. *The Myth of Mirror Neurons.* New York: Norton.

Hobson, Peter. 2004. *The Cradle of Thought.* London: Macmillan.

Hobson, P., and J. Hobson. 2005. "What Puts the Jointness into Joint Attention?" In *Joint Attention: Communication and Other Minds,* edited by N. Eilan, C. Hoerl, T. McCormack and J. Roessler, 185–204. Oxford: Oxford University Press.

Hobson, P., and J. Hobson. 2011. "Joint Attention or Joint Engagement? Insights from Autism." In *Joint Attention: New Developments in Psychology, Philosophy of Mind, and Social Neuroscience,* edited by A. Seemann, 115–135. Cambridge, MA: MIT Press.

Holmes, N. P., and C. Spence. 2004. "The Body Schema and the Multisensory Representation(s) of Peripersonal Space." *Cognitive Processing* 5 (2): 94–105.

Huemer, M. 2001. *Skepticism and the Veil of Perception.* Lanham, MD: Rowman and Littlefield.

Hume, D. 1740. *A Treatise of Human Nature.* Oxford: Clarendon Press.

Hutto, D. 2008. *Folk Psychological Narratives: The Sociocultural Basis of Understanding Reasons.* Cambridge, MA: MIT Press.

Hutto, D. 2011. "Elementary Mind Minding, Enactivist-Style." In *Joint Attention: New Developments in Psychology, Philosophy of Mind, and Social Neuroscience*, edited by Axel Seemann, 307–341. Cambridge, MA: MIT Press.

Ishida, H., K. Nakajima, M. Inase, and A. Murata. 2009. "Shared Mapping of Own and Others' Bodies in Visuotactile Bimodal Area of Monkey Parietal Cortex." *Journal of Cognitive Neuroscience* 22 (1): 83–96.

Jeannerod, M. 1997. *The Cognitive Neuroscience of Action.* Oxford: Blackwell.

Jeannerod, M. 1999. "To Act or Not to Act: Perspectives on the Representation of Action." *Quarterly Journal of Experimental Psychology* 52A (1):1–29.

Jeannerod, M., and E. Pacherie. 2004. "Agency, Simulation and Self-Identification." *Mind and Language* 19 (2):113–146.

Kaplan, D. (1977) 1989. "Demonstratives." In *Themes from Kaplan*, edited by J. Almog, J. Perry, and H. Wettstein, 481–563. Oxford: Oxford University Press.

Kaplan, D. 1979. "Dthat." In *Contemporary Perspectives in the Philosophy of Language*, edited by P. French, T. Uehling, and H. Wettstein, 383–400. Oxford: Oxford University Press.

Kaplan, D. 1989. "Afterthoughts." In *Themes from Kaplan*, edited by J. Almog, J. Perry, and H. Wettstein, 565–614. Oxford: Oxford University Press.

Kelly, J. W., A. C. Beall, and J. M. Loomis. 2004. "Perception of Shared Visual Space: Estblishing Common Ground in Real and Virtual Environments." *Presence: Teleoperators and Virtual Environments* 13:442–450. doi:10.1162/1054746041944786.

Kessler, K., and H. Rutherford. 2010. "The Two Forms of Visuo-Spatial Perspective Taking Are Differently Embodied and Subserve Different Spatial Prepositions." *Frontiers in Psychology* 1:1–12. doi:10.3389/fpsyg.2010.00213.

King, J. 2014. "Speaker Intentions in Context." *Noûs* 48 (2): 219–237.

Klatzky, R. L., J. M. Loomis, A. C. Beall, S. S. Chance, and R. G. Golledge. 1998. "Spatial Updating of Self-Position and Orientation During Real, Imagined, and Virtual Locomotion." *Psychological Science* 9 (4): 293–298.

Kopp, C. 1982. "Antecendents of Self-Regulation: A Developmental Perspective." *Developmental Psychology* 18:199–214.

Kripke, S. 1980. *Naming and Necessity.* Cambridge MA: Harvard University Press.

Krueger, J., and A. Taylor Aiken. 2016. "Losing Social Space: Phenomenological Disruptions of Spatiality and Embodiment in Moebius Syndrome and Schizophrenia."

In *Phenomenology and Science*, edited by J. Reynolds and R. Sebold, 121–139. New York: Palgrave Macmillan.

Laborie, S. 2017. "The Raft of the Medusa." http://www.louvre.fr/en/oeuvre-notices/raft-medusa.

Làdavas, E. 2002. "Visual Peripersonal Space in Humans." In *The Cognitive and Neural Bases of Spatial Neglect*, edited by H.-O. Karnath, A. D. Milner, and G. Vallar. Oxford: Oxford University Press. doi:10.1093/acprof:oso/9780198508335.003.0009.

Leavens, D. 2011. "Joint Attention: Twelve Myths." In *Joint Attention: New Developments in Psychology, Philosophy of Mind, and Social Neuroscience*, edited by Axel Seemann, 43–72. Cambridge, MA: MIT Press.

Lenggenhager, B., T. Tadi, T. Metzinger, and O. Blanke. 2007. "Video Ergo Sum: Manipulating Bodily Self-Consciousness." *Science* 317 (5841): 1096–1099.

Leslie, A., O. Friedman, and T. P. German. 2004. "Core Mechanisms in 'Theory of Mind.'" *Trends in Cognitive Sciences* 8:528–533.

Levelt, W., and S. Kelter. 1982. "Surface Form and Memory in Question Answering." *Cognitive Psychology* 14:78–106.

Lewis, D. 1969. *Convention*. Cambridge, MA: Harvard University Press.

Linkenauger, S. A., J. K. Witt, J. K. Stefanucci, J. Z. Bakdash, and D. R. Proffitt. 2009. "The Effects of Handedness and Reachability on Perceived Distance." *Journal of Experimental Psychology: Human Perception and Affordance* 35:1649–1660.

Liszkowski, U., T. Striano, M. Carpenter, and M. Tomasello. 2006. "Twelve- and Eighteen-Month-Olds Point to Provide Information for Others." *Journal of Cognition and Development* 7 (2): 173–187.

Liu, S., Y. Zhou, R. Palumbo, and J.-L. Wang. 2016. "Dynamical Correlation: A New Method for Quantifying Synchrony with Multivariate Intensive Longitudinal Data." *Psychological Methods* 21 (3): 291–308.

Luo, Y., and R. Baillargeon. 2005. "Can a Self-Propelled Box Have a Goal? Psychological Reasoning in 5-Month-Old Infants." *Psychological Science* 16 (8): 601–608.

Macdonald, H. 2014. *H is for Hawk*. London: Vintage Books.

Maister, L., F. Cardini, G. Zamariola, A. Serino, and M. Tsakiris. 2015. "Your Place or Mine: Shared Sensory Experiences Elicit a Remapping of Peripersonal Space." *Neuropsychologia* 70:455–461.

Markie, P. 2005. "The Mystery of Direct Perceptual Justification." *Philosophical Studies* 126 (3): 347–373.

Martin, M. G. F. 1992. "Sight and Touch." In *The Contents of Experience: Essays on Perception*, edited by T. Crane, 196–215. Cambridge: Cambridge University Press.

Martin, M. G. F. 2002. "The Transparency of Experience." *Mind and Language* 17:376–425.

Martin, M. G. F. 2004. "The Limits of Self-Awareness." *Philosophical Studies* 120:37–89.

Masangkay, Z. S., K. A. McCluskey, C. W. McIntyre, J. Sims-Knight, B. E. Vaughn, and J. H. Flavell. 1974. "The Early Development of Inferences about the Visual Percepts of Others." *Child Development* 45:357–366.

Matthen, M. 2005. *Seeing, Doing, and Knowing: A Philosophical Theory of Sense Perception*. Oxford: Clarendon Press.

Matthen, M. 2006. "On Visual Experience of Objects: Comments on John Campbell's 'Reference and Consciousness.'" *Philosophical Studies* 127:195–220.

McDowell, J. 1994. *Mind and World*. Cambridge, MA: Harvard University Press.

McDowell, J. 2008. "The Disjunctive Conception of Experience as Material for a Transcendental Argument." In *Disjunctivism: Perception, Action, Knowledge*, edited by A. Haddock and F. Macpherson, 376–389. Oxford: Oxford University Press.

McGinn, C. 1977. "Charity, Interpretation, and Belief." *Journal of Philosophy* 74:521–535.

McGinn, C. 1981. "The Mechanism of Reference." *Synthese* 49:157–186.

Meltzoff, A. N., and M. K. Moore. 1983. "Newborn Infants Imitate Adult Facial Gestures." *Child Development* 54:702–709.

Meltzoff, A.N., and M.K. Moore. 1997. "Explaining Facial Imitation." *Early Development and Parenting* 6:179–192.

Merleau-Ponty, M. (1945) 2002. *Phenomenology of Perception*. London: Routledge.

Metcalfe, J., and H. Terrace, eds. 2013. *Agency and Joint Attention*. Oxford: Oxford University Press.

Michael, J., T. Wolf, C. Letesson, S. Butterfill, J. Skewes, and J. Hohwy. 2018. "Seeing It Both Ways: Using a Double-Cueing Task to Investigate the Role of Spatial Cueing in Level-1 Visual Perspective-Taking." *Journal of Experimental Psychology: Human Perception and Performance* 44(5): 693–702.

Milner, D., and M. Goodale. (1995) 2006. *The Visual Brain in Action*, 2nd ed. Oxford: Oxford University Press.

Mole, C., D. Smithies, and W. Wu, eds. 2011. *Attention: Philosophical and Psychological Essays*. Oxford: Oxford University Press.

Moll, H., M. Carpenter, and M. Tomasello. 2011. "Social Engagement Leads 2-Year-Olds to Overestimate Others' Knowledge." *Infancy* 16:248–265.

Moll, H., and D. Kadipasaoglu. 2013. "The Primacy of Social over Visual Perspective-Taking." *Frontiers in Human Neuroscience* 7:558. doi:10.3389/fnhum.2013.00558.

Moll, H., and A. Meltzoff. 2011. "Joint Attention as the Fundamental Basis of Taking Perspectives." In *Joint Attention: New Developments in Psychology, Philosophy of Mind, and Social Neuroscience*, edited by Axel Seemann, 393–413. Cambridge, MA: MIT Press.

Moore, C., and P. Dunham, eds. 1995. *Joint Attention: Its Origin and Role in Development*. Hillsdale, NJ: Erlbaum.

Nagy, E. 2008. "Innate Intersubjectivity: Newborns' Sensitivity to Communication Disturbance." *Developmental Psychology* 44:1779–1784.

Nichols, S., and S. Stich. 2003. *Mindreading: An Integrated Account of Pretence, Self-Awareness and Understanding of Other Minds*. Oxford: Oxford University Press.

Nielsen, T. I. 1963. "Volition: A New Experimental Approach." *Scandinavian Journal of Psychology* 4:225–230.

Noe, A. 2004. *Action in Perception*. Cambridge, MA: MIT Press.

Onishi, K. H., and R. Baillargeon. 2005. "Do 15-Month-Old Infants Understand False Beliefs?" *Science* 308:255–258.

Pacherie, E. 2007. "The Sense of Control and the Sense of Agency." *Psyche* 13:1–30.

Pacherie, E. 2011. "The Phenomenology of Joint Action: Self-Agency vs. Joint Agency." In *Joint Attention: New Developments in Psychology, Philosophy of Mind, and Social Neuroscience*, edited by Axel Seemann. Cambridge, MA: MIT Press.

Peacocke, C. 2005. "Joint Attention: Its Nature, Reflexivity, and Relation to Common Knowledge." In *Joint Attention: Communication and Other Minds*, edited by C. Hoerl, T. McCormack, J. Roessler, and N. Eilan, 298–324. Oxford: Oxford University Press.

Peeters, D., P. Hagoort, and A. Özyürek. 2015. "Electrophysiological Evidence for the Role of Shared Space in Online Comprehension of Spatial Demonstratives." *Cognition* 136:64–84.

Peeters, D., and A. Özyürek. 2016. "'This' and 'That' Revisited: A Social and Multimodal Approach to Spatial Demonstratives." *Frontiers in Psychology* 7 (222): 1–7. doi:10.3389/fpsyg.201600222.

Perner, J., and A. Kuehberger. 2005. "Mental Simulation: Royal Roads to Other Minds?" In *Other Minds: How Human Beings Bridge the Divide Between Self and Others*, edited by B. F. Malle and S. D. Hodges, 174–187. New York: Guilford Press.

Perner, J., and T. Ruffman. 2005. "Infants' Insight into the Mind: How Deep?" *Science* 308:214–216.

Perry, S. 2016. *The Essex Serpent.* London: Serpent's Tail.

Pezzulo, G., P. Iodice, S. Ferraina, and S. Kessler. 2013. "Shared Action Spaces: A Basis Function Framework for Social Re-Calibration of Sensorimotor Representations Supporting Joint Actions." *Frontiers in Human Neuroscience* 7:1–16. doi:10.3389/fnhum.2013.00800.

Posner, M. I., C. R. R. Snyder, and B. J. Davidson. 1980. "Attention and the Detection of Signals." *Journal of Experimental Psychology: General* 109:160–174.

Povinelli, D., J. Bering, and S. Giambrone. 2000. "Toward a Science of Other Minds: Escaping the Argument by Analogy." *Cognitive Science* 24 (509–541).

Povinelli, D. J., and S. Giambrone. 1999. "Inferring Other Minds: Failure of the Argument by Analogy." *Philosophical Topics* 27:167–201.

Prinz, J. 2007. "All Consciousness Is Perceptual." In *Contemporary Debates in Philosophy of Mind*, edited by B. P. McLaughlin, 335–357. Oxford: Blackwell.

Putnam, H. 1973. "Meaning and Reference." *Journal of Philosophy* 70 (19): 699–711.

Pylyshyn, Z. 2007. *Things and Places: How the Mind Connects to the World.* Cambridge, MA: MIT Press.

Racine, T. 2011. "Getting Beyond Rich and Lean Views of Joint Attention." In *Joint Attention: New Developments in Psychology, Philosophy of Mind, and Social Neuroscience*, edited by Axel Seemann, 21–42. Cambridge, MA: MIT Press.

Rai, U., and I. L. Singh. 2009. "Spatial Cueing and Shift of Visual Attention: An Overview." *Indian Journal of Social Science Researches* 6 (2): 71–78.

Reddy, V. 2008. *How Infants Know Minds.* Cambridge, MA: Harvard University Press.

Reddy, V. 2011. "A Gaze at Grips with Me." In *Joint Attention: New Developments in Psychology, Philosophy of Mind, and Social Neuroscience*, edited by Axel Seemann, 137–157. Cambridge, MA: MIT Press.

Reimer, M. 1992. "Three Views of Demonstrative Reference." *Synthese* 93 (3): 373–402.

Rietveld, E. 2008. "Situated Normativity: The Normative Aspect of Embodied Cognition in Unreflective Action." *Mind* 117 (468): 973–1001.

Rizzolatti, G., L. Fadiga, L. Fogassi, and V. Gallese. 1997. "The Space around Us." *Science* 277:190–191.

Rizzolatti, G., and C. Sinigaglia. 2008. *Mirrors in the Brain: How Our Minds Share Actions and Emotions.* Oxford: Oxford University Press.

Rizzolatti, G., and C. Sinigaglia. 2010. "The Functional Role of the Parieto-Frontal Mirror Circuit: Interpretations and Misinterpretations." *Nature Reviews Neuroscience* 11:264–274.

Rizzolatti, G., and C. Sinigaglia. 2015. "Review: Curious Book on Mirror Neurons and Their Myth." *American Journal of Psychology* 128 (4): 527–533.

Scaife, M., and J. S. Bruner. 1975. "The Capacity for Joint Visual Attention in the Infant." *Nature* 253:265–266.

Schauer, G. 2012. "How Persuasive Is Wilby's Solution to the Problem of Common Knowledge in Joint Attention?" https://georgschauer.com/2012/04/13/how-persuasive-is-wilbys-solution-to-the-problem-of-common-knowledge-in-joint-attention/.

Schellenberg, S. 2007. "Action and Self-Location in Perception." *Mind* 116 (463): 603–632.

Schiffer, S. 1972. *Meaning*. Oxford: Oxford University Press.

Schmid, H. B. 2018. "The Subject of 'We Intend.'" *Phenomenology and the Cognitive Sciences* 17 (2): 231–243.

Schmitz, M. 2014. "Joint Attention and Understanding Others." *Synthesis Philosophica* 2:235–251.

Scholl, B. J., ed. 2002. *Objects and Attention*. Cambridge, MA: MIT Press.

Schweikard, D., and H. B. Schmid. 2013. "Collective Intentionality." *The Stanford Encyclopedia of Philosophy*. https://plato.stanford.edu/entries/collective-intentionality/.

Searle, J. 1990. "Collective Intentions and Actions." In *Intentions in Communication*, edited by J. Morgan, P. Cohen, and M. E. Pollack. Cambridge, MA: MIT Press.

Sebanz, N., and G. Knoblich. 2009. "Prediction in Joint Action: What, When, Where." *Topics in Cognitive Science* 1:353–367.

Sebanz, N., G. Knoblich, and W. Prinz. 2003. "Representing Others' Actions: Just Like One's Own?" *Cognition* 88:B11–B21.

Sebanz, N., G. Knoblich, and W. Prinz. 2005. "How Two Share a Task." *Journal of Experimental Psychology: Human Perception and Performance* 31:1234–1246.

Seemann, A. 2008. "Person Perception." *Philosophical Explorations* 11 (3): 245–262.

Seemann, A., ed. 2011. *Joint Attention: New Developments in Psychology, Philosophy of Mind, and Social Neuroscience*. Cambridge, MA: MIT Press.

Shoemaker, S. 1968. "Self-Reference and Self-Awareness." *Journal of Philosophy* 65 (19): 555–567.

Shoemaker, S. 1994. "Self-Knowledge and Inner-Sense." *Philosophy and Phenomenological Research* 54:249–314.

Shope, R. K. 1983. *The Analysis of Knowing. A Decade of Research.* Princeton: Princeton University Press.

Siderits, M., E. Thompson, and D. Zahavi, eds. 2011. *Self, No Self?* Oxford: Oxford University Press.

Siegel, S. 2002. "The Role of Perception in Demonstrative Reference." *Philosophers' Imprint* 2 (1): 1–21.

Siegel, S. 2010. *The Contents of Visual Experience.* Oxford: Oxford University Press.

Siegel, S., and N. Silins. 2014. "Consciousness, Attention, and Justification." In *Scepticism and Perceptual Justification*, edited by Dylan Dodd and Elia Zardini, 149–169. Oxford: Oxford University Press.

Soliman, T. M., R. Ferguson, M. S. Dexheimer, and A. M. Glenberg. 2015. "Consequences of Joint Action: Entanglement with Your Partner." *Journal of Experimental Psychology* 144 (4): 873–888.

Spelke, E. S., K. Breinlinger, J. Macomber, and K. Jacobson. 1992. "Origins of Knowledge." *Psychological Review* 99 (4): 605–632.

Sperber, D., and D. Wilson. 1995. *Relevance: Communication and Cognition.* Oxford: Blackwell.

Sperry, R. W. 1950. "Neural Basis of the Spontaneous Optokinetic Response Produced by Visual Inversion." *Journal of Comparative and Physiological Psychology* 43:482–489.

Steup, M. 2009. "Are Mental States Luminous?" In *Williamson on Knowledge*, edited by Patrick Greenough and Duncan Pritchard, 217–236. Oxford: Oxford University Press.

Stich, S., and S. Nichols. 1992. "Folk Psychology: Simulation or Tacit Theory?" *Mind and Language* 7 (1–2): 29–65.

Strawson, P. F. (1959) 1996. *Individuals: An Essay in Descriptive Metaphysics.* London: Routledge.

Stueber, K. 2011. "Social Cognition and the Allure of the Second-Person Perspective: In Defense of Empathy and Simulation." In *Joint Attention: New Developments in Psychology, Philosophy of Mind, and Social Neuroscience*, edited by Axel Seemann, 265–292. Cambridge, MA MIT Press.

Suddendorf, T., and A. Whiten. 2003. "Reinterpreting the Mentality of Apes." In *From Mating to Mentality: Evaluating Evolutionary Psychology*, edited by J. Fitness and K. Sterelny, 173–196. Hove, UK: Psychology Press.

Surian, L., S. Caldi, and D. Sperber. 2007. "Attribution of Beliefs by 13-Month-Old Infants." *Psychological Science* 18:580–586.

Taffou, M., and I. Viaud-Delmon. 2014. "Cynophobic Fear Adaptively Extends Peri-Personal Space." *Frontiers in Psychiatry* 5. doi:10.3389/fpsyt.2014.00122.

Teneggi, C., E. Canzoneri, G. di Pellegrino, and A. Serino. 2013. "Social Modulation of Peripersonal Space Boundaries." *Current Biology* 23:406–411.

Tomasello, M. 1999. *The Cultural Origins of Human Cognition*. Cambridge, MA: Harvard University Press.

Tomasello, M. 2008. *Origins of Human Communication*. Cambridge, MA: MIT Press.

Tomasello, M. 2014. *A Natural History of Human Thinking*. Cambridge, MA: Harvard University Press.

Tomasello, M., J. Call, and B. Hare. 2003. "Chimpanzees Understand Psychological States: The Question Is Which Ones, and to What Extent." *Trends in Cognitive Sciences* 7:153–156.

Tomasello, M., M. Carpenter, J. Call, T. Behne, and H. Moll. 2005. "Understanding and Sharing Intentions: The Origins of Cultural Cognition." *Behavioral and Brain Sciences* 28:675–735.

Tomasello, M., and J. Farrar. 1986. "Joint Attention and Early Language." *Child Development* 57:1454–1463.

Treisman, A. 1988. "'Features and Objects': The Fourteenth Bartlett Memorial Memorial Lecture." *Quarterly Journal of Experimental Psychology* 40A:201–237.

Treisman, A., and G. Gelade. 1980. "A Feature-Integration Theory of Attention." *Cognitive Psychology* 12:97–136.

Trevarthen, C. 1980. "The Foundations of Intersubjectivity: Development of Interpersonal and Cooperative Understanding in Infants." In *The Social Foundations of Language and Thought: Essays in Honor of J. S. Bruner*, edited by D. Olson, 316–342. New York: Norton.

Trevarthen, C., and P. Hubley. 1978. "Secondary Intersubjectivity: Confidence, Confiding and Acts of Meaning in the First Year." In *Action, Gesture and Symbol*, edited by A. Lock. London: Academic Press.

Tronick, E. Z., H. Als, L. Adamson, S. Wise, and T. B. Brazelton. 1978. "The Infant's Response to Entrapment Between Contradictory Messages in Face-to-Face Interactions." *Journal of American Academy of Child Psychiatry* 17:1–13.

Vaishnavi, S., J. Calhoun, and A. Chatterjee. 2001. "Binding Personal and Peripersonal Space: Evidence from Tactile Extinction." *Journal of Cognitive Neuroscience* 13 (2): 181–189.

Van den Bos, E., and M. Jeannerod. 2002. "Sense of Body and Sense of Action Both Contribute to Self-Recognition." *Cognition* 85 (2): 177–187.

Vanderschraaf, P., and G. Sillari. 2014. "Common Knowledge." In *The Stanford Encyclopedia of Philosophy*.

von Holst, E., and H. Mittelstaedt. 1950. "Das Reafferenzprinzip. Wechselwirkungen zwischen Zentralnervensystem und Peripherie." *Naturwissenschaften* 37:464–476.

Warren, R. M., and R. P. Warren. 1968. *Helmholtz on Perception: Its Physiology and Development*. New York: Wiley.

Watzl, S. 2017. *Structuring Mind*. Oxford: Oxford University Press.

Wellman, H., D. Cross, and J. Watson. 2001. "Meta-Analysis of Theory of Mind Development: The Truth about False-Belief." *Child Development* 72:655–684.

Wettstein, H. 1984. "How to Bridge the Gap Between Meaning and Reference." *Synthese* 58:63–84.

Wilby, M. 2010. "The Simplicity of Mutual Knowledge." *Philosophical Explorations* 13 (2): 8–100.

Williamson, T. 1995. "Is Knowing a State of Mind?" *Mind* 104 (415): 53–565.

Williamson, T. 2000. *Knowledge and Its Limits*. Oxford Oxford University Press.

Williamson, T. 2005. "On Being Justified In One's Head." In *Rationality and the Good: Critical Essays on the Ethics and Epistemology of Robert Audi*, edited by M. Timmons, J. Greco, and A. Mele, 106–122. Oxford: Oxford University Press.

Wimmer, H., and J. Perner. 1983. "Beliefs about Beliefs: Representation and Constraining Function of Wrong Beliefs in Young CHildren's Understanding of Deception." *Cognition* 13:103–128.

Witt, J. K., D. R. Profitt, and W. Epstein. 2004. "Perceiving Distance: A Role of Effort and Intent." *Perception* 33:577–590.

Wittgenstein, L. 1958. *The Blue and Brown Books*. Oxford: Blackwell.

Wright, C. 2008. "Comment on John McDowell's 'The Disjunctive Conception of Experience as Material for a Transcendental Argument.'" In *Disjunctivism: Perception, Action, Knowledge*, edited by A. Haddock and F. Macpherson, 390–404. Oxford: Oxford University Press.

Wu, W. 2011. "Attention as Selection for Action." In *Attention: Philosophical and Psychological Essays*, edited by C. Smithies, D. Mole, and W.Wu, 97–116. Oxford: Oxford University Press.

Zagzebski, L. 1994. "The Inescapability of Gettier Problems." *Philosophical Quarterly* 44 (174): 65–73.

Zahavi, D. 2014. *Self and Other: Exploring Subjectivity, Empathy, and Shame.* Oxford: Oxford University Press.

Zajonc, R. B., K. A. Adelmann, S. T. Murphy, and P. M. Niedenthal. 1987. "Convergence in the Physical Appearance of Spouses." *Motivation and Emotion* 11:335–346.

Index